WHAT'S THE ECONOMY TRYING TO TELL YOU?

WHAT'S THE ECONOMY TRYING TO TELL YOU?

Everyone's Guide to Understanding and Profiting from the Economy

DAVID M. BLITZER

McGraw-Hill
New York   San Francisco   Washington, D.C.   Auckland   Bogotá
Caracas   Lisbon   London   Madrid   Mexico City   Milan
Montreal   New Delhi   San Juan   Singapore
Sydney   Tokyo   Toronto

Library of Congress Cataloging-in-Publication Data

Blitzer, David M.
What's the economy trying to tell you? : everyone's guide to
understanding and profiting from the economy / David M. Blitzer.
p.   cm.
Includes bibliographical references and index.
ISBN 0-07-005939-X
1. Economics.   2. Finance, Personal—United States.   3. Finance—
United States.   4. United States—Economic Policy.   I. Title.
HB171.B357   1997
330—dc21   97-7891
                                                                  CIP

McGraw-Hill

*A Division of The **McGraw·Hill** Companies*

3 4 5 6 7 8 9 0   DOC/DOC   9 0 2 1 0 9 8

ISBN 0-07-005939-X

*The sponsoring editor for this book was Allyson Arias, the editing
supervisor was Caroline Levine, and the production supervisor was
Suzanne W. B. Rapcavage. This book was set in Fairfield by
Victoria Khavkina of the McGraw-Hill Professional Book Group
composition unit.*

Printed and bound by R. R. Donnelley & Sons Company.

CONTENTS

CHAPTER FIVE. HOW THINGS CHANGE   185

CHAPTER SIX. KEY PLAYERS IN THE GAME   217

CHAPTER SEVEN. USING THE ECONOMY
TO YOUR ADVANTAGE AS AN INVESTOR   249

PREFACE

The economy surrounds us almost every day and has a lot to do with how happy or sad, rich or poor, and successful or disappointed we are in various pursuits in life. In this sense the economy confronts almost all of us almost all the time. In several years of studying, watching, and forecasting the economy, three other aspects of it have become clear. First, the economy can be understood with a combination of common sense and good economic analysis. Second, when one *does* apply both the common sense and the analysis, it is often quite fascinating. Third, there are rewards to successful economic analysis that go beyond fascination—and often include profits! This book is an attempt to apply both the analysis and the common sense and to do so without a lot of jargon and complexity.

Economics is not a laboratory science. While some very limited experiments may be possible, one can not rerun the 1987 stock market crash or repeat the last recession to test out an economic theory or forecast. The only way to practice economics is in the real world with all the excitement, and messiness, that it entails. However, the closest thing economics has to a laboratory is the financial markets, which have the following characteristics: they move quickly so one doesn't have to wait long for the results. There are always plenty of buyers and sellers, so markets are competitive. The financial markets benefit from generous information flows, so conditions can react to new information rapidly. In short, the financial markets are the best of experimental labs—except there are no controlled experiments. Nevertheless, there are endless opportunities to learn, and profit.

In *What's the Economy Trying To Tell You?* I have tried to distill some of the lessons of the markets and the economy into some useful ideas about how to understand the economy and profit from the markets. Economics teaches that there is nothing wrong with profits and the profit motive—but the pursuit is more enjoyable if one views the adventure as intellectually exciting as well as potentially financially rewarding.

Writing a book, aside from being a more massive undertaking than predicted, leaves one with two kinds of debts. First, and most obviously, there is the debt to family for both providing the time and urging the project forward. Second, there are many intellectual debts to numerous colleagues, coworkers, associates, and others who have asked questions, challenged ideas, and offered theories of why the economy is the way it is.

David M. Blitzer

WHY WORRY ABOUT THE ECONOMY?

WHY YOU SHOULD READ THIS BOOK

Over 200 years ago economics was nicknamed the dismal science. To judge by the comments we hear, most of us think this is just about right. While it might make economists feel better if most people suddenly decided that economics was fascinating, exciting, or invigorating rather than dismal, this is not in the cards. However, like it or not, the economy is a fact of life for all of us. Is there anyone who didn't wish for more money, for his stocks to go up, for her mortgage payments to cost less? In short, is there anyone who didn't wonder at some point why the economic things in life couldn't be a little better or a little different?

If you're like most people, this book won't convince you that economics isn't such a dismal science after all. But if you are any person at all, you are part of the economy and you're subject to its ups and downs. How well the economy does has a lot to do with how well you do. This is true not just in your investments or your mortgage payments. The economy reaches into almost everything that happens in modern life. There is very little chance of escaping its pervasive influence. No matter how much we may wish that the world could run on love, or reason, or common sense, or altruism, it runs to a large extent on money, production, income, and wealth. So, rather than try to escape the economy and its influence, a better idea may be to understand it and use it.

The economy is trying to tell us something about what is going on and what might go on. The trick is to understand what that is and how to profit from it.

Economists, either because they make new forecasts or deny old forecasts, are often compared to meteorologists. At the risk of insulting weather forecasters, let me suggest some reason to the comparison. If you know it's going to rain, you can carry an umbrella or wear a raincoat and reduce some of the annoyance and pain of being caught in a downpour. The economy is not much different. If you know interest rates will rise, you can hurry and refinance your mortgage this year or even buy a new house sooner, not later. Maybe refinancing the mortgage in time doesn't sound like remembering the umbrella, but it is another case where knowing what's coming would make life a little nicer.

Maybe one reason economists don't mind the nickname *dismal* science is that a whiff of recession in the news always sparks more interest in economics. A rise in the unemployment rate will spur interest in economics, just as hurricane warnings will make people turn on the news. Of course, some people listen to the weather every day, no matter how blue the skies look. Many people do the same with the economy. They read the financial pages and listen to financial reports on TV and radio. Watching the weather takes some skill. After a while you figure out which TV station's forecaster is most reliable, who tells the best jokes, and who has the newest computer graphics. Depending on what you want—humor, technological wizardry, or the right moment to carry that umbrella—you choose your TV station. But there are other skills to watching the weather. Sometimes it pays to look out the window. Most TV studios are in windowless rooms with no direct connection to the outside. Occasionally what's happening outside your window is not what you see on TV. Or, if it's not time for the weather report, knowing what sudden winds and dark clouds might mean is a big help.

With the economy the details differ; the ideas are somewhat the same and the stakes are much higher. For most of us, misjudging the weather means a soaking and a dry-cleaning bill. Misjudging the economy can mean getting soaked in a very different—and more expensive—way. Knowing something about the economy can pay off. Besides the obvious profit from following, watching, and understanding the economy, there is another kind of payoff. Economy watching involves two eternal sources of fascination: money and the quirks of human nature. For people who trade stocks, bet on bonds, or play in any of a wide range of markets from Wall Street to art auctions to collecting antique cars, the thrill of the chase should not be forgotten. Watching the economy can be both rewarding and exciting.

WHY DOES THE ECONOMY MATTER?

The economy is all around us and it plays a large part in our lives. It has more impact than the weather on how we live and how well we live. After all, air conditioning and heating have partially conquered the weather, but we haven't even begun to conquer the economy. Looking for a job? It's much easier to find one when there are a lot to be found. Trying to buy a house? It's easier when prices and mortgage rates are both low. Of course, if you're trying to sell a house, you might want high prices and buyers afraid of missing out on a good thing. In either case, it makes a big difference if there are a lot of people trying to buy or trying to sell, or both or neither.

When it comes to Wall Street and stocks and bonds, the economy has a role to play as well. It may not be like buying a house, even though there is always some stock market seer who claims that stocks rose because there were more buyers than sellers. (What happens to all those disappointed buyers who can't find sellers?) The economy does other things to us as well. For one, that house or those stocks or anything else may be worth more or less next year depending on inflation. A vacation in Europe to celebrate good times might be a steal or cost a fortune depending on how the dollar fares in the world markets.

Economics runs through other parts of our lives as well. We all worry about money—usually not having enough of it. Suppose you read in the papers that the economy is in a recession, that economic activity (that's not what economists do—it's what we all do together) is falling. Should you panic? Worry about your job? Sell the house? Buy stocks? Panic is rarely a good idea; some concern about how well you're doing your job probably is a good thought. Selling the house just as a recession is announced is a bit extreme, while buying stocks at that time is likely to be a good idea. But only if you think you know what you're doing.

A SOURCE OF ANXIETY

Economics seems to be a great source of worry as well. People spend a lot of time worrying about the deficit—not the deficit between their own income and their spending, but the national budget deficit. Repeatedly, overspending is cited as a major problem that the government should fix. Whether or not the deficit is a problem, the government did cause it. Politicians are in the habit of comparing family budgets with the national budget and suggesting that it is (almost) a crime to run the country on debts and borrowed money. But precious few American families manage to buy a home without a mortgage and are therefore as "deeply in debt," as the politicians characterize our national budget picture. Further, some of the same politicians are responsible for those loopholes in the tax code that let the government give us a tax break on our mortgage payments and encourage us to go into debt to buy a house.

So, before you feel guilty about taking out a 30-year mortgage to buy a home, ask yourself when the government started borrowing. It was 1789, the same year the federal government started. Think 30 years is a long time for a mortgage? The last time the government ran a surplus—didn't add to its debts in a year—was in 1969, almost 30 years ago. The moral to the deficit tale may be to understand the economy a bit and be able to recognize some of the political talk.

The budget deficit is not the only source of economic worry. A major concern these days is trade, especially trade with Japan and Asia. A few years ago some economist or reporter coined the phrase "the twin deficits" to suggest a mystical link between owing too much to ourselves in the budget deficit and too much to others in the trade deficit. Trade deficits have something to do with the value of the dollar—another source of worry for anyone with nothing to do but wonder what to worry about next. But with trade, worry can extend to guilt as well.

We are told to buy American and keep jobs at home. Some people argue that we shouldn't buy Japanese cars or

French wine, while others merely moan about spurring global competition. Behind many of these arguments are questions about the dollar and other currencies. According to the *macho theory* of currency trading, every nation should want a strong currency and should never suffer the devastating shame of devaluing its currency. Yet a few years ago, when the British could no longer survive in the European Exchange rate mechanism, Britain pulled out and let the pound sink to levels that politicians only days before had claimed would spell disaster and ruin. A year later Britain's economy boomed and Europe's swooned under the weight of the German mark.

Despite much of the rhetoric, there are some benefits to a strong dollar. A strong dollar is an attractive reserve currency. That's econospeak for saying that other countries want to hold dollars. For one thing, it lets us borrow from anyone else in our own currency, a privilege granted to only a few nations. When the United States wants to borrow money, it issues bonds in dollars and everyone gladly buys them. When Mexico wants to borrow money, it can't market peso bonds, so it must borrow and repay the loans in dollars. Individual U.S. citizens get to borrow in dollars too, not in pesos or yen or marks. And only the U.S. government can print dollars if it wants to.

A more important aspect of the macho theory of currency is the "big stick." If the dollar is the reserve currency and everyone's wealth is tied to it, people are likely to pay attention to the United States. After all, if the dollar goes down, so does individual wealth. So, if you want to be the big player on the international block—and what nation doesn't?—it helps to have a strong currency. Asian nations are paying more and more attention to Japan because of the strong yen and its rising importance in other Asian economies. Maybe, then, the real worry about the dollar should not be the bills in our pockets but the ones *not* in some other nation's coffers.

Another lasting source of economic anxiety is inflation. No surprise. One day a dollar is a dollar, the next it is only 90 cents. What happened? Inflation is not as rampant as it was in Germany in the 1920s, when it took a wheelbarrow of German marks to buy lunch. Today inflation, unlike other problems in the economy, creeps in. But if you see it coming, you may be able to limit its damage to your own wealth and well-being.

HOW OLD IS ECONOMICS?

Modern economics—or political economy, as it used to be called—dates back to 1776. No, it didn't begin with the American Revolution. Rather, Adam Smith, a Scottish philosopher, published a book called *An Inquiry into the Nature and Causes of the Wealth of Nations.* Smith's work is considered the first example of modern economics. Many of the topics and concepts that appear in this book can be traced to his writings. In some quarters Smith is most famous for suggesting that businesses always try to monopolize markets and raise prices. Economists credit him with the theory of the "invisible hand"—the idea that a market economy will operate so that no one can be made better off without making someone else worse off. It is as if an "invisible hand" is guiding the markets when in reality the markets merely reflect the activities of those trading in them.

Of course, economics didn't spring forth with Adam Smith. Prices and economics were discussed long before Smith appeared. St. Augustine considered what a just price is. When prices for some widely consumed good or service surge or when some company's profits appear to reach stratospheric levels, the popular press seems to return to St. Augustine and ask what is the *just* price. Others maintain that economics began much, much earlier. The story is told of three learned professors debating whose science appeared first. The biologist, citing the Book of Genesis, argues that his field of study began within a week of Creation. The botanist promptly responds that her field preceded that of the biologist. They both turn to their colleague. The economist merely smiles and notes, "In the beginning, all was darkness, chaos, and a void." Surely, he suggests, chaos was the beginning of economics.

(*Continued*)

ECONOMICS AND THE ELECTIONS

Economics figures in most national elections. In 1992 Bill Clinton's unofficial slogan was "It's the Economy, Stupid!" In 1984 Ronald Reagan based his reelection on a simple question: "Are you better off than you were 4 years ago?" Both approaches struck a responsive chord and both men were elected. Examples extend to almost every presidential campaign. John Kennedy was elected during a recession that plagued the prior administration; the recession ended in the second month of Kennedy's term as he demonstrated a combination of timing and luck matched by few Presidents. Franklin D. Roosevelt's landslide victory in 1936—based on his efforts to turn back the Great Depression—set the course for the next several decades of U.S. politics.

The accompanying table shows a few economic indicators for each election year since 1948. The unemployment rate, in the second column, is always a politically sensitive number. Interest rates are also important to politicians, as well as to home buyers. The table shows the yields on Treasury bills and bonds. The T-bonds are an average of all issues with 10 or more years of maturity. From 1942 to 1951 the Treasury and the Federal Reserve controlled interest rates to ensure the sale of government debt, so the 1948 number should be taken with a grain of salt. Stocks have figured in the political picture since the 1920s (and the crash of 1929). The next two columns show the S&P 500 annual average and how much it rose or fell during the year. Inflation comes in and out of politics as it rises and falls, and is measured by the consumer price index. It was an issue in 1948 and then faded until the 1970s. The last column shows the misery index—the sum of inflation and unemployment. This measure was popularized by Ronald Reagan when he challenged Jimmy Carter in 1980; the number tells why.

(Continued)

Election-Year Economics

YEAR	INCUMBENT (PARTY)	INTEREST RATES			THE STOCK MARKET			
		UN-EMPLOY-MENT RATE (%)	T-BILLS (%)	T-BONDS (%)	S&P 500	CHANGE IN LAST YEAR IN S&P 500 (%)	INFLA-TION (%)	MISERY INDEX
1948	Truman (D)	3.8	1.04	2.44	15.53	2.42	7.7	11.4
1952	Truman (D)	3.0	1.77	2.68	24.50	9.68	2.3	5.3
1956	Eisenhower (R)	4.1	2.66	3.08	46.62	15.14	1.5	5.7
1960	Eisenhower (R)	5.5	2.95	4.02	55.85	−2.66	1.5	7.0
1964	Johnson (D)	5.2	3.55	4.15	81.37	16.47	1.3	6.4
1968	Johnson (D)	3.6	5.34	5.26	98.70	7.36	4.3	7.8
1972	Nixon (R)	5.6	4.07	5.64	109.20	11.10	3.3	8.9
1976	Ford (R)	7.7	5.00	6.78	102.01	18.40	5.7	13.4
1980	Carter (D)	7.2	11.61	10.81	118.78	15.30	13.5	20.7
1984	Reagan (R)	7.5	9.57	11.99	160.46	0.03	4.3	11.8
1988	Reagan (R)	5.5	6.67	8.98	265.79	−7.34	4.1	9.6
1992	Bush (R)	7.5	3.46	7.52	415.74	10.52	3.0	10.5
1996	Clinton (D)	5.5	5.14	6.65	621.91	14.82	1.6	7.2

SOURCE: U.S. Bureau of Labor Statistics, U.S. Bureau of Economic Analysis, and Standard & Poor's, a division of the McGraw-Hill Companies, Inc. Data for 1996 based on 12 months ending in July 1996; all other years based on calendar years. Calculations by the author.

AN OPPORTUNITY

At this point, hopefully, you have a sense that the economy does make a difference in how well you live. But before you put your trust in any book about economics, you may be tempted to remember that Civics I lecture you heard urging Americans to vote in every election. Yet even in a close election, the winner usually wins by hundreds of thousands, or millions, of votes. Can any single person really make a difference? Can you as an individual do anything about the economy?

The answer is a sort of "yes and no." The no part is easy. Unless you are the Chairman of the Federal Reserve or some other key government economic policymaker, or the CEO of a major financial institution, there is little you can really do singlehandedly to shift the direction of the economy. Even though what you buy, how much you save, and how you invest your money contribute to the overall results, they don't confer any control powers on you.

The yes part of the answer is more interesting. While you can't control the economy, you can make an educated guess as to what it's likely to do and how it may affect you. Forewarned is forearmed. Some knowledge may be wishful thinking—like knowing what the stock market will do tomorrow. Other considerations are more realistic, such as recognizing when the economy is in a recession and realizing that the downturn won't last forever. Equally possible, but more subtle, is recognizing when stocks are grossly out of line with their past history or when a major shift in the economy is coming. Most realistic is to be able to look at the turmoil that often greets a shift in the economy, a dive in interest rates, or a surge in the stock market and realize that something like this happened before and we all survived to see another day.

Moreover, using the economy to avoid the worst, or to profit a little, can work in all directions. Good Wall Street traders can make money in almost any market as long as their guesses about the market's next move or two are better, on average, than those of other traders. In fact, most successful investors know that they can play both the rises and the falls in a market and understand enough about the past and the possible future to keep both their patience and their confidence intact. Some understanding about the economy can't hurt alongside that.

There are few ways to get something for nothing, and virtually none of them work in the economy. Neither this book nor any other will tell you how to forecast the future flawlessly. There are too many uncertainties floating around to make that possible. But forewarned is indeed forearmed.

This book won't guarantee that your stocks never go down or that you always buy low and sell high. What it may do—and what some understanding of economics can do—is help you see why the economy and markets do what they do and make educated guesses about what they may do next. Getting some of the guesses, or forecasts, right can pay off in the long run.

One of the arguments against using what you see in the economy is that politics always gums it up. Politics (or should I say politicians) tends to mess things up from time to time. But the politicians don't stand separate and aside from the economy—they are part of it, a very big part of it. Like it or not, politicians are waist deep in what happens to us and our economy. One thing politicians enjoy is taking credit for any successes and laying the blame for any failures on someone else. Another thing they like is getting reelected. Both matter a lot when politics meets economics.

For a politician, having a good economic record is the right combination of brilliant timing and dumb luck. John Kennedy knew this well. The fact that the economy slid into a recession in mid-1960 as the presidential campaign heated up and that Kennedy's opponent, Richard M. Nixon, was Vice President when the recession hit didn't hurt Kennedy's vote. Most recessions run for a year or so, and that one was no exception. Kennedy was inaugurated in January 1961. The recession ended in February 1961. Since even an average expansion is good for about 4 years, if John Kennedy had lived to seek reelection, he could probably have pointed to a strong economic performance—ending a recession and sustaining the expansion. Lyndon B. Johnson, who succeeded Kennedy, did point to the administration's economic successes, though the poor showing of Barry Goldwater, the Republican challenger, did as much as the economy to ensure Johnson's victory in the 1964 election. Timing didn't end with the 1960s—we still have business cycles and we still have opportunistic politicians taking credit.

Among the recent loser and winner combinations are George Bush and Bill Clinton. Bush came into office at the end of a 6-year expansion. The chances of his making it through 4 more years without an economic downturn were slim. But Bush's real error may have been in not considering that the economy would turn sour and demand a leader who was compassionate about hard times and active in battling economic reversals. He did neither. Bill Clinton's timing has been second only to Kennedy's. Clinton took office just as the expansion was gathering speed. He has been able to ride the momentum straight through the 1996 elections. With a little less luck, he might have won a return ticket to Little Rock. It all depends on much more than the economy. Forewarned may be forearmed, but it is no guarantee.

WHAT'S AHEAD IN THE BOOK

The economy *is* telling us what's happening and what could happen next. If only we can hear what it's saying, maybe we can profit by the message. The first step is to define what the economy is and what economics is all about. If this seems obvious, try explaining the economy to a 6-year-old. It's trouble enough explaining it to a 36-year-old. The next step is to look at how the economy is measured, scaled, and gauged. How big is big, how rich is rich, and how fast is fast growth? Is 3 percent inflation a lot? What if your money is worth only 50 cents in 10 years, 15 years, or 20 years? Economists seem to have taken to heart Mark Twain's comment that there are lies, damned lies, and statistics. In the following pages we'll use very little math, but some numbers, as we try to see how it all gets counted.

The economy in the United States and increasingly throughout the world is organized into markets. Markets are where we trade things—my labor in writing this book for your money in buying it (with a toll exacted by the publisher along the way). Or, more likely, someone's labor, time, and effort for his or her wage; or hard-earned dollars for a car. Markets are rather old—maybe as old as civilization itself. They also appear whether someone wants them or not. "Black markets" for buying or selling the forbidden are almost as common as normal "white markets"—and usually more interesting. Before you presume that black markets arise only in socialist or communist nations that try to prohibit free economic activity, think about buying or selling illegal drugs. That's another black market. So is the "oldest profession," except where it may have been legalized.

Markets are crucial to understanding the economy. They include much more than the stock market, although that one is quite interesting. Markets exist for almost anything—time and labor, art, cars, things we make, services we buy. Most markets have common elements, patterns that make buying a car and getting a second opinion before surgery almost the same thing. As the axiom goes, the only constant is change. In the economy, changes occur all the time. They are what shift prices and give rise to opportunities. After we think we know a market when we see it, we'll look at how it changes.

Of course, economics involves more than changing markets. It is also about people and organizations. You can't tell the players without a scorecard. This chapter is the scorecard—a look at the key players in the game. Some players, such as the President and his advisers and the leaders of Congress, are in the government. Others, including the leaders of the Federal Reserve and the Fed itself, are almost in the government. Still others are businesses and the people who run them. Last, but most important, are the rest of us.

Subsequent chapters aim at putting it all together to advantage. We look at forecasting what happens next and figuring out which way the wind is blowing. Forecasting is both art and science, and there is just not enough of either to go round. But we will look at what the prospects are. One of the obvious places to put all this to use is in investing and watching Wall Street. How investors might use their understanding of the economy to advantage in determining which forecast to bet on, rounds out the discussion.

For the ever-adventurous reader, the Appendix includes some comments about other reading. This is certainly not an exhaustive list, and it is shaped by personal commentary. Hopefully, those who suspect that economics isn't quite a dismal science will find more places to explore here.

WHAT IS ECONOMICS AND THE ECONOMY

One of the more difficult questions posed to an economist is "What is economics?" Students of economics seldom confront this rather basic question until the second year of graduate school. It is often answered with an odd response like "the allocation of scarce resources" or "production, distribution, and stability." Looking up *economics* in the dictionary doesn't help; the word has a Greek root relating to household management. More often than not, the final answer is that economics is what economists do.

Economics is the rules of the game, how we organize society. Most of what we see as important in everyday life is organized by the economy. On a day-to-day basis, economics has to do with what kind of job we have or don't have; with how much money we earn; with what things cost; with whether we can save and invest enough for a comfortable future; with how much we will need tomorrow and with how well off our children will be in coming years.

Perhaps more important, economics is *why* we have jobs, why we work, why we earn incomes, why money matters, and why markets are important. In this book, it is also how to understand money, markets, and income to make them work for us.

Money and wealth certainly aren't everything; there is much more to living the good life. But at least some money and some wealth matters. While economics often tries to avoid the more philosophical, spiritual, or emotional questions of everyday life, it does deal with questions that concern most of us most of the time.

Economic ideas contribute to the way our society is organized. That the kind of organization we have today has evolved gradually doesn't make the principles behind it any less important. True, no one really decided how to organize modern American, Western, or global society. Rather, it evolved through history to the current arrangement, and is still changing and evolving. In fact, the social fabric is always likely to be changing. Many of the principles behind the current organization depend on economics and include such ideas as these:

- Private property—we can own land, houses, tools, books, and all kinds of other goods and use them, or dispose of them, as we wish.

- Jobs—we have jobs and earn income with our labor.

- Human rights—we do not own other people and don't have preemptive rights to someone else's labor and property.

- Markets—the way we exchange private property or exchange labor for income is through a voluntary bargaining process called a market.

• Money—we use money as a way to store wealth and to buy and sell things we own, including our own labor.

There are different ways to organize society. Private property is not essential. Many tribal systems have no private property. Socialist or communist regimes, such as those that dominated Eastern Europe and Asia for much of this century, oppose corporations and private ownership of factories, farms, or mines. While salary and wage earnings are the key sources of income in the United States today, there have been periods when inherited wealth was far more important to the overall economy and to the leaders of society. And while human rights may seem inalienable, slavery has been a feature of many different societies.

What distinguishes markets and money from other elements of the economy is that they are a little more fundamental. In almost any society based on private property, both money and markets are present. Not much private property is needed to give rise to markets and money—just enough so that people have some things to exchange and need a way to keep track of how much they have. Trading has been practiced since before recorded history. Ancient tribes traded with one another to get essential tools that were hard to make locally. Today economists speak of "gains from trade." I have something you need more than I do, and you have something I need more than you do. After some discussion and bargaining we swap and we're both better off. That is gain from trade. Trading also comes naturally and at an early age—whether it involves colored jelly beans, baseball cards, or just about anything else that can be carried around and exchanged. Anyone who doubts that gains from trade are important or that a shrewd trader of any age can get ahead need only reread Mark Twain's tale of Tom Sawyer painting the fence. Tom wasn't the first fast-talking salesman, but he was one of the best.

Money and having more of it are also rather basic to human existence. Many years ago, an op-ed writer in *The Wall Street Journal*—a literary bastion of capitalism—named the profit motive and the sex drive as two of the most basic aspects of human existence. Once we admit markets and trading to society, it is only natural to want to hold on to the results of our trading and be able to accumulate the results as easily as possible. That gives rise to money in a form that is convenient to use in transactions, hard to counterfeit, and easy to store and carry around. The next, and bigger, step in the evolution of money is lending money at interest to make more. This concept doesn't always follow quite as quickly, but is certainly a part of modern society.

Economics would be far less interesting if it covered only markets and money. Given a little time, economists will try to explain almost anything. Love, marriage, charity, what kind of jobs we have, where we work, where we live, and who our friends are have all been subjects for economists. The explanations are not always successful, but they almost always give some interesting insights into what is going on in society.

Economists also grapple with issues that may not seem to matter to the economy. Time is one of these; stability and change are others. Time does matter, because things are worth more if we have them right now than if we expect to get them sometime in the future. This is true even if we are absolutely sure we will get them in the future. In fact, the interaction of time and money—interest rates—is the basis for much of what happens in the financial markets. Stability and change also make a big difference in how the economy affects people's lives. Which is better, a boom-and-bust economy or a steady-growth economy? Supposing the steady-growth economy grows so slowly that after several years we are not as rich as we would be in the boom-and-bust world. Are we better or worse off?

Finally, at least to some of us, economics raises interesting issues—ones that matter to people. In the end, the idea of organizing things a little better is a challenge worth examining in detail.

THE MOST MISUNDERSTOOD PART OF ECONOMICS

Economics is a major source of misunderstanding in public debates. In recent years the political arena has echoed with arguments over the budget deficit and the national debt. We hear every possible opinion from claims that we are about to drown in our own red ink, to suggestions that we ignore the debt, to claims that cutting our taxes will lead to larger tax revenues for the government and a drop in the deficit. Or is it the debt?

While some of these arguments are rather involved, the difference between the national debt and the budget deficit is rather straightforward. Each year the government collects taxes and spends money. When expenditures exceed revenues, the government is left with a gap. This gap is the deficit. In fiscal 1996—the 12 months ended on September 30, 1996—the deficit was about $107 billion. Since money doesn't grow on trees, the government borrows money to fill the gap. The deficit is the amount by which government spending exceeds government revenues in a year. When revenues are greater than expenditures, we have a surplus. Government revenues come from income taxes, social security payroll taxes, various other taxes, and some miscellaneous fees such as entering national parks and buying government publications. Expenditures cover a wide range of items, including social security benefits, Medicare and Medicaid payments, salaries of government workers, foreign aid, and government purchases from paper clips to jet planes.

The total amount the government owes—the accumulation of all the past deficits—is the national debt. This figure is roughly $5.2 trillion, including funds invested in U.S. Treasury securities. The debt that is held by the public, including foreigners, is about $3.8 trillion. When the government spends less or collects more in revenues, the deficit will be reduced. If the deficit is smaller, the national debt will grow more slowly. To reduce the national debt, the deficit must be turned into a surplus. The last surplus was almost 30 years ago. A lot of confusion exists between the debt and the deficit. There has been a national debt since the beginning of the country. In fact, one of the original reasons for establishing a central government and the Continental Congress during the American Revolution was to borrow money to fund George Washington's army. The United States began borrowing money before it was even a nation!

The numbers and reports on the national debt have another important complication. The government "saves" some revenues by investing them in Treasury

(Continued)

bonds. For example, social security tax payments currently exceed social security benefit payments by about $53.4 billion per year. On its books, the government takes these extra revenues and "buys" T-bonds. These bonds are counted as part of the total national debt, even though this is merely fancy bookkeeping by the federal government. The bonds purchased with social security funds don't count in the same way as the Treasury bonds you buy, because the social security fund bonds are merely bookkeeping. True bonds comprise the *national debt held by the public.* This is the number that really matters. To the extent that the financial markets worry about the size of the national debt, this is the number they worry about. When the deficit is counted, the impact of the social security tax funds and the bonds bought with those funds is already removed. Therefore, if you add the national debt held by the public at the end of last year to this year's deficit, you will get the national debt held by the public at the end of this year.

Should you worry about the deficit or the national debt? Certainly not the national debt—it's been around as long as the nation. As to the deficit, it is also not worth much lost sleep. This is not to say that government policy on taxing spending isn't important or that how much we spend compared with how much we save doesn't matter—it all does. But the deficit is probably the wrong thing to focus on. What, then, should we worry about? One point of concern is the overall arrangement of government policies, including spending, taxes, and the level of the deficit or surplus. Not all deficits are bad, however. If the economy is slipping into

(*Continued*)

recession, the deficit—especially any increase in the deficit—represents a government stimulus to the economy that can help end the recession. But if the economy is booming *and* the deficit is getting larger and larger, the government may be overstimulating the economy and risking inflation.

Some longer-term issues related to the deficit are also legitimate concerns. Over the last few decades the proportion of total income that America saves and invests for the future has declined. If we invest less today, there will be less wealth tomorrow. One reflection of the decline in savings is the rise in the deficit. Simply worrying about the deficit, some politicians argue, is the wrong response. Increasing savings is the right response. Japan in its peak years of economic growth had far more savings and a far larger deficit (both measured as a proportion of GDP) than did the United States.

(*Continued*)

MEASURING AND TRACKING CONDITIONS

Putting economics to work almost always involves measuring or counting. To determine if a price is too high or too low, we have to measure the price. To gauge if we are being offered a good deal on a house, a stock, or a new job, we need to measure real estate, shareholder value, and salary, the job supply, or how good a suggested new employer will be. Even one step removed, measurement and counting make all the difference in the world. Your stockbroker calls up and offers you stock that "always soars when the economy does well." But how do you—or your broker—decide if the economy will do well?

Measurement has a venerable history in economics. Indeed, for a long time people thought the only "thing" to economics was measuring or counting. Nowadays, a lot of people seem to equate economics with forecasting. Forecasts almost always require numbers—at times to provide a forecast that really gets specific, at other times to make a vague forecast look specific enough to be worth paying for. Sometimes economics drives the way we measure. As we'll see when we look at the unemployment rate, deciding what we are measuring often involves understanding the economy and its various sectors and markets.

In the opposite direction, measurement often drives economics, as in figuring out what is important to understand or what really matters. Politicians and pundits argue a lot about reducing capital gains rates—that is, lowering taxes on the earnings from investments held for a long time. This morally uplifting policy is designed to encourage people to "invest in America's future." Economists are less than excited by it, however, because capital gains taxes are a tiny part of the taxes we all pay. Moreover, capital gains taxes are only a very small part of the numerous factors that drive long-term investment decisions.

We know that changes in the economy affect our investments and our lives. But just knowing that is not enough. We need to see patterns between the economy and our investments so we can figure out when we should buy stocks or sell bonds or search for a new job. Finding those patterns requires economic measurements of what is getting bigger or smaller.

Now that we have decided to measure the economy, what will we measure? To start with, money. It is something that most of us care about most of the time. From money, we move to interest rates—the price of money over time. Then we turn to prices in general and how they are measured and how they change. Next we take a short detour into stock prices and how some of those are measured. Stocks are certainly not the only prices which are measured or worth measuring. We also look at prices for commodities and other items such as homes. One price that matters to many of us, but goes under a different name, is the wage or salary we earn—that is a price definitely worth investigating. Next we consider employment and how we measure some other factors tied to jobs. Since jobs and workers produce services and goods, we can shift to how economists measure output from widgets to the GDP. Our tour of economic measurement wraps up with softer measures such as how consumers feel and whether they will keep spending.

This rapid tour may sound like an advertisement for *If It's Tuesday, This Must Be Belgium* or like a teacher's syllabus followed by the comment "There will be a quiz." Hopefully it is neither. The point of all these measurements is this: When you look at the economy, knowing how big is big is worthwhile. Is the President's promise to create 4 million jobs in his first term just falling off a log or can it truly be accomplished? The President makes $200,000 a year. Is that a lot, especially compared with the multimillion-dollar contract of a sports figure? Before you answer, remember that when Babe Ruth was asked why he earned more than President Hoover in 1929, he said that he had a better year. Of course, both made a lot less than the President does today. Also, 1929 was not Herbert Hoover's finest moment; the stock market crashed and the Great Depression began.

MONEY

Traditionally money has had a number of functions—store of value, unit of account, medium of transaction. Economist Edmund Phelps added a more common function—source of anxiety. While these cover the issues, the first three are probably far more often memorized than understood. Store of value means we use money to keep our wealth: cash in the bank. Unit of account means money is a way to measure other things in the economy in terms of a single standard.

Medium of transaction means that we can use money to pay for an item instead of trading something else we happen to own. Source of anxiety is all too clear.

Another way to look at money is as something needed for transactions, for speculation, and for liquidity. Transactions involve money as the medium of exchange. Speculation means holding money (or securities) in the hope that prices will change. Liquidity is a way to deal with risks and uncertainties. Sometimes being liquid is as simple as carrying "mad money" on a date so you can always get home alone. At other times it is more complex and refers to how much cash an investor wants to hold in an account against an unexpected opportunity or an unforeseen pitfall.

Unit of account is money as a measure: how rich we are, how much we make, how much something costs. We could, as in some ancient parable, count wealth by counting things we own—two cattle, one house, three spouses. Or we could take a giant step and assume we all know the exchange rates among these things. That is, we all agree that one house is the same as six head of cattle, so if a woman is paid one house we know that she earns as much as the man paid six head of cattle. That would get us to the point where one kind of physical object is used as money. Some Native American societies used shells as currency. Gold was a traditional currency in many early Western cultures. Before you look askance at shells, note that they are a lot smaller, lighter, and easier to carry and store than gold. And shells are probably no harder to authenticate or easier to counterfeit than gold bars.

It is as a medium of exchange that money serves its most common function. Using heads of cattle, houses, or even gold or shells to buy your morning newspaper or your weekly groceries isn't particularly convenient. Paper money and coins do facilitate commerce. Of course, most of us *don't* use paper money or coins for commerce. We use a check or a credit card or what might be called a virtual credit card—we simply mention a number and people agree we have paid them with a credit card. If that sounds far-fetched, think about a telephone credit card. You never really need to show it to anyone or anything. You just punch in the code numbers, the call goes through, and you get a bill at the end of the month. Except for the fact that most of us don't trust our memories, we could leave home without it!

Recently various ideas have cropped up about smart cards, electronic money, e-cash, and other electronic payment systems. What is used for currency is likely to change in the future, maybe the near future. But its key properties will remain the same. Money should be widely accepted as "legal tender for all debts public and private," to steal a line from the dollar bill. It should be convenient, portable, and easily divisible so we can make change. It should be reliable so we don't invest a lot of time spotting counterfeits. In some situations we may even want it to be anonymous so that a transaction doesn't have an audit trail.

The point is that what now serves as money is much more than just printed greenbacks. In economics, it is often important to know how much money there is in circulation. If there isn't enough, business will slow, because no one has any ready cash to make purchases or carry out business until the next payday. If there is too much money or if the amount is growing too fast, prices can get out of line. In all this, remember that money is different from riches or wealth.

In the United States, the federal government issues, or prints, money. It doesn't have to be done this way, and for a large portion of our history it was not done this way. The

Federal Reserve has been around since 1913; before then there were various printing arrangements at different times. Today, insofar as control is possible, the Fed controls the supply of money.

So far all this may seem a bit too simple, and why we should count money a bit too obvious. But measuring money, and measuring with money, turns out to be an important step in using the economy to our advantage. Measuring how the amount of money is growing or shrinking can help forecast the effects of different economic policies and programs. The widely followed theory of *monetarism* sees the money supply as the crucial variable in the economy. Even those economists who do not strictly follow monetarism agree that money is an important issue, particularly when inflation is involved. To understand how different monetary measures can be used to gauge the prospects of inflation and economic growth, we need to start with how money is measured.

Measuring money consists of defining its components and counting how much of each is outstanding. Table 3.1 shows the usual definitions and roughly how much of each money measure exists in the economy. These are often called "the M's," for obvious reasons. The abbreviations in the table are explained below. What is, and isn't, money may depend on what we are measuring and why.

Most of us think of money as that green stuff in our pockets. This is *currency.* There is almost $400 billion of it in the economy, including a lot that circulates in foreign countries. In fact, when local currencies were subject to extreme inflation during the first few years after the Communist collapse in Eastern Europe, the U.S. dollar was more readily accepted than many local currencies. There are more $100 bills circulating, or hidden in mattresses,

TABLE 3-1 **Concepts and Measures of Money**

M's	CONTAINS	RECENT QUANTITY
Currency	Currency outside of banks, the U.S. Treasury, and the Federal Reserve	$0.40 trillion
M-1	Currency, travelers checks, checking account balances	$1.08 trillion
M-2	M-1 plus savings accounts, savings deposits under $100,000, balances in money market mutual funds, certain overnight deposits between banks and other financial institutions, and certain deposits in foreign offices of U.S. banks	$3.85 trillion
M-3	M-2 plus large-denomination savings deposits and deposits of financial institutions	$4.96 trillion
L	M-3 plus nonbank holdings of U.S. savings bonds and short-term Treasury securities, commercial paper, and bankers' acceptances	$6.07 trillion
Debt	Outstanding debt of all nonfinancial parts of the economy	$14.61 trillion

SOURCE: Federal Reserve Release H6: Weekly Money Supply Report.

outside the United States than inside. Currency still plays a very important role in our domestic economy. Even in the modern world of credit cards we have not completely eliminated the need for good old-fashioned cash. In fact, cash has a number of desirable properties that characterize almost anything that can be used for money.

Cash is portable. Short of very large sums, your pocket will suffice for transporting what you're likely to need. Compared with some commodity moneys like gold bars, this is a major advance. Second, because it is difficult to counterfeit U.S. currency—and more difficult to do it without getting caught—cash is reliable. We may not be experts in spotting bogus bills, but we can expect the currency to be good. Third, money is divisible—we can make change if necessary. Fourth, it is widely accepted. British, French, German, or Japanese currency is portable, reliable, and divisible, but it is not too widely accepted in most American communities. To extend the currency's own motto: "In God We Trust"—all others pay cash. Finally, cash leaves no audit trail. There is no way to tell where the dollar in your pocket came from or who had it last. If you want to do business "off the books" to evade the IRS, cash is very convenient. If you are financing an illegal drug deal, cash is also convenient. Of course, in the drug deal the absence of the audit trail in the cash outweighs the inconvenience of needing several suitcases to carry home the money. In one sense there is a lot of cash in the economy—about $400 billion. With 255 million Americans, some of whom are too young to carry much money, that works out to a little less than $2000 each. The answer to why there is so much seems to relate to the illegal use of currency and to its acceptance in foreign countries where people don't trust the local stuff. Before any new form of money or electronic currency can really replace cash, it will need to provide all the services offered by old-fashioned greenbacks.

Money is not always convenient. First, for large sums it can be annoying. Second, because it is so widely accepted and leaves no audit trail, it is easy to use stolen money as one's own. And because it is easy to steal, people are reluctant to carry large amounts of it. Further, cash in your pocket may feel good, but it doesn't earn any interest. One answer to the problems of security and interest is a checking account. The money stays safely in the bank and you can use it whenever you want by writing a check. Now we are closer to what economists mean when they talk about money. Checking accounts are often called *demand deposits,* because the money is available on demand, right away now. It is liquid, meaning that it can be instantly converted to cash. There is one other form of money that is also easily used and widely accepted—traveler's checks. They are almost as well recognized as dollars, come in many of the same denominations, and in some places may even be more readily accepted. Some countries make it easier to cash traveler's checks than to change U.S. dollars for local currency. These three together—currency, checking account balances, and traveler's checks—are called M-1, or *narrow money,* by economists.

When we look at the economy and the transactions that comprise it—everything from buying a morning paper to selling a house—it is clear that a lot of money is needed to grease the wheels of commerce and keep the transactions rolling. All this money must be liquid and acceptable to everyone. M-1 fits the bill. Monetarist theories strongly emphasize the way money works and its importance to the economy. These ideas—usually associated with economists who either taught or were educated at the University of Chicago—enjoy some notoriety from time to time. Monetarism is straightforward and offers simple policy proposals, two attributes that make it popular with politicians. One of the basic ideas is wrapped up in the *quantity theory of money,* which holds that the amount of money available is related to economic growth and the price level. If the amount of money increases faster than the economy is growing, prices will rise. The catch phrase is "too much money chasing too few goods." So, if the money supply grows by 10 percent and the economy (as measured by the goods and services produced) grows by 3 percent, prices must rise by 7 percent. As with a lot of economic theories, this one turns out to be an oversimplification (not just a simplification), of the way the world works. The growth of money, the economy, and price inflation don't fit together quite as neatly as the theory would suggest.

More than currency and checking account balances can be used to keep the wheels of commerce turning. In fact, whether to keep money in cash, checking, savings, or even traveler's checks is merely a question of balancing safety, convenience, and the interest income derived from some forms of money. What passes as an easy and economical way to hold money varies from person to person and from time to time. When interest rates are high, the trouble involved in keeping money in savings accounts or even in certificates of deposit with specific maturity dates and early withdrawal penalties is offset by the interest paid. When interest rates are low, the interest isn't worth the trouble. In Table 3-1, M-2 includes a number of interest-bearing forms of money excluded from M-1. Over the last 15 to 20 years, the portion of M-2 that is not in M-1 rose and fell with changes in inflation. Because some inflation has become embedded in the economy and because restrictions on different savings accounts have decreased over time, M-2 has become an easier-to-use form of money than M-1. It is increasingly the measure that most economists use when they talk about money and the money supply.

The basic idea behind all this is that some consistency must be maintained among the rate of real (inflation-adjusted) growth, the growth in the price level, the growth in the money supply, and the change in the pace at which money is used. The last is called the *velocity of money*. Numerically, the percentage change in the money supply plus the percentage change in velocity should equal the percentage rate of real growth plus the percentage rate of inflation. If money is growing by 5 percent per year, velocity is steady, and the economy is growing by 3 percent, then inflation should be 2 percent. Most of these numbers do not change by large margins from one year to the next. If inflation is 3 percent this year, chances are very great that it will be no lower than 1 percent, or higher than 5 percent, next year. The same holds for the other measures. So here is a handy way to check on the consistency of economic forecasts and policy. If various government agency forecasts are way out of line, something is wrong. In the beginning of the 1980s the Reagan administration and Paul Volcker's Federal Reserve were on a collision course. Inflation was high—8 to 10 percent—and the Fed was sharply curtailing money growth. Either velocity would have to adjust dramatically or real growth would disappear. Although the politicians and pundits promised strong growth, velocity didn't change fast enough and a recession ensued. The inconsistency among the four key factors in the quantity equation revealed all. Unfortunately, this approach is much better at spotting a rotten forecast than making a razor-sharp forecast of its own.

Most elements of quantity theory and most economic policy analyses are based on M-2. While there is a good case to include M-2 along with M-1 in the popular definition of money, the case weakens when we get to M-3 and L. M-3 adds large (over $100,000) savings accounts and accounts that some banks or other financial institutions maintain at other banks. These are not funds likely to be used for a routine purchase. Rather, whoever owns these assets has probably made a decision to keep them in an almost-cash form for security, rather than for spending and transactions. To some extent, money in M-3 is being held for liquidity reasons, but it is pretty far from greasing the wheels of commerce.

L, which stands for *liquid assets,* also reflects liquidity concerns. It includes a lot of short-term investments that cannot be spent without first converting them into money (of the M-1 or M-2 variety). As a result, neither M-3 nor L is likely to be regarded as money in the usual sense of the word.

How the economy is performing also plays a role in determining what is and isn't money. If inflation is high and prices are rising rapidly, cash money is losing value— unless it can pay interest. Interest isn't paid on cash or on some checking accounts. Other kinds of money, such as savings accounts or money market funds, do accumulate interest and become more popular if inflation rises. When the popularity of different kinds of money changes, people shift their habits. They keep less in checking and more in savings, even if doing so may be less convenient. They carry less cash. In periods of extreme inflation—so-called hyperinflations, as in Germany during the 1920s—people plan their shopping on payday so that the money doesn't lose value overnight. Even in more moderately inflationary economies the best places to preserve value are in real assets like real estate or in commodities or even gold. These may replace money to some small extent. In the late 1970s U.S. real estate became a very popular store of value for many people.

There is a reverse trend as well: deflation. The last major deflation in the United States occurred during the Great Depression of the 1930s. But, to some extent, Japan in the first half of the 1990s suffered from deflation. Deflation turns everything on its head and is even worse than inflation. In deflation, prices fall and money grows in value by just sitting still. Interest rates may be minuscule, but cash rises in real (deflation-adjusted) value, so people earn interest for pocketing their money. The difficulty is that in periods of deflation most people are nervous and worried and do nothing but keep the cash in their pockets. When money is not put to work in commerce, the economy stalls and deflation rapidly becomes depression.

INTEREST RATES

Money today is not the same as money tomorrow or next year. Money today is worth more than money next year. It is also worth more than money tomorrow, but if this is taken literally, tomorrow is so close that we sometimes doubt that one day makes a big difference; so we talk in terms of years. The difference between money today and money next year is the interest rate. Looked at differently, how much does someone have to offer to pay you next year for you to give up $100 today? If the answer is $110, then the interest rate is $110 divided by 100, or 10 percent. Today's dollars are more valuable than next year's, since it takes more of next year's dollars to replace a given amount of today's.

Why is this true? It may be as simple as the old proverb of a bird in the hand is worth two in the bush. It may be a case of following the market. If the bank pays 10 percent interest, it makes no sense to accept less than 10 percent interest. It may be that we are implicitly comparing the growth in money to growth available in some other investment like bonds that mature, wines that age, or trees that grow. Or, since the future is uncertain and we are not sure we'll get our money back if we loan it to the bank, or to a neighbor, we want some reward for putting it at risk and waiting for a year.

Not all interest rates are the same. Economics textbooks often talk about *the* interest rate. But if you search through the financial pages of the newspaper, you may find several interest rates, all for different things done with U.S. dollars. A lot of factors determine interest rates, but when it comes to measuring what interest rates are and how much you might be paid for lending your money to someone, two points stand out. First, how good are the chances of getting your money back? If you lend it to Uncle Sam by investing in a Treasury bond, the chances of being paid back are very good. (After all, the government can always print money to pay off its debts.) If you lend out your money by buying a bond from a small company with shaky finances, you might not get your money back on time, or even at all. But you will probably be promised a lot more interest than if the borrower were the U.S. government.

When you are doing the borrowing, the same principle applies. It probably costs more for you to borrow for a home mortgage than it does for the government to borrow—even though you have to put your house on the line and the government doesn't promise anything, except maybe higher taxes. Like it or not, the government poses a better risk than you or I do. After all, it can print more money to pay off the loan, and you or I can't. Corporate borrowers also pay more than the government does for loans. In most of the 1980s, investors rushed to buy "junk bonds"—securities issued by companies with very shaky finances that offered very high rates of interest. These bonds weren't nicknamed junk for no reason. What all this means is that when you compare interest rates, it pays to check on the creditworthiness of the borrower. As a rule of thumb, interest paid by a reliable, creditworthy corporate borrower is likely to be 1 to 3 percentage points higher than the rate paid by the U.S. Treasury. Interest paid by a less than creditworthy corporation will be another 1 to 4 percentage points higher. Home mortgage rates are usually 2 to 4 percentage points above the Treasury rate—and we do have to pledge our houses as collateral if we don't pay on time.

Another key issue in borrowing is how long the loan is for. In most situations, the shorter the time period, the lower the interest rate. Thus, lending money for 1 year, yields less interest than lending it for 5 years. Why? Because a lot more can happen in 5 years and the risks are much greater than in 1 year. Of course, the risks are even less in 6 months than 1 year, and less still in a month or just overnight. Overnight lending may sound strange but banks do it all the time. Under Federal Reserve regulations, banks are required to have a certain amount of money on hand at all times. If they don't have as much as they need under the Fed's rules, they borrow it from another bank. Often the loans are done overnight. Since the time period is short and the bank's credit rating is usually fairly good, and the Federal Reserve is watching over all this, the rates tend to be very low. But even in this market, things can go awry. When they do, interest rates for the offending banks will rise quickly.

Table 3-2 shows different kinds of interest rates, the leading factors in determining them, and some typical values as of late 1996. These figures only scratch the surface of what's out there and are far from enough information to really guide an investor. Still, the table is a start to what might be worth measuring. A brief review of the data will

TABLE 3-2 Kinds of Interest Rates

Instrument	Explanation	Key Factors	Typical Level (as of 9/96) (%)
Discount rate	Rate Fed charges banks for loans	Federal Reserve policy	5–6
Fed funds	Overnight loans between banks	Federal Reserve policy	5–6
T-bill	Short-term Treasury security	Federal Reserve policy	5
10-year T-note	10-year Treasury security	Federal Reserve policy, inflation	6
"The long bond" or "The bond"	30-year Treasury security, the longest readily tradable bond	Inflation, Federal Reserve policy, strength of the economy	6–7
Prime rate	Rate banks charge good corporate customers	Bank's cost of borrowing, Federal Reserve actions	8
Adjustable mortgage	A home mortgage whose rate adjusts every year or so	Mortgage market conditions, Treasury note rates	7–9
Fixed-rate mortgage	A home mortgage whose rate is fixed for the loan life, usually 15 or 30 years	Mortgage market conditions, Treasury note rates	7–9
Corporate bond	A loan to a creditworthy corporation, most often for 10 years	Treasury rates, economic conditions, inflation	8
Junk bond	A loan to a less creditworthy corporation	Corporation's financial stability, Treasury rates	8–11
Muni bond	A bond issued by a state or local government or agency where the interest is tax free	Treasury rates, tax exemption	4–6
Credit card loan	Interest consumers pay when they borrow on their credit cards	Rarely changes	12–18
Real interest rates	The *expected* return after inflation is removed	Can't be measured directly	Probably about 3

be useful, especially when we talk about the Federal Reserve and how policy is made.

At the top are two rates which regular folks like you and me never pay but which drive the entire structure of interest rates. Both of these are controlled by the Federal Reserve and are crucial to its role in setting monetary policy. The first is the *discount rate*—the rate paid by commercial banks when they borrow directly from the Federal Reserve. While there are times when these loans are for a few months, most are for 1 or 2 days only. Periodically, the Fed will adjust the discount rate so that it is consistent with other money market rates. The adjustments are also used as a signal to the financial markets. If the Fed feels interest rates are too low, it may emphasize its point by raising the discount rate. Usually the discount rate is changed only a few times each year, and it is possible for more than a year to go by without a rate change.

While the discount rate may be the more famous figure, in the last few decades the *Fed funds rate* has been the more important. Commercial banks must keep a certain amount of money available as either cash or on deposit with the Federal Reserve. (One function of the Fed is to be a bank's bank.) The amount is a percentage of the total deposits in the bank. When a bank needs more cash to meet these reserve requirements, its first choice is usually to borrow the money from another bank. The loan is made by asking the Federal Reserve to move money between the accounts that the two banks have at the Fed. Since the funds are at the Fed, they are called Fed funds. The interest rate is determined by bargaining among the banks. When money is tight and funds available for meeting reserve requirements are limited, the Fed funds rate rises. When money is relatively easy to get and funds are plentiful, the Fed funds rate falls. The Fed can easily change the availability of funds to meet reserve requirements. By adjusting the available funds, the Fed can then "target" the Fed funds rate. On a day-to-day basis the Fed can keep the funds rate within one-eighth of a percent of its desired goal. In recent years funds rate "targeting" has been the Fed's principal tool to adjust monetary policy and manage the economy.

INTEREST-BEARING SECURITIES

The rest of the economy, including ordinary investors, can get into the act starting with the T-bills row in Table 3-1. T-bills are short-term loans to the government. Every Monday the Treasury borrows money by selling T-bills that mature (pay off) in either 91 or 182 days. Every fourth Thursday it sells 1-year T-bills. Anyone can go to a branch of a Federal Reserve bank and buy T-bills. The minimum size is $10,000. Of course, a lot of the money comes from large institutions buying in $1 million or $10 million lots. A typical auction is for $20 billion, split between 91-day and 182-day bills. Because T-bills are widely sold and traded, because everyone knows the terms of the loan, and because the government's credit is above reproach, T-bills are the benchmark rate for the short-term money markets. Most other short-term rates are set with reference to Treasury bills.

The interest rates discussed so far cover short periods of time and borrowers who should be able to pay off the loans. For better or worse, that does not include a lot of borrowers or lenders. Some borrowers want the money for longer periods of time, or represent less secure risks than the U.S. government or a major bank. Some lenders want to earn more than what can be had by investing in T-bills and are willing to bear some risks to earn those higher rewards. The federal government typically borrows short term with T-bills that last 3 or 6 months, intermediate term with T-notes that last 3, 5, 7, or 10 years, and long term with T-bonds that last 30 years. (There is no real difference between Treasury notes and bonds other than the convention that instruments of 10 years or less are usually called notes, and those of longer maturity are called bonds.) In the past few years a few corporations have sold bonds for much longer than 30 years. The Tennessee Valley Authority, a government agency, issued 50-year bonds and Walt Disney Corporation issued 100-year bonds. These long periods may be unusual today, but they once were quite common. Around the turn of the century, railroads sold debt issues that were scheduled to last 100 to 300 years. If that seems extreme, the British government paid off some of its debts from the Napoleonic wars by selling perpetual bonds that never mature. They pay interest as long as there is a British government willing to honor the bonds. These issues still trade; prices can even be found on some electronic information services.

The Treasury sells new notes and bonds several times a year at regular auctions. Prices are quoted at a percentage of "par," which is usually taken to be 100, and in thirty-seconds of a point. When you buy a Treasury bond at issue, you typically pay par or a fraction less, say $99^{16}/_{32}$. The bond will pay interest twice a year and the par amount or principal is returned to the investor on the last interest date, when the bond matures. If the interest rate is 6 percent, the bond pays $3 per half year period per $100 of par value. That $3 per half year is $6 per year, or 6 percent.

Except for the fact that most of us don't compute easily in thirty-seconds of a point, it is all pretty simple. Nothing else is straightforward about bond pricing. Possibly the most important, and often the hardest point to understand is that when interest rates go up, the prices of all bonds go *down*. And vice versa. The trick is to remember that notes and bonds have a *fixed* rate of interest. Suppose you buy a 10-year T-note paying 6 percent interest at par. A month goes by and interest rates have risen. If you buy another 10-year note, it would now pay a higher rate of interest (say, 7 percent) and would sell at par. The 7 percent note should be worth more than the old note paying only 6 percent. Since the price of the new note is par, the price of the old one will fall.

How far will the price fall? The new note offers a return of 7 percent over its 10-year life. The price on the old note will fall until it, too, can offer a return of 7 percent over its remaining life. (Since the old note is now a 9-year, 11-month instrument instead of a 10-year note, the price will adjust slightly to reflect the shorter life.) To convert to numbers, you can either work out the mathematics or get a bond calculator. Even the pros use computers or calculators, not the pencil-and-paper method. The reason is that bonds trade daily and interest rates change. The time has long since passed when investors bought bonds and locked them away in the vault for up to 50 years.

BOND PRICES

Over the last 15 years, as the space program wound down after the excitement of the moon landings and the end of the cold war meant less defense spending on research, the rocket scientists shifted to Wall Street. What attracted them, besides the money, was the mathematics of bond pricing. While the basic pricing formulas have been around for decades, if not centuries, the development of computers has made all kinds of analyses practical for the investor and fast enough for the bond trader.

A bond is a promise to make regular payments in the future. Further, a dollar today is worth more than a dollar next year, and the answer to "How much more?" is the interest rate. The price of a bond is the value of all those promised future payments. The longer in the future they are, the less they are worth today. When the interest rate changes, the value of all those future payments change. As we saw, higher interest rates mean that a dollar today has a bigger premium compared with a dollar tomorrow. In other words, tomorrow's dollar is worth less. Consequently, the price of the bond will fall.

Figuring out how much it will fall for different kinds of changes in interest rates is a challenge in itself. To complicate matters, many bond investors use the income they get from bonds to buy more bonds. Now, if interest rates rise, forcing the price of bonds down, investors lose money. But because of the higher interest rates, when investors reinvest the income from those bonds they get a better return on their money. One of the interesting mathematical questions is whether the losses from falling bond prices can be balanced against the gains from rising returns on reinvested income. The answer, called immunizing bonds against the impact of changing interest rates, is yes. This, and many other variations of pricing bonds, as well as futures options and those infamous derivatives, have kept the rocket scientists busy on Wall Street.

(Continued)

Bonds trade because their prices change and people believe they can profit by buying bonds now (if they think the price will rise) or selling bonds now (if they expect the price to fall). Not all investors are likely to be right at the same time, but they will keep trading. One factor that plays a major role in setting the prices at which bonds trade is *credit risk*. Credit risk is how confident investors are that the bond issuer will pay interest and principal on time. If the bond issuer is the U.S. government, most investors will assume that the government will absolutely pay on time. For large, well-known, and profitable corporations selling bonds, there is also a high probability that the interest and principal will be paid on time. But investors don't have to examine the details of every bond issuer around; they can look at the bond rating. Bond ratings are expert opinions of whether the bond will pay interest on time.

Consider three kinds of bonds in terms of creditworthiness: U.S. Treasuries, investment-grade securities, and junk.

BOND RATINGS

For investors, a key question is whether the company or government that issued a bond will pay the interest and the principal on time. Traditionally, the biggest risk in buying a bond has been that the issuer would go out of business or vanish before payments were made. Stories are told about Imperial Russian war bonds and other infamous (or even fictitious) issuers, and even about investors who used worthless bonds as wallpaper. The chance that a bond issuer will fail is called credit risk. Of course, such risk is not limited to bonds. If you apply for a mortgage, the bank will check to see if you have enough income to make the payments—if you're credit-worthy.

A typical investor doesn't have the time or information to make a thorough review of the creditworthiness of a company or a government before buying a bond. But to a large extent the investor doesn't have to. In the United States virtually all corporate and municipal bonds have ratings, which look a little like school grades. The best is AAA, then comes AA+, and on down to BBB− , and then to BB, and into the C's. The lowest rating is a D—for default, not an F for failure—although it means the same thing. The rating is the result of a detailed review of the bond's creditworthiness performed by a rating agency. The two leading U.S. rating agencies are Standard & Poor's and Moody's.

Rating agencies are paid fees by the bond issuers for publishing their ratings. The fee depends on how complicated the issue is and how much work is involved. The success of the rating agency depends on its reputation; it will remain in business only as long as the financial markets and investors trust its analysis and ratings. The absolute need for this trust ensures that the rating agency will do its best.

Bond ratings are often divided into two broad categories: investment grade and junk. In some states, regulations prohibit certain investors, such as insurance or pension funds, from buying junk bonds. But junk bonds may not be quite as bad as their name suggests. At the other end of the scale, U.S. Treasuries are backed by the federal government and have an AAA rating.

(*Continued*)

JUNK BONDS

The takeover madness of the 1980s featured a seemingly new instrument in the financial markets: junk bonds, issued by companies with far less than gold-plated blue-chip credentials and with very questionable chances of meeting the bonds' principal and interest payments on time. Actually, junk bonds have been around for decades, but only in rather obscure form. Until about 1980 almost all junk bonds were "fallen angels"—securities that had once been respectable investment-grade issues until the issuer fell on hard times and the bonds were downgraded to junk status. For a diligent investor who took the time to research junk bonds, there might be some unrecognized jewels waiting to be rediscovered and upgraded to investment level. These could be very rewarding investments.

Two things came along to change the image and role of junk bonds. First, financial research showed that junk bonds weren't as disastrous an investment as most people thought. In fact, if an investor purchased a portfolio of a number of issues, the hidden jewels would more than offset the truly junklike bonds and the investor would make money. That way, the returns on the jewels would pay for the whole portfolio with ease. Once it became clear that junk bonds might have some value, all that was needed was a market. In the fallen-angel days, trading was limited to a relatively small club of pros who did most of their business among themselves. What was needed was a market where one would be ready and willing to buy or sell junk bonds.

About the same time, there was increasing interest

in a kind of corporate takeover called a *leveraged buy-out* (LBO). In an LBO, a group of investors (later called corporate raiders) choose a company to buy—ideally, a company with very little debt and some well-hidden or at least supposed value. Then they borrow money from investment bankers and buy the company. Of course, the bankers want to be paid back. So the raiders issue bonds for the company they just bought and use the proceeds to pay off the bankers. Since the bonds probably stretched the company thin and raised more money than what any reasonable or prudent investor would borrow, the bonds usually got a junk rating. Selling the bonds required an underwriter and a market for junk.

In the competition for LBO business, one investment bank led the way to underwriting junk bonds and making more LBOs possible. The bank was Drexel Burnham Lambert, piloted by junk bond king Michael Milken. The original idea behind the bonds was to polish a company's hidden assets and do an equity offering—sell stock to the public and use the proceeds to pay off the bonds. There were relatively few LBO round trips: Many companies vanished, even though diversified junk bond portfolios did pay off for a lot of investors. In later years, Milken and junk bonds became mired in turmoil, with insider-trading scandals and criminal lawsuits brought by the federal government. Eventually the combination of LBOs and junk bonds collapsed and was finished off with the stock market crash of 1987. Still, the legacy lives on. Mutual funds specializing in junk bonds are a successful part of the industry today.

(*Continued*)

U.S. Treasuries are presumed to be of the highest credit quality. After all, the government can always print money to pay off its debts. This argument isn't precisely true, but almost. Certainly there should not be much doubt about the ability of the government to meet its obligations in its own currency. Investment-grade bonds are a bit less secure than Treasuries, but still quite reliable. These are usually broken into a series of ratings categories, from AAA (for the best) to D (for default). Junk bonds are far from a sure thing. Many junk bonds turn out to earn their name and do not pay in anything close to a timely fashion. It should be no surprise that the market usually demands higher interest rates on lower credit issues. For a given maturity or lifetime of the bond, Treasuries offer the best security and the lowest returns, investment-grade the next, and junk the last.

Another important factor in bond pricing is the *maturity* of the bond. Think about two different investments—both in Treasury notes, so that credit risk is not an issue. One is for 3 years and the other is for 10 years. The difference is how long until the principal—the money you put up—comes back to you. In the case of the 3-year note, it is a relatively short time and all the payments are fairly close to today. There is less time for interest rates to rise and for your investment's price to sink than with the 10-year note. Less time for something strange to happen to price translates into less risk. So the 3-year note typically offers a lower yield or rate of interest than does the 10-year note.

Because Treasuries are as close to being free of credit risk as anything and because the market for them is very liquid, they are a benchmark for most other interest rates in the economy. A liquid market means you can buy or sell a Treasury quickly and easily without having your transaction change the price. The opposite is true when selling a house. You bargain extensively before a single sale and the price depends on your bargaining and that sale. Further, houses are seldom sold quickly. The market for selling a house is not liquid; the investment in your home is not a source of liquidity. In the Treasury market, where literally billions of dollars change hands daily, one trade rarely moves the price much.

When you go to the bank for a mortgage loan, the bank decides on the loan rate by looking at the Treasury market. The T-note figures show what the yield is for a bond the same maturity as the mortgage—with one proviso. The average 30-year mortgage loan lasts less than the 30 years because homeowners may sell the house or refinance the loan. Further, in today's financial markets, the bank probably won't hold the loan until it is paid off. Rather, the bank will sell the loan to another firm which will package it for resale as part of a "mortgage-backed" bond. The price of that bond is figured by looking at Treasury notes of similar maturities and making an adjustment for credit risks, for differing payment schedules, and for the chance that the loan will be paid off before the end of its 30-year life. Mortgage lenders aren't the only ones using the Treasury market as a benchmark. When an investment bank brings a new corporate bond to market, it bases the price of the bond on the Treasury market.

Because of its widespread use as a benchmark, the Treasury market is a good place to look for indicators of the economy. Rising, or falling, yields on 10-year T-notes are a good guide to trends in mortgage rates and the future condition of the housing and home-building industries. The level of T-bill rates (for 3- to 6-month instruments) tells a lot about short-term borrowing costs and the state of the economy. If T-bill rates are high, chances are that many investors will keep their money in short-term investments rather than the stock market. Stock prices are much less likely to rise when short-term rates are high. Moreover, high short-term rates mean that short-term loans are expensive and may be avoided by many borrowers, including business.

When business does borrow money for short time periods, the two most common sources are bank loans and the "paper" market. Traditionally bank loans have been based on the prime rate—an interest rate that the banks announced from time to time. The best customers paid prime; lesser customers paid more, such as "prime plus 2," meaning 2 percentage points more than the prime rate. While changes in the prime rate still make headlines, it is less widely used as a benchmark today. In the last two decades more and more corporations have turned to direct borrowing in the securities markets. To remain competitive, banks have found it necessary to price loans by using a market rate (usually the Fed funds rate) as the benchmark rather than a rate they establish themselves. The differences in borrowing costs are probably rather small.

Even so, more and more corporations borrow in the money markets rather than only from banks. The corporations sell short-term debt, called *commercial paper,* to investors. Some large corporations that are frequent borrowers will set up their own programs to borrow money directly from large institutional investors like pension funds and money market funds. Other corporations will work through a commercial paper dealer, often a major investment bank, to borrow from large investors. The typical loan can involve hundreds of thousands or even a few million dollars. It is not a place for the average investor to put away a few dollars each week.

WHAT THE RATES TELL US

For most of us, the various interest-paying securities in the economy have two related uses. First, they represent possible investments, either directly or through mutual funds or pension plans. As potential investors, we want to understand the safety, the return, and the tax treatment of a bond or other investment. At the same time, the interest rates can tell us a lot about the economy and what is going on in the financial markets. When we look at interest rates as a way to see what's happening in the economy we tend to look at three things: how high or low they are, whether the rates are rising or falling, and what the differences are between certain key pairs of rates. The last measure is often called the *spread,* as in the spread between junk and investment-grade bonds.

Rising or falling rates can tell us something about the economy's strength and about attitudes at the Federal reserve. Normally, falling interest rates suggest that the economy is either slumping or just emerging from a slump and that the central bank is trying to encourage growth. This hint that economic conditions could be better (and may get better) is usually a very strong plus for the stock market. Rising interest rates typically point to a strong economy that is on a roll. They suggest that people and businesses are borrowing money. Most of the time investors borrow because they are optimistic about the future and expect to be able to repay the loans easily. Saving for a rainy day is not part of the American economy. Spending and borrowing when times are good is.

How high is high? It is often difficult to say whether interest rates are very high or very low at any given moment. At the start of the 1980s interest rates reached heights that hadn't been seen since the Civil War. The prime rate touched 22 percent, and 30-year Treasuries paid coupon interest of 14 percent. (That bond issue, still outstanding, and is due in November 2011. Its early 1997 price was around $150^{20}/_{32}$, and it yielded 6.95 percent.) Over the next decade interest rates came down, though with some interruptions. Obviously, since interest rates can't fall below zero, the wonderful idea of ever-lower interest rates can't go on forever. But everything is relative. In the early to mid-1990s we reached levels which were considered to be *high* in the late 1950s. So what seems high may be low, and what seems low may be high. The lesson here, for both economists and investors, is this: Investors who started looking at bonds only in the 1980s should not think they experienced an average period. The 1980s were the single best decade for bond investors in this century.

There is another way to judge how high is high or how low is low. We can remove inflation from interest rates and look at what the bond pays after adjusting for changes in the value of money. If we subtract the inflation rate from the bond yield, we have the return after inflation is netted out, sometimes called the *real interest rate*. Economists use the word *real* to mean that inflation and the impact of changing money values are excluded from the measure. Real interest rates may not be more stable than regular interest rates, but their typical range is smaller and more telling. A real interest rate calculated for a 10-year Treasury is usually around 2 to 3 percent. If it is under 2 percent or even negative, there is probably a lot more inflation than anyone expected, and bond holders may be about to lose their shirts. If you calculate a negative real rate on your bonds, check the numbers. If the numbers are right, sell the bonds. If real rates are really high, 5 percent or more, the economy is probably sliding downhill. Bonds may be very attractive with unusually good real returns, but stocks should be looked at skeptically unless interest rates have begun to fall. Unfortunately, these rules are not flawless guides.

Spreads between interest rates can tell a lot. The spread shows the relative value of one kind of instrument or investment over another. Take the difference between junk bonds and investment-grade corporate bonds. Because the difference reflects the quality or a company's creditworthiness, it is sometimes called a quality spread. In good times when everyone is prospering, investors worry less about weaker companies going bankrupt. The extra borrowing costs for weaker companies are relatively small. The difference between AA and BB bonds may be only 2 to 3 percentage points. But in a recession, when everything looks like it is collapsing, this spread could easily double or even triple. Watching the spread between investment-grade bonds and junk can tell you how much the markets fear economic recession and bankruptcy.

Spreads between short-term and long-term issues are another key indicator. They can reveal a lot about government policy and the strength of the economy. When the spread between T-bills and 10-year T-notes is half a percent or less, policy is probably trying to slow the economy to restrain inflation. When the spread is over 2 percentage points, policy is trying to spur growth. Pro-growth policies usually make for better stock markets. Chapter Eight examines the yield curve and how it can be used as a crystal ball for the economy.

INFLATION

Almost anyone can tell a tale of how years ago everything was cheaper. Part of the tale that is often forgotten is that years ago wages and salaries were smaller too. Nevertheless, the value of money does change over time. Inflation is how we measure and talk about changes in the value of money. We start by defining something called the price level, which is what things cost right now. Inflation is the rate of change in the price level. If prices go up by 10 percent in a year, we have inflation of 10 percent. That sounds high these days. But in many Eastern European nations, and in parts of Latin America, inflation rates have reached 10 percent or more *per month*. Even in the United States, we have seen some high numbers within recent memory. During the late 1970s, when the economy was reeling from the OPEC oil shocks, inflation settled firmly into "double digits" above 10 percent and almost touched 20 percent for a while.

More recently, the way we measure inflation has become an issue. Inflation measures are often used to adjust different payments to neutralize the impact of inflation. Social security payments, income tax rates, and wages under some union contracts are all adjusted for inflation. What a price index counts, and doesn't count, makes a difference. Like many other economic measures, inflation can be a guide to future events. If inflation is high or rising, real estate is often a far better investment than bonds. But if inflation is coming down, bonds are more attractive. Stocks also behave differently depending on the inflation rate, but in more subtle ways.

The two most widely followed price indexes in the United States are the consumer price index (CPI) and the producer price index (PPI). Old-timers may remember the producer price index as the wholesale price index. The CPI and the PPI are set up on the same general basis but cover different things, as their names imply.

The Consumer Price Index

The items measured by a price index comprise its market basket. For the CPI there is a market basket of goods and services. The basket is based on surveys of consumer expenditures conducted by the federal government. Because our buying habits change, the CPI should be revised every few years to keep it up to date. For example, 5 or 10 years ago, relatively few people had home computers. Nowadays, almost a third of American households have computers. If the market basket weren't updated, it would not take into account computers, software, and services like Compuserve and America Online. The market basket also specifies how much of total spending goes to each different item. Since on average we spend almost nothing on caviar, it doesn't matter much if the price goes up by 300 or 400 percent. But most of us spend a lot of money for energy—electricity for our house, gasoline for the car, maybe natural gas for cooking or heating. If energy prices rise by 10 percent, that can make a big difference to our finances. The market basket for the CPI is extensive and covers well over 100 items, assembled into major groups. (There is a separate price index for each item or group of items, so the CPI isn't really one number. Rather, it is a system of indexes.)

When the newspapers headline "Consumer Prices Rise Scant 0.1 Percent in October," there are pages and pages of supporting data, including price changes in major spending categories and various details. For many years the price index for medical care always climbed faster than the overall CPI. If consumer prices rose 5 percent in a year, medical care rose 8 or 10 percent. In the CPI details, one can see how much of that increase is for drugs, for hospitalization, and for doctor's fees. When oil prices surge because of political turmoil in the Mideast, the CPI will show how much the average American household budget will be put into its own turmoil.

Clearly one of the difficulties with the CPI is how accurate the market basket is. If the market basket is out of date and doesn't reflect what Americans spend their money on, it won't reveal how much damage inflation is doing. This might seem like a minor annoyance, but it isn't. Government economic policy is based on the CPI and similar measures. If the CPI ignores areas where prices are falling and gives too much weight to areas where prices are rising, it will overstate inflation. What if the Federal Reserve misunderstands the CPI and raises interest rates to curtail this phantom inflation? The higher interest rates slow the economy and dampen job creation. Those slightly incorrect numbers are suddenly very expensive. This may seem farfetched, but it is a key topic in congress's semiannual review of Federal Reserve policy.

The market basket raises some other issues as well. Even if the CPI's basket of goods is perfect, it is right only for that mythical average American family with 2.2 children, 2.4 cars, and 0.4 pets. Almost certainly, the market basket doesn't reflect what *you* spend each month. Even though there are actually two complete market baskets—the CPI-U and the CPI-W—your spending is not quite the same. This can be an issue when we use the CPI to adjust for inflation. The CPI is used to adjust social security payments once a year to keep up with inflation. Social security payments go to people over 65 years old. The way senior citizens spend their incomes is different from the way the average American family spends its income. For instance, senior citizens probably spend more on health care and less on children's clothes. There are certainly many other differences. Yet the average American's market basket is being used to adjust the senior citizen's social security payment. Some mistakes are almost certain. Who comes out ahead is not clear, although most analysts think the understatement of how important health care in the average senior citizen's budget is a key factor. In any event, if the idea of adjusting social security for inflation is to protect senior citizens from the damage of rising prices and be fair to everyone, we are missing the mark.

Other difficulties with the CPI have to do with the way price indexes are constructed. Once the government has determined what the market basket is, the Bureau of Labor Statistics sends out data collectors who go through stores recording prices. They figure out what it costs to buy the market basket. The data are collected and a new cost for the market basket is determined each month. The monthly cost of the market basket is used to build the CPI by selecting a base period (currently the average value for 1982–1984) and then dividing each monthly number by the base period. Table 3-3 shows how this works and what the inflation rate would be for a hypothetical market basket.

An obvious problem is that the same market basket is used each month, based on what people bought in the first year or base period for the index. What we buy changes over time and with the seasons—swimsuits and sunglasses in June and July, skis and snow parkas in November. These seasonal shifts are handled statistically. But the more important shifts are changes in what is available and in our overall spending habits. The increasing availability of CDs rather than records and audio tapes, rental videos instead of movie theaters, and frozen pizzas rather than home delivery—all affect our purchasing patterns. Over a year or more, these changes begin to add up. But the CPI market basket is frozen as it was in the base year.

Table 3-3. Sample Price Index

Date	Market Basket Costs	Index	Monthly Percentage Change
January 1996	$4,000.00	100.00	—
February 1996	4,012.00	100.30	0.3
March 1996	4,020.02	100.50	0.2
April 1996	4,036.10	100.90	0.4
May 1996	4,028.03	100.70	−0.2
June 1996	4,032.06	100.80	0.1
July 1996	4,044.16	101.10	0.3
August 1996	4,052.24	101.31	0.2
September 1996	4,048.19	101.20	−0.1
October 1996	4,064.38	101.61	0.4
November 1996	4,076.58	101.91	0.3
December 1996	4,084.73	102.12	0.2
January 1997	4,105.15	102.63	0.5
February 1997	4,109.26	102.73	0.1
March 1997	4,117.48	102.94	0.2
April 1997	4,125.71	103.14	0.2

The biggest problem with the frozen market basket is the way we respond to changing prices. As personal computer prices fell and prices for televisions, stereos, and other home entertainment equipment remained almost stable, consumers began to shift their buying to computers. All of us watched the prices and used our hard-earned dollars more effectively to satisfy our desires. We kept the old TV but bought a new computer. We subscribed to an online service and dropped our magazine subscriptions. If gasoline prices fell but airline bargains were harder to find, we even considered buying a bigger car and driving to vacation spots instead of flying. All these changes, in response to price fluctuations, affect the quantities of things we buy. We are smart enough to get the best bang for our bucks. But the CPI doesn't reflect our wisdom, because the index uses the market basket of what *we used* to buy. This kind of error means the CPI overstates inflation. It presumes that we continue buying things that become more expensive and do not switch to buying more of things that get cheaper. The problem is in the way the CPI is concocted.

This problem is well known in economics and even has a name, the index number problem. If the market basket is the base period (known in economics as a Laspeyre index), the index overstates inflation. If, instead, the basket is the current period (a Paasche index), the index understates inflation. (Using the current period for the market basket also means that every month we need to recalculate the entire history of the index, because how much is spent on each thing changes. This task is rather onerous, even with fast computers.)

There are seasonal changes not only in how we spend our money but also in prices. Snow shovels are cheap in March and April because the hardware shop doesn't want to store them over the summer. These seasonal changes can be caught and adjusted for by various mathematical devices. But some seasonal shifts are difficult to capture.

Easter, for example—which follows a lunar calendar and has no set timing—affects a lot of consumer spending and tends to confuse some of the data. Similarly, the "end of the school year" creates difficulties for such data as unemployment figures, which include students looking for summer jobs. But these problems are different from the index number construction that leads the CPI to overstate inflation.

The CPI is sometimes called the cost of living—probably a misnomer. The index does tell us what the average American family's market basket of the base year would cost today. It doesn't tell us how much it costs, or how much more it costs, to live well in the United States than it did a year ago.

Now that you have waded through the theory of the CPI, there are a couple of practical issues that can help in understanding monthly consumer prices reports. Suppose you read in the paper that inflation is about 3 percent. The next day the CPI is released, and the press reports that economists are concerned because the CPI rose 0.4 percent compared with an expected rise of 0.2 percent. What gives? Isn't 0.4 percent a lot lower than 3 percent? Obviously, the CPI is being quoted as a monthly percentage change. But most of us think in terms of annual rates, like a money fund that yields 5 percent per year. The inflation rate of 3 percent is an annual figure. One way to compare the 0.4 percent monthly rise with the 3 percent rate is to annualize the 0.4 percent figure by compounding the rate. That is, 0.4 percent is an annual rate of 4.8 percent. Now we know why the economists were worried: Inflation jumped from 3 to 4.8 percent—almost 5 percent—in a month.

ANNUAL RATES AND COMPOUNDING

When we examine inflation rates or interest rates from different countries, it is important to compare like periods of time. Two percent per month may sound like less than 10 percent per year, but we can see why it would be a lot more. If you simply add 2 percent each month for a year, you reach 24 percent. But it is even a bit more than that, because the 2 percent each month compounds on the previous month. Suppose you start with a price of $10 and it rises at 2 percent per month. A month later it is $10.20. A month after that it is $10.40. After another month it is $10.61, and after a year it is $12.68, not $12.40. At 2 percent per month for only a year, compounding makes very little difference. But over long periods of time compounding makes all the difference in the world. An investment of $1000 compounded annually at 10 percent per year is $6,727.50 after 20 years. Without compounding, it would be $3000.

Because it is important to compare percentages over the same period of time, many economic calculations use "annual rates." Numbers and growth rates are stated as the amount that would occur over a period of 1 year. Percentages—inflation, interest, economic growth, and so forth—are all stated as the amount over a 1 year period. If we convert from one time period to another, the rates are compounded. For instance, a growth rate of 2 percent per quarter is compounded to 8.24 percent per year. The calculation to annualize a quarterly rate is:

$$[1 + (2\% \div 100)]^4 = 1.0824$$

$$(1.0824 - 1) \times (100) = 8.24\%$$

If the calculation is being done between monthly and annual data, the exponent 4 is replaced with 12. The reverse can also be done. Suppose we have a rate of 10 percent per year and we want to know what the quarterly equivalent is. It is a bit less than 2.5 percent:

$$[1 + (10\% \div 100]^{(1/4)} = 1.0241$$

$$(1.0241 - 1) \times (100) = 2.41\%$$

All these fractional exponents are easily handled on most calculators. Again, the 4 can be replaced by a 12 to handle monthly data.

There is another situation in which annual rates are important. Amounts other than percentages are often stated in that way. It is common to read a news report claiming that last month's housing starts ran at an annual rate of 1.2 million. That does *not* mean that 14.4 million (12 times 1.2 million) houses were started in the United States last year. Rather, it means that if the monthly rate continued for a year, there would be 1.2 million houses started. The same is true of the quarterly GDP numbers, which are always stated as quarterly data at annual rates. This may seem like an odd way to handle data, but it has its advantages. Suppose you are looking at data for April and you want to know if the economy is growing faster or slower than a year ago. Which line for housing starts would you use?

	1994	1995	1996 1st Qtr.	April
Annual rate	1.446	1.358	1.469	1.511
Annual, quarterly, and monthly rate	1.446	1.358	0.367	0.126

(Continued)

One other important calculation is often made with annual rates. The numbers are "seasonally adjusted." Everyone knows that more toys are sold around Christmastime, that almost no houses are built in Maine or North Dakota in January, and that air conditioners sell best in spring and summer. A statistically based computer routine is used to calculate what the month-to-month (or quarter-to-quarter) change due to the calendar would be. The size of the change is usually based on the last 3 to 5 years of data. This way we can tell whether the increase in housing starts from January to June is due merely to the warmer weather or to a strong housing market. Beware that sometimes the results sound strange. We might say that, *before seasonal adjustment*, housing starts fell from a monthly rate of 20,000 to 38,000 from January to June. The idea is that, if adjusted for the seasons, the number would have gone down. This is so nonsensical that seasonally adjusted annual rates are commonly used.

(Continued)

Or did it? Inflation reports can bounce around a bit, and measuring things in tenths of a percent may disguise or lose sight of some small changes. An increase of 0.4 percent might really be 0.36 before any rounding off, or almost half a percent lower than the annualized 4.8 percent it seems to represent. More importantly, the 0.4 percent may be a 1-month blip that will be reversed next month. Often some volatile item, such as fresh vegetables, will spike upward 1 month and then collapse the next. The monthly reports could be up 0.4 percent, up 0.1 percent, and then up 0.2 percent. Annualized, this looks like a roller coaster: 4.8 percent, 1.2 percent, and then 2.4 percent. To smooth out the roller coaster, many people measure annual inflation rates as the change over the last 12 months. The advantage of this method is that some of the random bumps are flattened out. One problem is that if the inflation rate is truly changing very rapidly, the sliding 12-month approach will tend to turn up, or down, a bit after the inflation pattern actually shifts.

The CPI isn't the only inflation measure. Sometimes it is the best one to use; other times it isn't. If you want to see whether consumers are better off, comparing inflation as measured on the CPI to wage increases is a good way to go. But if you're looking at a business and want to see if its price increases are keeping up with changes in raw materials costs, the CPI may be a very poor choice. Part of the art of measuring the economy is to use the right tool. Two inflation measures that are built in a similar way are producer prices and the employment cost index. Another measure, built quite differently, is the GDP deflator. Some commodity prices are also used as measures of inflation. We will look at each of these in turn.

The Producer Price Index

The PPI refers to producer or wholesale prices. The construction is similar to that of the CPI, with market baskets and weights based on a single base year. The producer price index is divided into three broad categories related to different steps in the manufacturing cycle: raw materials (such as crude oil or timber), intermediate materials (petroleum feed stocks or lumber), and finished goods (lubricants or wooden crates and barrels). While some of the finished goods are things consumers buy, the prices reflect wholesale and distributor transactions, not retail purchases. Moreover, a number of service items included in the CPI—travel costs, medical care, school tuition, and so forth—never appear in the PPI. Producer prices tend to be more volatile than consumer prices, but often see smaller rises than consumer prices over several months or longer. Overall moves in producer prices are not a good leading indicator of consumer prices trends. However, in some narrowly defined sectors, such as oil and gasoline, movements in producer prices will foreshadow consumer price moves.

Another price index of some interest is the employment cost index (ECI). Published quarterly by the Bureau of Labor Statistics, the same agency that does the CPI and PPI, the ECI measures how much it costs to hire a worker. The index reflects the employer's perspective and includes wages or salaries, social security taxes, and other benefit costs. The ECI is broken into sectors, like the other indexes. In the ECI's case it is not health care, transportation, and energy (as in the CPI) or finished, intermediate, and crude goods (as in the PPI). The ECI shows employment cost trends for private sector versus public sector, for union versus nonunion, and for white collar versus blue collar. The ECI is one place to look for some hints on why employment is growing faster or slower.

Now, step outside the confines of index number systems for a different approach. Gross domestic product (GDP) measures the total value of what is produced in the economy. As we will see below, the details of the measurement are not always transparent. The GDP yields a measurement not only of the overall economy but also of price.

Gross Domestic Product

Toward the end of 1995 the process for measuring GDP was revamped, largely to eliminate many of the biases discussed earlier with the CPI. The idea was to use a moving base year rather than be a prisoner of the way the economy worked in some frozen arbitrary period. For the GDP two sets of output indexes are calculated. The first is a measure of the total value of output without any inflation adjustment. This index reflects the value of goods and services produced each year in that year's dollars. If inflation reduces the value of a buck, it won't get reflected in this index. The second output index reflects changes in quantities produced but excludes changes caused by prices. It is created by calculating the percentage change in production from one year to the next using prices averaged over the two years. These annual changes are strung together to build an index.

The ratio of the first index (before any inflation adjustment) to the second index (which excludes inflation) gives us an inflation index. It is often called the *implicit price deflator,* because it is implied by the rest of the GDP calculations and it can deflate, or remove inflation, from GDP estimates. One advantage of this unusual approach is that there is no bias from whatever was chosen as the base year because the base year is always moving. Also, it reflects the entire economy in proportion to the size of each part of the economy. There is no worry about measuring stuff that makes little difference. Possibly because the implicit price deflator is hard to fathom, the GDP also includes measures that look a lot like the CPI or the PPI. These are interesting, but add less to the complete picture than the implicit price deflator does.

Commodities Prices

Specially developed indexes are not the only inflation measures worth looking at. Some of us may remember the two oil crises of the 1970s. In 1973 and again in 1979, oil prices doubled and then almost doubled again. To a large extent the jumps in oil prices explain a lot of what happened to the economy and the financial world in the 1970s and the 1980s. Simply measuring oil prices can be very important as part of an inflation early-warning system.

To most of us, oil is oil is oil, and the only different kinds of gasoline are regular and premium. But to the oil trade, oil is not just oil and there are many many varieties. To measure oil prices, we need to choose a few benchmark varieties of oil and follow those prices. The high cost of shipping also has to be considered. Many of us have experienced buying gasoline cheaper in a major industrial center near refineries than in some remote vacation spot where gasoline is trucked in. (Of course, competition, taxes and knowing where to find a cheaper gas station may also play a role.) Because of the shipping costs, oil prices are identified by both the specific chemistry of the kind of oil and its location. West Texas Intermediate is crude oil available at production fields in western Texas. Intermediate refers to the sulfur content. In some areas where air pollution is a problem, regulations require that only low-sulfur oil be used. Another common benchmark is Saudi Light, referring to a particular grade of oil produced in Saudi Arabia. A third is Brent, referring to oil produced in the North Sea. Brent is often priced FOB Rotterdam, Holland, a major oil-trading and shipping center in Europe.*

Oil prices are reported in various newspapers and news services and are compiled and published by the U.S. Department of Energy. While the price of crude oil is the best guide to how oil prices may be playing havoc with the economy, some measures of refined products—such as

---

*FOB stands for freight on board. The term means that the price includes all fees and expenses that must be paid before the oil is loaded on a tanker.

home heating oil, gasoline, aviation fuel, and residual fuel oil—may be useful for other purposes.

Oil is not the only commodity that can be used to track inflation. In fact, at one time or another, most any commodity has been used. There are a few of specific interest that seem to crop up more often than most. One is food prices. Certainly food is important. When oil prices were creating turmoil for the economy in the 1970s, food prices weren't too far behind. But in more recent years food price inflation has been less of an issue in the United States, though unfortunately not in many other nations. Lumber prices are often cited as an indicator of home-building activity and important to the economy. Another measure is liner board, used in corrugated boxes. Some analysts argue that when the economy booms and production rises, there is a shortage of boxes and liner board prices climb.

The oldest of all commodities as an inflation measure is gold. Gold is probably more mystical than reasonable as an inflation gauge. Outside of its political, psychological, and mystical role, it plays a very small part in our economy. But gold is still widely used as an inflation yardstick. If any of the measures noted above—the CPI, the PPI, the GDP deflator, or even employment costs—is anywhere close to the right inflation measure, gold is probably very far wrong.

Once upon a time, monetary policy was based on gold, and money—dollars—were convertible into gold bullion or coins on demand. In the United States, that ended in 1934. In fact, from 1934 to 1973 American citizens were not permitted to own gold bullion, although coins and jewelry were legal. Part of gold's mystique comes from that part of its history. Part also comes from the idea that it is the ultimate store of value. All this may make some sense, but gold today does not play a big enough role in the economy for its price to be a crucial driving force. In recent years investors have made more money, and made it with more safety, in such bits of paper finance as the Standard & Poor's 500 or Treasury bills. Gold has proved to be a bad bet. As a measure of inflation, gold is at best misleading. Nevertheless, its mystique is not likely to vanish soon and it will continue to be widely followed and discussed.

When we opened the discussion of inflation we talked about moments in history when inflation soared tens or hundreds of percent per month. In the last 20 years, various countries in Latin America and Eastern Europe have suffered such price increases. At various times currencies have been renamed and rebased in efforts at resuscitation. These bouts often end in failed governments as well as failed economic policies. If rampant or hyperinflation is disastrous, deflation can be almost as terrifying. In a deflation, prices fall and money—cash—gets ever more valuable. In inflationary times, people search out real assets, keep as little money as possible in bank accounts, and rush to spend before money loses value. In a deflationary period, everyone hoards cash and buys nothing. You get richer just for biding your time.

But don't think that deflation is the way to go. The economy will quickly grind to a halt as no one spends any money or buys much of anything at all. Deflations become a ticket to recession and depression. The last substantial deflation in the United States was during the Great Depression of the 1930s. Prices fell, wages were cut, and money rose in value by just sitting there—no one spent any money or invested. The result was a massive collapse and unemployment rates reported (probably underreported) at 25 percent.

Is there any right inflation rate? Probably nothing precise, but a reasonable target is a rate between 0 and 3 percent per year. To some extent, inflation targets are a case of the grass is always greener in some other pasture. Ignoring inflation is as hazardous as developing a fixation on it to the exclusion of all other policy issues. We have seen both happen in the United States in the last two or three decades. Hopefully, being able to measure inflation will limit the hysteria.

STOCK PRICES

Thus far, we have seen how much poorer we can get by letting our money gather dust in the bureau draw during an inflation. Now we will turn to seeing how much richer, or poorer, we may get by investing in the stock market. Stock market reports seem to be second only to the weather forecast as a staple of the evening news. Both the market and the weather have enjoyed a technological revolution in the last two decades. Once upon a time, the weather forecasters made do with a few temperature and rainfall observations collected by calling colleagues in other cities or reading the National Weather Service bulletins. Now the weather reports sport satellite photos and three-dimensional radar and computer projections. Stock market reporting and forecasting have also enjoyed the fruits of technology. The only hitch is that whereas weather forecasting may have improved and become more accurate, the stock market remains a gamble.

The stock market is fascinating. Probably many more people find stocks exciting than find the weather even mildly interesting. By watching stocks or investing some money, we can feel virtuous about planning for the future and saving for a rainy day while simultaneously getting a bit of a gambler's thrill. Winning is always more fun than losing, and looking at the market's long-term trends suggests that winners tend to be more plentiful than losers. Since 1926—through the Depression, a number of market crashes, and several wars—the stock market has given investors a long-term return of close to 10 percent per year (or even 6.6 percent after inflation is removed). And since money is closer to stocks than to the weather, stocks make better cocktail conversation too.

KEEPING SCORE

In any great challenge, keeping score is important. Stock prices and compilations of stock prices into averages and indexes are how we keep score in the market. Ask a reporter what the market did and he will quote the change in the Dow-Jones Industrials (known more simply as "the Dow"). Ask a professional money manager how the pension funds she manages are doing, and she will compare their performance with the S&P 500 index. Moreover, this is not a purely American game. In England there is the FT-SE 100 (called the "Footsie 100"), in Germany there is the Dax, and in France there is the CAC. Tokyo has the Nikkei, and Hong Kong has the Hang Seng. Wherever there is a stock market, indexes are sure to follow. Indexes are built from stock prices and related data. To start we look briefly at stock prices and then examine how some of the widely used indexes are calculated. Lest the indexes seem too academic, you will find them useful in choosing a mutual fund or judging a stock's performance. You can even trade indexes themselves on the futures and options markets. In fact, you don't actually need to own any stock to make money (or lose money) in stocks. All you need is some money, a little (dangerously little?) knowledge, and an appetite for risk.

Sometimes it is hard to find out what the price of something is. If you want to sell your house, you'll get lots of estimates of what it will bring, but all of them may be wrong. Stocks are different. The prices, at least for widely traded U.S. stocks, should be easy to find. Just look in the daily paper. Stock prices are quoted in dollars plus some number of eighths. (If you read that a stock closed at $42.375, that means the last trade was at $42\frac{3}{8}$. The newspaper's computer just doesn't do fractions.)

But stock brokers will tell you that there is also a bid price and an ask price at any moment. The *bid* is what someone is willing to pay for the stock, and the *ask* is what an owner wants. The difference is the bid-ask spread. Typically the asking price investors would pay to get the stock is higher than the bid price they would get if they sold the shares. (If not, investors could buy and sell a lot of shares and virtually print money.) For a stock to trade, someone must want it enough to pay the asking price and close the spread. Likewise, someone who really wants to sell a stock can accept a slightly lower bid price. On a heavily traded stock on the New York Stock Exchange, the spread may be an eighth of a point. On a thinly traded stock, the spread could be more. One result of the bid-ask spread is that a small change in the price of a stock may not mean much at all. Stocks may seem to rise or fall an eighth or a quarter when it is merely a question of which side of the spread happens to be reported in the last trade in the newspaper. Moreover, percentage changes in stocks can be deceptive. Since stocks are almost always priced in eighths, an eighth will look like more volatility in a $10 stock than in a $100 stock.

While the stock prices reported in the paper reflect the way stock values are tracked, there are usually other costs the investor must deal with. Stock brokers get paid for trading stocks for investors. They get a commission or fee for making the trade. Commissions can vary from a few cents to several tens of cents per share of stock. If a large institutional investor, and very big brokerage client, is trading a large block of a heavily traded stock, the commission will be a few cents a share or less. Moreover, the bid-ask spread is at most an eighth for the institutional investor's business and may be half a point or more for the odd-lot trader.

The newspapers will usually report four different prices for a stock, taken at different times of the day. But these are not 10 a.m., noon, and so on. Rather, the paper will report the opening price, the highest price of the day, the lowest price of the day, and the last, or closing, price during the day. The price you get when you call a broker and put in a buy or sell order should be between the high and the low. How close to one or the other depends on how prices moved during the day, what special instructions you might have given the broker, and how lucky you got. Most investors place orders for trades "at market," meaning whatever the price is at the moment. Moreover, most investors are not trading in blocks of 10,000 shares or more, and many of these trades are executed through one or another computer system. Some professional investors who deal in large amounts of money and use the fastest computer information systems may be able to consistently make money on in-and-out trading within a few days or less. But most of us should look for stocks that we think are worth holding for a while. If we just trade in and out every day, the brokers are likely to get much richer from the commissions long before we get rich from the trading.

Sooner or later, most market watchers and stock owners want to know how their stock is doing compared with the rest of the market. They will recognize that most of the time most stocks move the same way, so that a big part of whether their stock is rising or falling may be simply whether most stocks are rising or falling. Moreover, things far removed from the market—politics, oil prices, and even the weather—may be an important driving force behind yesterday's stock prices. Measuring the results of the overall market is important to understanding the stock market and how it interacts with the rest of the economy. That's why we have stock averages and indexes.

For the U.S. stock market alone, there are probably enough stock indexes to fill a book. They vary by the way they're calculated, by the kinds of stocks they cover, and by how often they are reported. In this review, we will survey a handful and then look with some care at one or two. Although we are only scratching the surface, we will cover some of the most widely quoted and followed U.S. indexes.* We also look briefly at some indexes that cover other countries.

THE DOW JONES INDUSTRIALS

The most widely quoted stock market measure, and one of the oldest ones, is the Dow Jones Industrials. Currently this average is based on the prices of 30 widely held blue-chip stocks, including such companies as General Motors, IBM, and Exxon. There may be some argument as to the 30 most important corporations in America, but the 30 in the Dow would make most lists of leading businesses in the United

---

*As a member of the committee at Standard & Poor's that manages S&P's indexes, including the ones discussed here, I hope that my experience will make a few extra insights possible without introducing any untoward biases. In the end you, the reader, will have to be the judge.

States or the world. The list does change from time to time, but the changes are relatively rare and are not made lightly. The calculation of the Dow consists of averaging the prices of these 30 stocks and dividing by a special number called the divisor. The divisor is used to keep things in line. For instance, if a stock is dropped from the Dow and a new one is added, the index would ordinarily take a jump or a dive. Instead, the divisor is adjusted to make sure that the first reported index value after the change and the last reported index value before the change are the same. The same thing happens if a stock splits. (In a split the company decides it would be better if the stock were trading at, say, $50 per share instead of $150. To make the change without hurting anyone, it announces a 3-for-1 split, after which each shareholder has three times as many shares as before. In terms of money, no one is any better or worse off, since each shareholder's stock is worth the same as before.)

The Dow dates from 1896, and there have been a lot of changes. When it began there were only 12 stocks, not 30. Over time the divisor has dropped as well. Currently it is a bit less then 0.50. That means that if a Dow stock rises 1 point, the average rises 2 points. If every Dow stock rises 1 point each, the average will climb 60 points. Sixty points is probably enough to spark headlines on the 6 o'clock news—even though seeing 30 stocks rise a point each would be a big yawn to most reporters.

Some people get very excited about movements in the Dow. At recent levels, around 6500, almost any change tends to sound big. After all, the Dow didn't even touch 1000 until the middle 1960s and then took another few years, to the early 1970s, to stay solidly above the millennium level. In the two to three decades since then, the Dow has added some height and now sounds rather grand.

Some perspective can be added if we remember that a typical day sees the market move close to 1 percent. A Dow of 6000 means that anything less than 60 points is probably not worth much noise—and even that may not be very big given the comment above.

If 60 points is a small move, what's a big move? The stock market crash in 1987 saw the Dow lose about 22 percent (507 points) in a single trading day. The crash of 1929 was comparable, and the panic of 1907 was actually bigger, in percentage terms. On the somewhat less frightening side, the market took a big tumble in October 1989 when the then-proposed buyout of United Airlines collapsed on a Friday afternoon. That tumble—which made plenty of headlines on the evening news and the morning papers—saw the Dow drop about 6.9 percent.

THE STANDARD & POOR'S 500

While the Dow may be the most famous stock measure, it is not the one most professionals use. The more popular index for the pros is the Standard & Poor's 500. Whereas the Dow follows 30 stocks, the S&P 500 follows 500; that alone gives it much broader coverage of the markets. The number of stocks is probably not the key difference between the two measures. The more important one is that the S&P 500 doesn't measure just the price of the stock. Rather, it measures the total market value of the stocks in the index. Instead of an average of prices adjusted by a divisor, the S&P 500 is an average of market values adjusted by a divisor. The market value is the price of the stock multiplied by the number of shares outstanding.

If two Dow stocks both rise a point, they both have the same impact on the Dow Jones Industrial average. Suppose these two stocks have the same price but one has 10 times more shares in the market as the other. The more-shares stock is a bigger company as measured by the value that the market places on it. Yet the 10-times-larger stock has no more impact on the Dow than its little brother. The S&P 500 is different. Because the index is measuring total market value, the stock with a market value (sometimes called a market capitalization) 10 times larger has 10 times the impact on the index.

Most investment professionals prefer to look at the market the way the S&P 500 does. Moreover, the ideas underpinning the modern economic and financial theories of the stock market use measures based on the same market-capitalization average as the S&P 500 does. Since the S&P 500 has a long history—almost as long as that of the Dow—it is a convenient measure.

Like the Dow, the S&P 500 has a divisor, but with the 500 it has more uses. For the S&P 500 the divisor was set so that the index's average value from 1941 to 1943 was 10. Its recent value was around 750, as of early 1997. For the S&P 500, the divisor is used to convert the market value of a portfolio of all the shares of all stocks in the index to the index. Think of the divisor as the conversion factor to move from a total market value to index points. This is the same arithmetic as moving from the market capitalization of a company to the value of a share of its stocks in dollars or share points where the conversion factor is the number of shares outstanding. This probably sounds a little obscure, so an example will help. We often talk about a company's profits in terms of earnings per share (EPS). Suppose a company has 50 million shares outstanding and earned $150 million. Its EPS is $150 million divided by 50 million, or $3 per share. If its earnings grow to $165 million (10 percent) and the shares outstanding don't change, then its EPS rose 10 percent. Is that good?

One way to find out is to compare it to the market by calculating the EPS for the Standard & Poor's 500. This is done (usually by a computer, often by Standard & Poor's) by adding up the earnings of all 500 stocks in the S&P 500 and then dividing by the divisor. The divisor is like shares outstanding for the index. Once you see this, you can compare any company-level data to S&P 500 data. After a couple of readings this seems fairly straightforward. Yet most stock analysts on the "Street" argue endlessly about the prospects for the EPS on the S&P 500 without having the foggiest idea how it is really calculated. By the way, a rise of 10 percent per year is good, but not great. The divisor for the Dow won't work quite the same way because the Dow is based on prices only, not market values. One other difference between the S&P 500 and the Dow is that stock splits aren't a concern for the 500, because they don't change the market value of the company.

A broad market index such as the S&P 500 can provide various kinds of useful information for investors in particular and economy watchers in general. For those who watch the market, the index provides a benchmark of what the market returns in good years, bad years, unusual years, stupendous years, and horrendous years. It does more, though. It chronicles the ups and downs of the market and lets an analyst separate the bulls from the bears. The S&P 500 also provides a link from the stock market to the rest of the economy. As the market's gauge, it lets us link the fortunes of the stock market to the progress of the economy. The S&P 500 is one of the 11 series in the Leading Economic Indicators, developed by the Commerce Department's Bureau of Economic Analysis and now published by the Conference Board.

When the S&P 500 is used to gauge investment returns in the stock market, analysts calculate the returns investors would earn if they held the stocks in the index in the same proportions as the index and reinvested the dividends in the index itself. The resulting numbers are called the *total return* to holding the S&P 500. Total means the combination of price changes and reinvested dividends. The dividends make a huge difference. Over the 20 years ended December 1995, the annualized total return for the S&P 500 was 14.6 percent, while the price-only return for an investor who didn't reinvest the dividends was only 10.1 percent. (These returns are larger than those of the last 30, 40, or 50 years, reflecting the strong market in the 1980s.) While these calculations may sound theoretical, the results would be almost the same as any of a number of mutual funds that are managed to track the index.

The index is not just a way to measure the market; it is also a benchmark to beat. Probably because beating the stock market consistently is very difficult—and certainly not because of the way Standard & Poor's selects stocks for the index—it is not an easy bogey to outdo. Of the almost 400 mutual funds that have been around for 10 years or more and that have portfolios at least 75 percent in stocks, only 84 did better than the Vanguard 500 Index Portfolio, a fund that is managed to track the S&P 500.

Another use of the index in watching the stock market is to identify the bull markets and bear markets. One of the few things the vast majority of economists have agreed on is the dates of recessions and expansions in the U.S. economy. Stock market analysts have no similar level of agreement on the dates of bull and bear markets. Nevertheless, the index can teach us some valuable lessons. For investors with memories as long as 10 years or so, the market crash of 1987 is probably one of the most remembered events. It was the largest short-term drop since the crash of 1929, and most of the numbers (as noted earlier in this chapter) in 1987 are comparable to those in 1929.

Many investors look at the data for the month of October 1987, and wonder what could have happened to take 22 percent off the value of America's publicly held corporations. Extend the horizon slightly and note that the drop from late August, when the S&P 500 peaked, to the October 19 close was 33 percent. But another look at the index reveals that the drop was only one of the unusual aspects of the 1987 stock market. Investors who bought the index on the last day of 1986 and went off on a safari without the benefit of radio, television, or telephones would have returned home at the end of 1987 to find they had actually made about 2 percent, including reinvested dividends. Not much, and less than the investors could have gotten in a mundane money market fund, but nothing like the 33 percent loss of August to October. What happened? There were two amazing aspects to the 1987 market—as seen from the index's vantage point. First, the market roared skyward for 8 months without looking backward. Then, it paused in the heat of summer and collapsed.

An analyst armed with the numbers from the S&P 500 rather than the hype of those October headlines might have recognized it was a case of easy come, easy go rather than a signal for a new Great Depression.

One of the longest-running questions for both economy watchers and stock market forecasters is how the economy and the stock market affect each other. A strong economy and rising corporate profits should be good for stocks, while a strong stock market makes people wealthier and more likely to boost their spending. On the dark side, recessions should be bad for stocks, and falling stock prices won't spur either consumer spending or business investment. As plausible as these connections sound, the truth is often more complicated. Getting at more reliable relations between stocks and the economy requires good ways to measure both stocks and various parts of the economy. On the stock side, the S&P 500 or some other broad-based stock index can provide a gauge of how the market is doing.

These analyses usually show that two economic factors play an important part in driving the stock market: interest rates and corporate earnings. Lower interest rates and higher corporate earnings are good for stocks. However, once we dig into the timing of the movements, some interesting results appear. In the bottom of a recession, interest rates fall because both consumers and business have lost confidence and don't want to borrow money. Falling interest rates will spark new life in stocks, and the stock market may rally and begin to rise despite the economy's poor condition. *The moment to buy stocks is not when the next expansion is clearly under way—it is when things look the worst.* The "official" arbiter of when recessions begin and end is a group called the Business Cycle Dating Committee of the National Bureau of Economic Research (NBER). Because the committee often waits for all the numbers to be reported, it finds itself dating recession starts and finishes a number of months after the fact. One slightly offbeat method of timing the stock market is to buy stocks when the committee announces that the economy *is in* a recession. In 1990 the recession began in August and was announced by the NBER in October. The stock market bottomed in October as well. But be warned. This approach is no more flawless or reliable than any other method of market timing or fortune telling.

The interaction between stocks and the economy can run both ways. Rising, or falling, stock prices can also affect the economy, though again the timing and size of the impacts is not always what we expect. Rising stock prices mean stockholders are wealthier, and wealthier people do spend more money. But a huge boost to the economy or consumer spending is not a likely result. Most studies suggest that the "wealth effect" is quite small. A dollar of stock market wealth might add a nickel to consumer spending. In contrast, a dollar of income adds almost a full dollar to spending. Rising stock prices have other impacts as well. A strong stock market can make companies wealthier. One result is an increase in mergers done with stock. The strong stock markets in the 1980s and again in the mid-1990s both fed, and were fed by, corporate merger and acquisition booms. Strong stock markets also make it attractive for rising companies to go public and sell stock. This new-found wealth has been a key ingredient in many recent booms, including our infatuation with biotechnology, computer technology, and the Internet. We will return to stocks and economic booms, busts, and cycles in later chapters.

INVESTMENT RETURNS

Measuring how high or low stocks are is one thing; measuring how much you earn on an investment is something else. Yet in investing and in playing the economy, it is the return that really matters. Returns are how you keep score. Which would you prefer—to buy a stock at 10 and sell it at 14 or buy it at 100 and sell it at 120? The first stock gains 40 percent, the second gains 20 percent. But suppose you bought the second one by borrowing half the money (on margin). That is, you put up $50, borrowed $50, and bought the stock at $100. You sold it for $120, paid off the $50 loan, and held $70 back for your $50 at risk. You made $20 profit on $50, or 40 percent, just as with the first stock. The game gets to be more fun with bonds. First, when interest rates fall, bond prices rise. Second, with bonds the interest earned is often a large part of the return so it needs to be figured in as well. Then there are taxes to account for. Most people don't escape the tax collector, so the return that matters is the return after taxes. The role of borrowed money—as shown in the second example of the $100 stock investment—is also important. Borrowing money can magnify the returns, but it also magnifies the potential losses and risks.

In measuring investment successes or failures, what matters most is a comparison of the value put in with the value that can be taken out of the investment. The goal is to have, not a valuable stock portfolio, but a valuable portfolio that cost very little. Comparisons among investments, links between the economy and investments, and financial advice should all be thought of in terms of returns, not prices.

In general, measuring returns consists of comparing the value of an investment on two different dates and seeing how it has changed. There are a few things to be wary of in the arithmetic. First, any interest payments, dividend checks, or expenses must be accounted for. With a stock or bond, the income is an important part of the return. A hidden, but very important part of the total is the earnings over time on the interest or dividends received. Most analysts argue that returns should be calculated by assuming that the interest or dividends are reinvested in the basic investment. With stock returns, assume that the dividend is used to buy more stock. This method is used in developing total-return indexes for the stock market, as described in the previous section. When the yield on a bond is calculated, the same assumption is buried in the mathematics.

Second, some investments consume money as well as

returning it. A real estate investment may require that taxes be paid or property be repaired. These costs should be figured into the overall return. If an investment is made with borrowed money, the cost of borrowing needs to be included. Income taxes are another cost of the investment that must be included. You should base returns on market prices as much as possible. It is not what you think (or wish) your stock or house is worth. It is what you can sell it for on the market that matters. Setting a price, or "marking to market," is easy for things like stocks and bonds, but potentially very difficult for other things like real estate.

A general (and not all too useful) formula for figuring returns is to divide today's price plus any income from interest or dividends by yesterday's price and then to subtract 1 from the total. The result, expressed as a percentage, gives the return. For instance, a stock that sold for $10 yesterday, sells for $11 today, and pays a dividend of 25 cents gives a return of:

$$(\$11 + 0.25) \div (\$10) = 1.125$$

$$1.125 - 1 = 12.5\%$$

If the same investment has a string of daily returns of 12.5 percent, 2 percent, -5 percent, and 10 percent, the figures can be compounded to get a return of 17.79 percent over the 4 days. The idea is more important than the arithmetic. Your goal is to compare what you invested with what you got back. This is one of those economic points that sounds obvious but still bears repeating. All the economic and financial theory of stocks, bonds, investing, and the economy is based on returns, not on prices. Prices can always be made to look larger or smaller by changing the currency. The Japanese talk about billions and trillions of yen—never a mere thousand and rarely even a million—not because Japan is somehow richer than the United States (it's not) but because there are about 120 yen to the U.S. dollar. The flip side is Britain, where the pound is worth about $1.65 and things may sound cheaper than in the United States. In the first half of the 1990s the high numbers of the Japanese stock market with an index around 20,000 gave terrible returns, while the U.S. markets were very rewarding with indexes measured in hundreds, not tens of thousands. Enough said belaboring the obvious—returns are what counts.

GROSS DOMESTIC PRODUCT OR GDP

When most people think about measuring the economy, they probably wonder about counting how much of what is produced. In many textbook explanations and anecdotal tales as well, economists seem to spend all their time counting widgets or some other universally produced—and universally useless—device. Since no one has ever seen, bought, sold, or used a widget, it is best left uncounted for now, especially with so many better ways to look at the economy.

The basic measuring rod for the economy is the gross domestic product. GDP is both the most used and the most maligned of economic measurements. When used in the way it was designed, GDP can be very helpful in understanding the economy. But there are a range of issues that GDP has nothing to say about despite efforts of critics to claim otherwise.

Just as the S&P 500 gives a single measure of how far up, or down, the stock market is, GDP gives a single measure for the economy. One number cannot cover every little variation and adjustment in something as complex as the entire economy. But a carefully measured number can tell a lot about the economy—and GDP does tell a lot. Before delving into how it is measured, we need to look at how GDP is used and what it tells us. As the total of everything produced in the U.S. economy, GDP shows whether the country is getting richer or poorer from one year to the next. Over the last 30 years, the average annual growth in GDP, adjusted for inflation, has been about 2.7 percent. The average masks some turmoil. There were times when the economy shrunk, the country got poorer, and people saw their income fall or lost their jobs. These recessions stand out in any long-term chart of GDP growth, such as that in Fig. 3-1.

GDP MEASUREMENT

In 1995 and 1996 the government made some major changes in the way the impact of inflation is removed from GDP and the way "real" GDP is calculated. Real GDP means the amount of goods and services the economy produces in inflation-adjusted terms. The most important measures of how fast the economy is growing are real GDP growth and real GDP growth per person. The latter is sometimes called real growth per capita. Under the old system, GDP was adjusted for inflation in about the same way as the CPI. A base year was chosen, and that year's prices were used to convert current dollars to real dollars. For GDP that system has problems. Over long periods of time price changes cause major

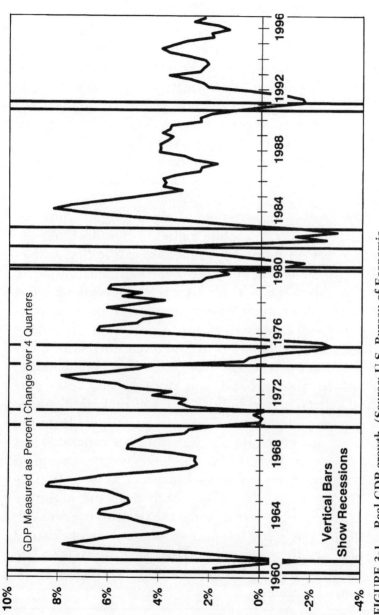

FIGURE 3-1. Real GDP growth. (*Source:* U.S. Bureau of Economic Analysis Recession, based on NBER Business Cycle Chronology.)

89

shifts in the economy. If these price changes are ignored, the data tell the wrong story. Imagine trying to explain the effects on the economy of the oil crises of the 1970s without allowing for adjustments in oil prices. Also, in the last 10 to 15 years computer prices have plummeted by 15 percent to 20 percent *per year*. This alone created so much distortion that the share of GDP going to investment was substantially different when one used current dollars than when one used real dollars to do the measuring.

The answer was a system of chain-weighted indexes. For jargon lovers, these are called Fisher-ideal indexes. (Fisher was an American economist of the first half of this century. While he made a lasting contribution to index numbers, he is better known for his work on interest rates and monetary theory and for failing to predict the 1929 stock market crash.) In any event, the secret of calculating real GDP is to find a year-to-year or quarter-to-quarter percentage change for each component of GDP. With this in hand, you can take any year's current-dollar GDP and build a series of real GDP values. Earlier on we saw how a price index is built from the prices of different things people buy, with the amounts they buy as the weights. For the GDP, we are making an index of *quantities* and using the prices as weights. This is the reverse of the CPI, which uses the amounts bought in a single year as weights. Also, we use an average of this year's and last year's prices as weights instead of some arbitrary base year. That way, the weights are always up to date and the data tell the correct story for any period of time.

(Continued)

Understanding the ups and downs of GDP growth and other aspects of the business cycle is crucial to using economic information to advantage. The more one studies the ups and downs of the GDP, the clearer it becomes that few things in the economy can escape the business cycle or the impact of the overall growth pattern of the economy. In fact, the changes and turmoil of the last 10 to 15 years of downsizing are largely the story of one economic sector after another discovering that it is not immune to the economy and the business cycle. Examples include medical professionals who now confront issues of falling prices and defense workers who now realize that federal spending is as much a creature—or victim—of the ups and downs of the economy as anything else.

We can also use GDP to get a quick picture of whether the average American is better off by comparing the growth in GDP with population growth. In the United States over the last 30 years, GDP growth has outstripped population growth and, on average, Americans are richer. It can also give us some idea of how we compare with other countries. Our GDP growth has lagged behind that of the developing countries and, until recently, behind a few notable industrial nations such as Japan. But we have done better than other nations. Moreover, the United States is at, or close to, the top of the GDP per capita tables. If we exclude some of the oil-rich nations that got wealthy by virtue of location as much as hard work, the United States is in an enviable position.

GDP is the sum total of what is produced in the economy. It encompasses products—including cars, trucks, computers, loaves of bread, and bushels of wheat—as well as services—including financial services, car rentals, video rentals, restaurants, and pizza deliveries. Since a common measure is needed to add up cars, trucks, video rentals, and the rest, GDP is measured by the market value of all these products and services. A $20,000 car counts the same as 10,000 $2 movie rentals.

There is a serious double-counting problem if you simply add up all the cars, trucks, steel, tires, and so forth produced somewhere in the economy. When you buy a car, you buy the steel, tires, engine, seats, glass, and other items that are in it. You also buy the value added in the assembly line by the workers who put the car together. No one would want a pile of steel, rubber, and oil instead of a car. But if you added the steel output to the cars, you would count steel twice. To avoid counting things many times over, GDP sums up "value added." Valued added means the value added to the raw materials in the production process. If a car sells for $20,000 and the materials included in it cost the auto manufacturer $12,000, then the value added in the production is the difference, $8000. If there are a string of processes, the value-added calculation ensures that each part is counted only once, not twice and not missed altogether. In the car example, if the auto company buys sheets of steel for the car and the steel mill in turn buys iron ore and coking coal, the iron ore and the value added by turning it into steel sheet are both counted only once. The sheet steel for the car is added in when the steel mill sells it to the car company and then subtracted out from the value of the car so it is not double-counted. The result of all this adding and subtracting of value added and raw materials is that GDP counts the total value of the final products, not all the intermediate products that go from one thing into another. In figuring total GDP, we add up the value of these final products.

The D in GDP reminds us that the measure applies to

one country. When GDP is calculated, the production included is anything located in the United States. Cars built in a manufacturing plant located in the United States but owned by a Japanese auto company are counted in GDP. Cars built in Canada or Europe in a factory owned by a U.S. company are not included in U.S. GDP. An older measure, the gross national product (GNP), did the reverse. It excluded domestic production of facilities owned by foreigners and included production in foreign facilities owned by U.S. companies and citizens. Neither way is absolutely right or wrong as long as we keep it straight.

Not everything produced in the United States is consumed domestically. The GDP does include exports as well as products and services consumed here. Service exports can be important. They include things like air travel and financial and business services. Imports are treated differently. Since imports represent products or services that are consumed but not produced here, they are subtracted from domestic production in figuring GDP. The rough idea is that imports could have been, but weren't, produced at home. Besides imports and exports, GDP is broken into a few broad components. These are consumer spending, business investment, and government purchases of goods and services.

The part of business spending that counts in GDP is investment that remains in the business. Raw materials that become part of the product contribute to value added counted in the GDP total. For businesses, final products bought are things like new buildings, factories, and machines. Included here are offices, furniture, personal computers, and all the other trappings of a modern business enterprise. Business investment also includes inventory investment. If goods are produced but not sold, they still count as part of GDP. Unsold production is added to inventory and the increase in inventories is counted in GDP. Sometimes, companies sell more than they produce in a year by reducing their inventories. When this happens, the drop in inventories is subtracted from GDP. For the mathematicians, the net change in inventories is part of GDP.

Consumer spending is part of GDP and, by definition, anything consumers buy is considered a final product so there are no value-added, double-counting, or inventory issues to worry about. People working in a home office are considered a business for GDP calculations. The government component in GDP often raises some questions. While federal government spending in the United States is about $1.3 trillion, the federal government portion of GDP is only about $350 billion. Most of what the government does with our money is move it from one pocket to another. When the government makes social security payments or covers someone else's medical bills, it is not buying any goods or services. Rather, it is making what economists call a transfer payment. Transfer payments don't count in GDP. What does count are wages and salaries for government workers and items bought by the government for its own use, including war planes, ships, tanks, cars, trucks, computers, paper, and red tape.

The calculations just described provide information on GDP for a particular year. The challenge is to use these figures to track GDP quarter after quarter and year after year and to be able to exclude the impact of inflation from the analysis. If inflation were not an issue, we would simply total GDP in each year and compare one year with the next. Unfortunately, inflation is a concern in tracking the economy. It is a concern whether it is 1 percent, 3 percent, 10 percent, or more. Moreover, inflation often blurs the shifts in prices that go on all the time when some things become more expensive and other things get cheaper. If all you bought were personal computers, you would conclude that inflation was running at about -15 percent per year. If all you paid for was college tuition or medical bills, you would estimate inflation at about twice the overall rate. The vagaries of inflation reporting were discussed earlier. For the GDP, adjusting for both inflation and changes in one price compared with another can be difficult.

Until recently, the government chose a base year for producing inflation-adjusted or real GDP numbers and then recalculated the data in base-year dollars. Lately the divergence between falling prices for computers and technology and rising prices for other, more service-intensive items added distortions to the inflation-adjusted data. The distortions appeared as the time between the base year and the current year widened and the differences in price movements grew. Eventually, the errors became sufficiently significant that a change in the measurement approach was necessary.

The new calculations begin very differently from the ones some of us grew up with, but they cover much the same ground. First, everything is calculated as index numbers rather than in dollars. All that's changed is the unit of measure. Index numbers are the same familiar idea used for stock indexes. In fact, just as people talk about the Dow Jones or the S&P 500 as if it were counting dollars and not points, GDP can be thought of as either dollars or points. When an index is built combining different products and services, the dollar values of those products are used in the mix. This lets us add cars to medical care in totaling up GDP. But, with index numbers instead of dollars, we can make more adjustments in the base year with less trouble.

The new GDP calculations measure the real growth in GDP from one year to the next by calculating the growth with last year's dollars and this year's dollars and averaging the result. The result is a growth rate—almost like a total return to owning the economy for a year. Then, in the same way that a number of returns can be linked to figure a return over a range of years, we can generate an index from the series of real GDP returns. Despite this, the results are translated to dollars for easier reporting.

GDP does not measure everything. However, people often think it does and then complain about it. Common objections include arguments that GDP can rise but people may be sadder, not happier; that GDP does not measure how well off we are or how happy we are; that GDP ignores environmental degradation and ecological disaster; and that GDP is misguided because when a hurricane destroys a community and we rebuild the lost houses, stores, factories and roads, GDP rises. All these complaints are true. All miss the point. GDP is not intended to measure happiness, welfare, psychological well-being, environmental resources, or natural disasters. Yes, these issues are important—in fact, so important that they should be measured in their own right rather than tucked under the GDP umbrella.

Measuring happiness may be beyond the scope of either economics or this book (more likely the latter than the former). Nevertheless, some of the comments below do touch on consumer sentiment surveys. GDP does not measure the common welfare either. One of the largest areas that GDP avoids is the distribution of income. Most would agree that part of the American Dream is the chance to strike it rich. Most would also agree that the distribution of income should not be too unequal—that there should not be a few billionaires and a large pool of paupers.

Beyond these two generalizations there may be little agreement. Moreover, preventing or eliminating some of the inequality in income distribution may make it more difficult for some to strike it rich. Certainly income distribution is an important issue. But trying to measure it with GDP will lead only to confusion, or worse.

GDP is basically a measure of production and income—how much is produced or becomes available over time. It does not account for abrupt changes in our stock of wealth. A hurricane or an earthquake that destroys a city does not figure into GDP. Building new houses after the disaster is part of the economy's production is rightfully part of GDP. Some of the ecological issues are missed by GDP for similar reasons. GDP measures will count the value of oil extracted from the ground and the value of work done to locate new oil wells. But GDP does not include a balance sheet for oil in the ground, whether or not we know where it is.

Other ecological issues are also missed by GDP. When a utility produces electricity, it may also produce air pollution. The pollution damage reduces GDP but is quite difficult to measure. Moreover, expenditures to reduce pollution increase total GDP even if some pollution remains. Likewise, when you drive your car, the gasoline you buy is part of GDP, as was the catalytic converter on the car when the automobile was purchased. But the smog your car produces may not affect total GDP. The issue here is not GDP; it is the way we organize the economy. GDP counts things that move through markets and have prices. The problem is not GDP; it is the absence of any market for a clean environment or pollution control. Complaining that GDP is a poor measure because it ignores ecological damage is a case of shooting the messenger—in fact, the wrong messenger. The real issue is that environmental issues have been either ignored or attacked by regulatory fiat. The regulations pretend that someone knows how much we are all willing to pay to avoid pollution and can order us to make the payments.

OTHER PRODUCTION MEASURES

GDP is not the only broad-based measure of output or production, although it is one of the most comprehensive. Economy watchers will encounter a number of others which deserve at least a brief mention here. The big-picture measure is something called *industrial production*. This is an index, or actually a large collection of indexes, published by the Federal Reserve. It shows how much is produced each month in terms of an index or average. Unlike the GDP, which is based on the value of production, the industrial production index is based on physical quantities. When an individual index measures cars or steel or electric power, it is counting cars produced or tons of steel or kilowatt hours of electricity. GDP counts dollars. Neither is better, but at times the industrial production index is more useful.

Since the industrial production index does not cover services, it reaches only a portion of the economy. If we look at specific sectors within the index, the data reliability can vary. In some areas the figures are very useful and reliable. It should be easy to track the production of raw steel or finished cars and count the results. Other areas are harder. Tracking production of magazines where the real value of the product depends on the number of readers reached by advertisers, not on the tons of paper or kilowatt hours of electric power used, is more difficult. Yet, in some cases, the measures are based on things like electric power consumption if there are no good direct-output measures. Despite these issues and the fact that less than half of GDP is covered by the industrial production index, it has proved useful, particularly because the areas included in the index tend to be among the more volatile sectors. Moreover, some analysts believe the index carries extra weight in shaping Federal Reserve Board policy, since it is compiled by the Fed.

At the other end of the spectrum are output measures that cover only one or a few industries. A few sector measures are widely followed. These include auto sales and housing starts, both key economic indicators. Auto sales are usually reported each month and are counted at seasonally adjusted annual rates. This mouthful means that the number is adjusted for normal seasonal variation. Few snow shovels are sold in the summer and few bathing suits are sold in the winter (in most parts of the nation). By adjusting for seasonal variation we don't let the slump in December swimsuit sales convince us that no one will ever go swimming again. Annual rates means that instead of saying 1.2 million cars and trucks were sold last month we multiply the number by 12 and talk about how cars sold at an annual rate of 14.4 million last month. Sounds complicated, but annualization makes it easy to compare this month with all of last year.

Auto sales in the United States include cars and what the government statisticians call light trucks. The latter group covers pick-up trucks, vans, and most four-wheel drives. These are counted separately because they are subject to somewhat different safety regulations, but they are considered to be cars by most buyers. In 1995 car and light-truck sales in the United States were 14.8 million units, down 2 percent from 1994. Car sales are also broken down by foreign and domestic producers, a topic of some political interest.

Auto sales tell us two important things about the economy. First, they give a reading on how well, or poorly, the auto industry is doing. Autos are a major force in the U.S. economy, with 3.3 million workers building and selling cars and helping service them. Second, auto sales say a lot about American consumers. For most of us, buying a car is one of the larger purchases we make and one that we can often put off for a while if we're worried about losing a job or taking a beating in the market. As a result, auto sales give some hint of how willing people are to spend money.

Housing starts are another key output measure. Home building is a major industry in the United States and is widely watched because it is very sensitive to both interest rates and general economic conditions. When times are good, people buy homes. When times are tough they don't. Moreover, since most people pay for houses with a mortgage, the level of mortgage interest rates makes a big difference. There are a number of economic indicators for the housing industry, but the two most widely followed are housing starts and housing permits.

"Starts" mean that construction was started on new houses. Starts count single-family homes, buildings with two to four units, and buildings with five or more units. Single-family homes—what carpets America's suburbs— are the largest part of the total. In the first half of 1996, a generally good time for home building, total starts (at annual rates) were 1.48 million units. Of these, 1.17 million were single-family homes, a scant 37,000 were in the two- to four-unit category, and the other 267,000 were apartment houses with five or more units. There are probably a lot of reasons to count starts when building is begun rather than "finishes" when the construction is completed. The biggest reason may be that starts are easier to identify and pin down than finishes, which can be deferred if the market turns soft or the buyer gets cold feet. In many communities, builders need to apply for a permit before construction can be started. Since permits are issued by local government offices, counting house construction permits should be a way to get an early indication of housing starts. The theory is good and the government does collect and publish data on housing permits. However, it is not much of a leading indicator for housing starts. With single-family homes the planning period is too short for permits to provide a lot of extra information. Nevertheless, some analysts like to track housing permits rather than starts. Both are published each month in the same press release from the U.S. Bureau of the Census.

Some portion of new housing construction replaces old homes that are lost to fires, floods, or hurricanes or are abandoned when neighborhoods become less attractive. But the majority represent net additions to the stock of housing. While the month-to-month or year-to-year shifts in home building depend on interest rates and the state of the economy, the longer-term shifts depend on changes in the population—how many of us there are and where we live. Most of the time, we still think that bigger is better and that growth must continue. Home building is a successful industry. But its best year ever was back in the 1950s. The number of new homes built in the United States rises and falls, but with slower population growth in coming years, we may see slower home building as well.

Figures 3-2 to 3-8 show how some of these measures have shifted over time. A little perspective reveals that both

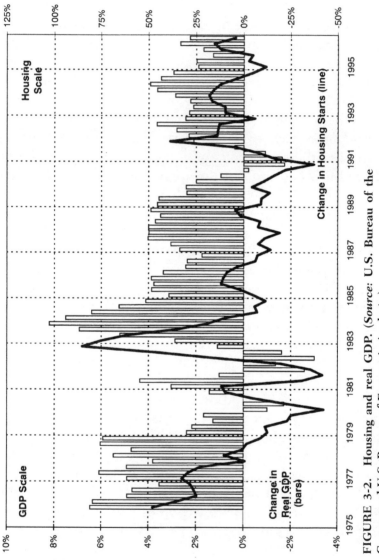

FIGURE 3-2. Housing and real GDP. (*Source:* U.S. Bureau of the Census and U.S. Bureau of Economic Analysis.)

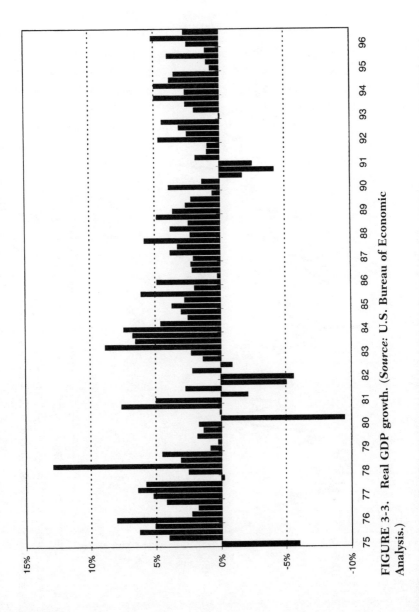

FIGURE 3-3. Real GDP growth. (*Source:* U.S. Bureau of Economic Analysis.)

103

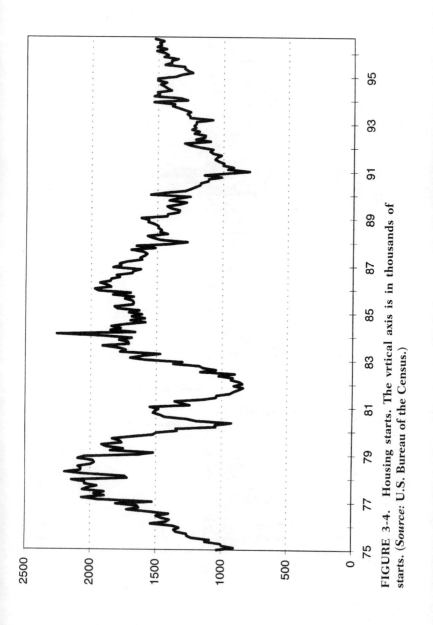

FIGURE 3-4. Housing starts. The vrtical axis is in thousands of starts. (*Source:* U.S. Bureau of the Census.)

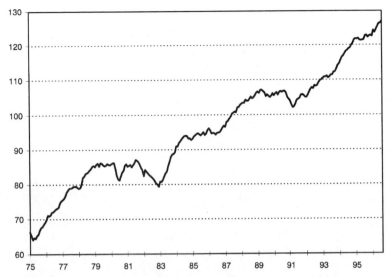

FIGURE 3-5. Industrial production index. (*Source:* Federal Reserve Board.)

autos and homes follow the ups and downs of GDP, but that at times there is little positive trend.

EMPLOYMENT AND UNEMPLOYMENT

Of all the things that go on in the economy, the two that concern most people are probably holding a job and paying taxes. Each month, usually on the first Friday of the month, the federal government's Bureau of Labor Statistics releases the employment data for the previous month. Partly because these numbers are available quickly and partly because they are generally reliable, employment data are some of the most closely followed statistics among Wall Street economists and analysts.

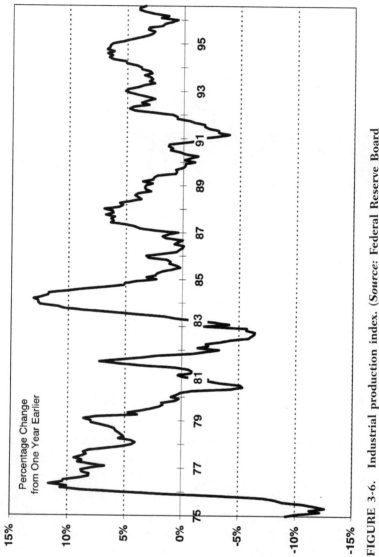

FIGURE 3-6. Industrial production index. (*Source:* Federal Reserve Board of Governors.)

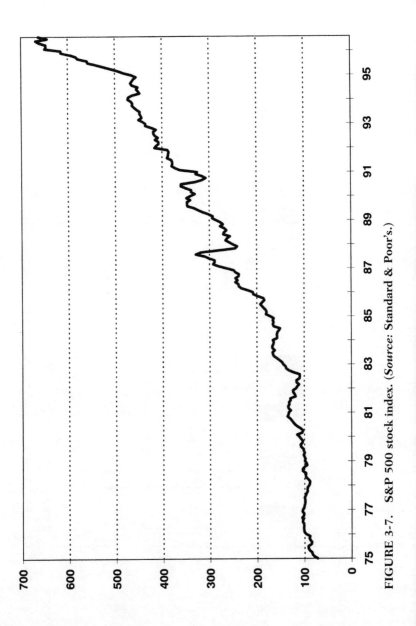

FIGURE 3-7. S&P 500 stock index. (*Source:* Standard & Poor's.)

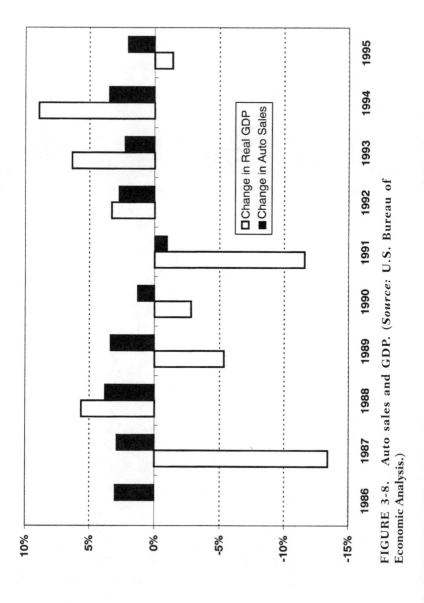

FIGURE 3-8. Auto sales and GDP. (*Source*: U.S. Bureau of Economic Analysis.)

There are two different sets of numbers. One counts jobs and employment and the other counts unemployment. The employment numbers are simpler and represent a monthly payroll survey of businesses. The results show how many people are working in which industries, how many hours a week people are working, how much over-time they are working, and what the average wages are on an hourly and weekly basis. The interpretation is straight-forward—the more people working, the better for the economy. Some kinds of employment are not included. Among these are self-employment and domestic employ-ment in people's homes, including nannies and less formal day-care workers. Since many small businesses are not covered in each monthly survey, the Bureau of Labor Statistics adds an adjustment factor to include them. At times this factor seems to push the totals up or down rather than improve the overall accuracy of the report. Also, the survey counts jobs, not people. If workers are moonlighting, they are counted twice. Because the payroll survey is fundamentally different from the other survey done to measure the unemployment rate, the two parts of the report can often tell different stories from one another.

The other part of the monthly report is the unemploy-ment rate. Here things get more complicated, because not everyone who is not working is unemployed. Moreover, some people work part time but really want to work full time and feel at best half employed. To see how this all works, begin by dividing the population into some different groups. From the total population in the United States— about 260 million people—we define people who could be working. This is the labor force. It consists of people between the ages of 16 and 64 who are living in the United States and who are not in prison or hospitalized. In 1996, this figure was about 133.5 million. Military personnel stationed in the United States are included in the labor force and are counted among those employed. The difficult part is that some people are not in the labor force even though they are eligible on the basis of age and location. One category of people not in the labor force are full-time students. Another is people who have chosen to do other things, such as care for their children full time. The difficult ones to define are the workers who have given up looking for jobs because they don't expect to find work. They are called discouraged workers. While they are not in the labor force—and not considered to be unemployed—they are counted separately once each quarter. However, few people really pay much attention to the numbers of discouraged workers. Data are also collected on people working part time because they can't find full-time work.

The figure most widely followed is the unemployment rate. It is the ratio of how many people are in the labor force but not employed to how many are in the labor force in total. Discouraged workers, students, homemakers, and others are not in the labor force and are ignored by the unemployment rate.

These calculations raise a number of difficulties for many people. Most agree that there are some people who choose not to work (and who can afford to make that choice) and should not be covered in the unemployment rate. But there are others who would work if the pay and conditions were right. This is certainly true of discouraged workers. It is also true of some homemakers who may decide that the costs of child care and the lost involvement in raising their own children are not really compensated by what they could earn in a job, especially on an after-tax basis. There may even be some students who would leave school and work if the wage and promotion prospects were right.

Some students, homemakers, discouraged workers, and others may belong in the labor force and some may not. The current Bureau of Labor Statistics survey divides those who are in from those who are out. A few years ago the bureau substantially revised the survey. In the process, more people were classified as in the labor force and fewer were either discouraged workers or out of the labor force by choice. The largest shift involved women at home with young children. In the old survey, an answer involving child care almost always eliminated someone from the labor force. In the new survey, there are additional questions to determine if someone would work for the right wage.

The unemployment data are widely followed and are some of the more politically sensitive economic numbers around. Figure 3-9 shows the ups and downs of the unemployment rate. The highest rate ever reported was in the Great Depression, when it reached the mid-20 percent range. However, those numbers probably significantly understated the true state of affairs. Lots of people were not counted and plenty of people had given up looking for jobs but were clearly willing to do almost any kind of work to survive. The highest figures since the end of World War II were reached during the 1981–1982 recession, when the unemployment rate touched 10.7 percent. The lowest figures were fractions of a percent in 1942 and 1943, during World War II. The lowest "modern" numbers were slightly under 4 percent in the second half of the 1960s, during the Vietnam War, and a long-running economic boom. As we might expect, unemployment rates are lower in good economic times and higher in bad economic times.

The unemployment rate never goes to zero. There are always a few people who quit their jobs to look for something better and some who get fired for cause rather than

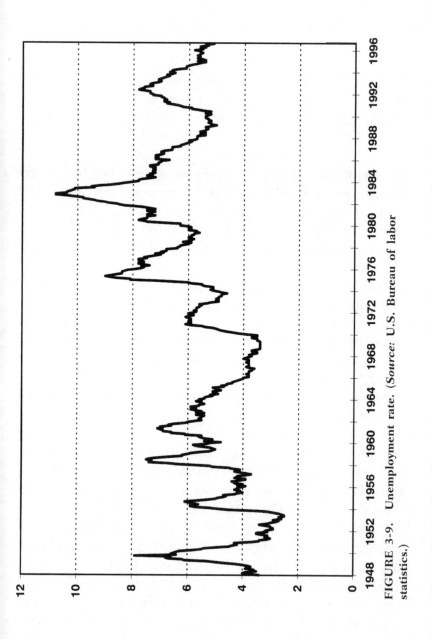

FIGURE 3-9.   Unemployment rate. (*Source:* U.S. Bureau of labor statistics.)

laid off because business is poor. In the United States it is not uncommon for young people to switch jobs a few times before finding something that they see as a career and long-term commitment. All this generates some moderate amount of unemployment, often called *frictional unemployment*. If the bottom for the unemployment rate isn't zero, what is it—2 percent, 4 percent, 6 percent, or more? This number, the *full-employment unemployment rate,* is a hotly debated topic. If the number selected is fairly high, the President and other policymakers might declare economic victory with a lot of people still searching for jobs. If the number is set too low, they might try to stimulate the economy much too much and leave us with inflation. In the 1960s and early 1970s, the then-recent experience suggested that the unemployment rate could get down to 4 percent before labor shortages or sharp increases in wages and salaries occurred. But in the late 1970s and early 1980s, the unemployment rate crept upward and then failed to fall even close to the old lows. This spawned various studies claiming that the full-employment unemployment rate had increased and the right number was really 5 or 6 percent. Some of the arguments for a higher rate were that an increasing number of new entrants in the labor force meant fewer experienced workers sticking with one job. The fact that a disproportionate number of the new entrants were women gave many of the debates an unwanted tinge.

Whatever the arguments about the 1980s, the first half of the 1990s has seen unemployment rates slip lower. Arguments about a full-employment unemployment rate of 6 percent faded as the rate moved to about 5.5 percent. Moreover, with inflation low, the target rate is likely to be moved down to 5 percent, or even below.

The employment data include some other information that also sparks both economic and political debates. In addition to reporting an overall unemployment rate, the Bureau of Labor Statistics reports figures for different groups within the population. Old-timers may remember when analysts looked at the unemployment rate for married men as a guide to the economy. The increasing importance of women in the labor force ended that idea. Today, rates for different age and ethnic groups are often followed closely. Teenage unemployment is typically three or more times the overall population rate.

For economy watchers other data may be more interesting than the unemployment rate, though they have much less political clout. The length of the workweek (measured in hours) is one item of interest. When business conditions improve, companies will ask people to work longer hours or pay overtime before they hire new workers. Hiring more workers costs money and the workers must be screened and trained. If business isn't sure the good times will last, it is better off paying overtime than rushing out to hire new workers who might just end up being laid off a few months down the road. Increases in the workweek and overtime can tell a lot about what is happening in the economy. The hourly and weekly wage data are sometimes watched as early indicators of inflation. However, these may not be reliable signals, since they only track wages rather than overall business costs and income. A better measure is the employment cost index, discussed earlier under inflation.

INCOME AND REAL WAGES

Having a job is nice, but what it pays matters a lot too. That goes for the economic numbers as much as it goes for each of us. Measurements of incomes, wages, and salaries are not quite as detailed as measurements of jobs, employment, and production. But there are a number of measures and they can be used to improve our understanding of the economy. Broadly speaking, the income measures fall into two general classes: aggregate and individual. Aggregate measures for the entire economy are useful in deciding if there is enough money out there to make for a good Christmas season. More individual and employment-related numbers can help us compare fortunes in one line of work with those in another, or get some hint about which people might be happier than which other people.

The aggregate measures of interest cover three broad figures: personal income, disposable personal income, and real disposable personal income. These also provide some widely followed but very misleading data on the savings rate. *Personal income* covers anyone whose activities are involved in producing what goes into GDP. It is the total of what we all earn as a group, including wages, salaries, interest payments, dividends from owning stock, income from owning a business or a farm, and transfer payments like social security and Medicare. The numbers are reported in the aggregate and are in the trillions. This is the big pie available for dividing among all of us. How it grows or shrinks says a lot about how much richer or poorer Americans are as a group.

Of course, we don't get to keep all this. In particular, we don't keep what goes to the government as taxes. Personal income less tax payments and some similar non-tax payments is called *disposable personal income*. The name means that people have it at their disposal, not that the government has disposed of most of our income through taxes. In any event, this is what is available for spending. It is the figure that most analysts use when they try to decide if people should feel richer or poorer. It might be thought of as national take-home pay. Some economy watchers deduct some fixed expenses (not part of the official data) from disposal income to get a figure called discretionary income. The fixed expenses include mortgage and car payments as well as basic medical and living expenses. The idea is to figure what's left in the cookie jar before the next payday. These ideas have some merit, but before they lead us to conclude that the entire country is in hock and can't spend a thing, we need only look in at the local shopping mall to find an error in the analysis.

Another use of income data is to gauge whether Americans as a group are keeping up with inflation and the economy over time. This is often measured by inflation-adjusting the disposable personal income data over time. The resulting figures on *real disposable income* give some idea of how much better or worse off people are as a group. Of course, the group has grown in size so some increase is needed to merely stay even on a per capita basis. Figure 3-10 shows shifts in real disposable income, real disposable income per capita, and real wages. The last measure is discussed below.

The same data used to calculate the personal income numbers are also used to calculate the personal savings rate. For the economy's long-time progress, savings are important. Savings funds and investments help us grow richer over time. Among those economy watchers who like to claim we are falling behind the Japanese, nothing is a better number than the savings rate. It allegedly shows that Americans never save anything and that the Japanese save everything. Let's leave the argument aside for a moment and look at the commonly reported savings rate, now 4 to 5 percent of disposable personal income. Despite its name, this does not mean that at the end of the year

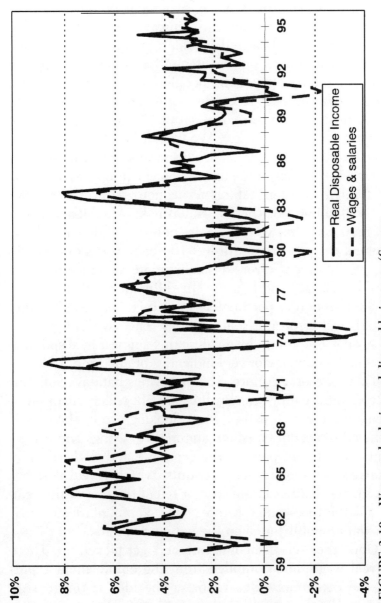

FIGURE 3-10. Wages and salaries and disposable income. (*Source:* U.S. Bureau of Economic Analysis.)

your savings account is up by 5 percent of your after-tax income. Whether it means anything at all is unclear.

Savings are calculated by taking disposable personal income, deducting a figure for total consumer spending, a figure for interest payments people make to others, and a figure for funds sent to foreigners (such as supporting an elderly relative who moved to Mexico for the climate or to Europe for old times' sake). What's left is called savings. In round numbers, we are taking disposable personal income (about $5.3 trillion) and subtracting consumption, interest, and foreign transfers (about $5 trillion). However, neither the $5.3 trillion nor the $5 trillion is known with absolute accuracy. So what we are really doing is taking two large numbers that we know within $100 billion or so (1 part in 50, or a 2 percent error—probably more accuracy than we should presume) and figuring the difference. The answer is not $300 billion in personal savings. It is really $200 billion in statistical error and some savings. The savings figure, or the savings rate found by dividing this amount by disposable personal income, is not very indicative of anything at all.

There are other, more reliable savings data available for the economy. Unfortunately, they are not widely reported or discussed. The two places worth looking are in the details of the GDP accounts, which summarize savings and investments in different parts of the economy, and in the Federal Reserve's "flow of funds" accounts, which reveal whether that savings bank account rose or fell at the end of the year. But for the foreseeable future, most commentaries on savings will probably hinge on the wrong numbers.

One other set of income numbers get picked up. These are real wage data compiled from the employment report and the consumer price reports. The idea is to measure wages and salaries adjusted for inflation. These numbers have gained some notoriety lately because they paint a rather dismal picture of the economy and show people getting slowly poorer over time. Most measures of real or inflation-adjusted wages show a lack of substantial gains in the last 10 to 15 years. While these may be close to the truth, they probably overstate the dismal side of things. Most workers received raises on the basis of a combination of existing skills, new skills, seniority, and the overall business as well as a factor for keeping up (somewhat) with inflation. The data on real wages tend to ignore the fact that people's wages change because they become better at what they do. As a result, the data overstate the negative to an extent.

SENTIMENT, CONFIDENCE, AND SURVEYS

Most of the economic measures discussed so far are based on what happens in the economy—how much something costs, how many people are working, what is being spent, and so forth. However, what happens in the economy depends more on what people think will happen than on what has happened. You buy a stock because you think it will go up. True, you may believe that because the stock has gone up already—but you are buying it in hopes of future appreciation. The same thing is true of almost everything that happens in the economy. You accept a job on the basis of promises you and your future employer make to one another about wages, salaries, working conditions, hours, promotions, and so forth. You buy a house on the basis of your expectations about the neighborhood and your future needs.

It is much easier to count the number of people working than to discover which employees are satisfied with their jobs and which ones think they are underpaid. (It is a safe guess that few think they are overpaid.) One way that expectations can be explored, checked, and measured is through surveys. Market researchers are big on surveys. Most of us have probably been interviewed on the phone or even in person at one time or another. Political campaigns also rely on surveys—although in politics they are called polls. "If the election were held today, would you vote for Jones for dog catcher? Are you a dog owner? Are you a friend of animals?" Economists use polls and surveys to explore market conditions.

A number of widely followed polls and surveys are reported on a regular basis. In a few cases, the reports are carefully watched in the financial markets and are considered as important as major government statistical releases like unemployment rates and GDP. Among the more widely followed are the National Association of Purchasing Managers (NAPM) survey, different surveys of consumer sentiment, and various surveys of economic forecasts. These only scratch the surface, but they give a sample of what is available.

Members of the NAPM are typically purchasing agents in large corporations. Their job is to supervise purchases of anything and everything for their employers. Because they are continuously in the market buying raw materials and supplies, they are the first to know if prices are rising or falling or if it is easier or harder to get deliveries on time. Each month the NAPM surveys its membership and publishes a series of indexes showing the results.

The survey is a "diffusion survey" that measures the proportion of purchasing agents seeing signs of a strong economy and the proportion seeing signs of weakness. The numbers reported are the percentage seeing gains less the percentage seeing losses plus 50. The plus-50 part means that when half see gains and half see losses, the index is reported as "50 percent." Without the plus 50, a 50-50 split would be reported as zero. This bit of statistical legerdemain makes the results easier to understand. The questions cover a range of issues, including some things that many purchasing agents may not have direct knowledge of, such as their company's recent hiring patterns. Among the different items is a series called vendor performance—a report of purchasing agents experiencing slower deliveries of goods on order. (The vendors selling to the purchasing agents are not performing as quickly.) This useful series is included in the official compilation of leading indicators as an early-warning signal for the economy.

Although the NAPM is widely watched on Wall Street, the darling of the 6 o'clock news is probably consumer confidence or consumer sentiment. There are a number of surveys of consumers' opinions about the economy. The two most widely followed are published by the Conference Board and the Survey Research Center at the University of Michigan. The Conference Board, a nonprofit business research group, releases the new figures to the press each month. Its figures cover consumer confidence and measure opinions about current and anticipated economic conditions and buying plans. The Survey Research Center's reports are similar, except that they are not released to the press or the public. Rather, the reports are offered to clients as annual subscriptions. Nevertheless, the Survey Research Center results spread through Wall Street and are usually on the major wire services within an hour or two of release.

The consumer attitude surveys give some indication of whether consumers are happy or sad or whether they are in a mood to buy more or less. Falling inflation and unemployment should lead to improved consumer attitudes and increased consumer spending. However, at times other issues may intervene. If a major political or social issue dominates the nation and the news, it will seep into the consumer sentiment surveys. In some presidential elections—when the campaign issue becomes how well off voters are compared with 4 years earlier—the consumer sentiment surveys often track the political polls closely. Likewise, a major political disruption, like the Iraqi invasion of Kuwait in the summer of 1990, will worry consumers no matter what the hard economic numbers show.

One other type of survey deserves mention here. In recent years collecting surveys of economists' forecasts has become a growing business. During the Reagan administration, the budget analysts responded to criticisms that they were using "Rosy Scenario's" economic forecast by using a widely followed compilation called the *Blue-Chip Economic Indicators,* a survey of about 50 forecasts widely read on Wall Street. Currently there are surveys of economic growth, inflation, interest rates, and other variables. Some are published in newspapers or specialty newsletters. Contributors range from professionals who make their living by tracking and forecasting the economy to magazine editors who are more interested in boosting circulation and poking fun at forecasters.

This review of how the economy is measured and what happens in it has barely touched on many topics. Measuring the economy is the starting point for forecasting, for comparing today with yesterday, and for trying to analyze what happened yesterday as well as what might happen tomorrow. There will be changes and improvements in many of the economic measures, including some of the measures discussed here. Computers, communications, and media will all affect the way we measure and study the economy in years to come. But in the end we will always be trying to measure and then outguess human behavior. Given what the real goal is—figuring out what we'll all do next in the economy—there is little chance these problems will either get boring or be completely solved any time soon.

MARKETS

WHAT MARKETS ARE

We keep reading that one of the great events of the end of the twentieth century was the collapse of communism and the triumph of market economies. While some of us may think that the real triumph of the end of the twentieth century will be surviving to see the twenty-first, we are at least a little curious about what a market economy might be. We live in one. Increasingly, other nations live in market economies and there is no escaping them. In fact, when people have tried to overturn a market economy, they were often confronted with forbidden or black markets or with something worse—nothing to buy or sell at all.

"Markets" are places where we buy or sell stuff—there are food markets, farmers' markets, stock markets, and so forth. But markets aren't just a place to meet and haggle. They do two very important things. First, they establish prices and values. Second, they communicate those prices and values.

Someone has just smiled and said, "An economist knows the price of everything and the value of nothing." What the value of nothing really is might be best left to a philosopher. But, like it or not, economists do use markets to put prices on practically anything and everything. There are studies about what a human life is worth based on how much we typically spend on health and safety or the environment to save a life. The rough answer in 1997 dollars is between $1 and $2 million. Lives aren't the only thing economists have tried to price. True love has also been studied, but with somewhat less recognition by economists than by others.

The market's ability to price almost anything is important. The way we tell if something is worth doing is by comparing the price for it with what we are willing to pay or what we would give up to get it—what it would cost us to lose the opportunity to do something else. Markets are about supply and demand. Let's start with a case where the supply is fixed at one. Suppose an art collector looks at a painting by Picasso. Is it really worth $1 million or $2 million or even $5 million? How can we tell? If it's sold for $5 million then that's the price, or value, that the market puts on it. Why not more than the $5 million it brought at the sale? Because being worth more in the market means that someone would have paid more for it, but no one did. Sure, you may say that you think it's worth $12 million, or you know of someone who would have paid $12 million for it, or your brother-in-law certainly knows someone who would have paid almost $12 million for it. One answer to these questions is to offer you a great deal on a certain very famous bridge in New York City—between Brooklyn and Manhattan. More to the point, the market couldn't justify the price above $5 million because no one was willing to pay more than that for the painting.

On the other hand, some art collectors don't value Picasso's work and wouldn't dream of paying even $5000 for it, to say nothing of $5 million. They may argue that the market is all wrong and the painting can't possibly be worth $5 million. To them, it certainly isn't worth anything like $5 million. One reason markets work so well is that anything in the market ends up with whoever places the highest value on it. It wouldn't make much sense for an art patron to be saddled with a Picasso she despised while someone who really wanted it, or wanted to donate it to a museum, lost out. In effect, the person who is willing to pay the most for this one-of-a-kind Picasso will get it. The buyer will determine the price, by placing the highest value on it.

Is the painting still worth the same $5 million the next day, the next week, or a year after the sale? What if it hangs in someone's home for 10 years instead of being sold again and again? How much is it worth then? To some extent, we don't know. But certainly, if the owner turns down an offer of $7 million, it is worth at least that much. If times change and the owner accepts an offer of "only" $2 million, the painting's value has fallen.

Markets for art can be difficult for economists to track because each painting is unique and because paintings aren't sold and resold every day. In fact, most paintings are rarely sold and it can be difficult to set a value that everyone can agree on without placing the painting on the open market. The art world is not the only arena where values are set by changing opinions of buyers. There are some very big examples of such markets—stock exchanges.

The stock market is one thing we can all agree really is a market. We buy and sell shares on it and the price of the last trade is easy to find. There are some similarities between art and stocks. In both cases, the supply is fixed over some moderate period of time. While there probably won't be another Picasso, there will be other famous

Impressionists. In the stock market, the number of shares of General Motors stock to be had is fixed unless (or until) the company decides to issue some new shares. In both art and stock, people's opinions and their willingness to put up money determine what something is worth. Just as the Picasso went to the buyer who valued it most highly, a share (or 100 shares or 1000 shares) of General Motors will go to whoever values it the highest. The investor who buys 100 shares of GM at $50 per share thinks it is worth at least that much, and the person who sold it thinks it is worth less than $50.

Who's right the next week? If there are plenty of people who think that $50 is cheap for GM, they will probably start buying. The price will rise as the market runs out of people willing to sell at $50 and a buyer offers $51 or $52 per share. Then the buyer was right. But if no one else wants to buy at $50, some owner may suggest a sale at "only" $49 and the price will fall.

Return for a moment to the art market to see how this might work. First, markets set a price or find a value for a rare painting. It may not be a value which every critic agrees on, but it is one for which someone made a sale and staked real money on the outcome. (Nothing impresses market economists more than betting real money on something!) Second, markets spread information. The mere fact that a price is set for a Picasso becomes news and the information is spread. In markets where goods are not unique and there are repeated sales, the information becomes very valuable. Look at the stock market. Suppose a company has 100 million shares outstanding. Not only is no share unique, all 100 million are exactly the same. If you own 100 of them and need to know their value, you simply turn to the stock market or business section of the newspaper and look up the number determined in the market. The same thing goes for most anything else that is sold. If you want to know how much it would cost to build a new outside deck on your house, you find out the market prices for lumber, nails, carpenter's labor, architect's fees, and so on. You check the markets involved.

Finally, markets make sure the right stuff gets to the right place. You might say markets are like giant traffic directors for the economy. Think about building that deck on your house. Suppose you consider what it will be worth to you once it's finished, figure how much you would pay for the lumber, and come up with a budget of $1000. The only problem is that when you get to the lumberyard you discover that you really need to spend $2500 on lumber. Then what? For one thing, the lumberyard thinks that there are other customers out there who would pay two and a half times more than you for the same wood. Maybe those customers are going to build a house and sell the house, and when they figure the value of the house, they *are* willing to pay $2500 for the wood. The wood is worth more to them, and they buy it.

Not fair! You should have been able to get the lumber for $1000. Economics is *not* about what is fair. Anyone who says it is, is probably running for public office and doesn't deserve our votes. Markets don't ensure fairness. They do ensure that the person who puts the highest value on something will get it. There is one little proviso, however. You have to be able to afford it. Few people worry about affording Picasso paintings, but many of us do worry about the cost of food, clothing, and shelter. Leftover food from restaurant kitchens may be worth more to the homeless than to anyone else. But often they can't afford the small sums required to buy the food. When that happens, the market has failed. When, and why, markets fail is important. Before dealing with that, let's look at when they work. To paraphrase Winston Churchill's comment, "Democracy is the worst form of government except for those other forms that have been tried from time to time." In a similar vein, markets are a messy and possibly unfair way to organize an economy—but they are far far better than anything else ever tried or considered.

WHY MARKETS ARE SO IMPORTANT

What markets do that is so important is organize who gets what and how it is used. This involves setting values, spreading information, and making sure that resources are put to their most highly paid use. The last is usually called efficiency or resource allocation. It means that a farmer who has harvested wheat can find rail cars to ship it to market. And if barges are a better way to ship the wheat, the farmer can find barges instead. Of course, most farmers don't buy or rent barges themselves. They sell the wheat to someone who hires the shippers and the barges and then sells the wheat again to someone else who mills it into flour and so forth. All these interconnections are guided by the market. If there is a lot of wheat this year and wheat prices fall, some farmers will switch to other crops that they think will pay better.

How do we know which farmers will switch to something else—say, corn or soybeans? You and I and economists in general don't know who will switch. The farmers know—they know by figuring out where they'll make the best profit next year. In the same way, the railroad and the barge company watch the grain markets, the cost of fuel and labor, and decide whether to buy more rail cars or barges. When all is connected by prices spreading information from one market to another, the system works pretty well.

COMPLEXITY THEORY, SELF-ORGANIZATION, AND ECONOMICS

One of the more recent developments in mathematics, physics, and related sciences is a collection of studies alternately referred to as "complexity theory," "self-organization," and "chaos theory." While some commentators may argue that economics has a special claim on chaos, there are interesting parallels between many of these studies and economics. One of the ideas behind these theories is that at times a collection of objects—animals, computer programs, people, or almost anything else—will seem to become very well organized without any systematic communication or planning. A common example is migrating birds. For a long time many scientists believed that migrating birds must need a leader and a plan to fly in a V-shaped formation. More recently some complexity theorists have shown that if each bird has a simple set of rules about how to position itself compared with the bird next to it, a neat V can easily result. The birds merely all use the same set of intuitive (or genetic) rules. The birds don't have any grand plan or a chosen leader to fly in a V.

There are similar issues in economics. Markets are large collections, almost a flock of buyers and sellers. On one hand, the markets are unorganized—each buyer or seller is out to do the best for himself or herself and no one else. On the other hand, the markets manage to come to a single price. Moreover, a large dose of theoretical economics and mathematics will show that no combination of buying and selling other than what the market price produces will make more people better off unless some others are worse off. In this sense, the market gives the best solution there is. On a less theoretical note, experience has shown that the seemingly self-aggrandizing market economies of capitalism produce more wealth and growth than the centrally organized markets that once flourished in Eastern Europe and Soviet Russia. It seems as if markets are self-organizing and benefit from some deep version of complexity theory.

These ideas are interesting, but as yet not even close to being proved. There is a growing body of work on complexity and chaos and their interaction with economics. So far the only sure conclusion is that there is a long way to go before the mathematics of complexity theory will explain why the economy is exactly the way it is. The curious reader, after wading through the books on complexity theory that now crowd the science shelves of bookstores, might turn to the one piece on economics: Paul Krugman's *The Self-Organizing Economy* (1996). It is fascinating, but it is not beach reading.

(Continued)

OTHER FORMS OF ORGANIZATION

Of course, all these notions of an "invisible hand" guiding the markets, and negotiating prices can sound a bit flaky. Others have come along who think they have a better way. The answer that these people give is to centralize control and decision making so everything can be properly guided to the right spot. We have direction from the top instead of markets (and direction from the bottom). We all spend some time in command-controlled economies. When was the last time a family decided where to eat dinner out together by running an auction to see who would pay how much of someone else's dinner in exchange for the right to choose the restaurant? That negotiation would be the free-market version of the decision. More likely one or two members decided where everyone would eat and that was that. (Whether it was the parents or the children who decided—or should decide—is best left to a book on popular psychology or restaurant marketing.)

CENTRAL PLANNING

The most infamous command-directed economies are the centrally planned nations. With the collapse of communism in many nations of Eastern Europe and Asia, these economies are getting to be less common. Under communism or socialism, market prices were set by the government, not by buying and selling. A central planning agency tried to gather all the information needed to run the economy and then issued orders on who would make what for whom. If the country wanted to build a lot of expensive armaments, no matter what the cost, central planning would get that done. But it would probably cost a lot more than if the economy had been organized by markets. Moreover, in the centrally planned economies, workers got ahead and got paid more by keeping the bureaucrats happy, not by making a better product at a lower cost. The result was often poor-quality goods and a lot of bribed bureaucrats.

Even today, a lot of us work in miniature centrally planned economies—they're called modern corporations.

The internal operations of a large company are run on a central-planning approach even though the company's leaders are most likely firm believers in free markets and capitalism and the company itself operates in one or more free markets. Think of some simple examples. If you need office supplies to get your job done, you don't go out and buy them. Rather, you order them from some centralized supply department that employs a supply specialist to know what kinds of things you need, how much you need, and when you need them. It usually doesn't stop there. The company knows what kinds of office furniture to buy for you, what computer software you should use, and even when you should come to work—all centrally planned through the greater knowledge of an all-wise bureaucrat.

There are times when this system works very well. By avoiding a market for internal operations, the corporation can achieve some results that it wants, even if its employees may not always agree. Some results are obvious. By buying stationery centrally, the corporation may save money and can certainly ensure that everyone uses the same kind of paper with the right logo, name, and address. Of course, some employees would rather spend more for really fancy stationery and others would cut corners, buy cheap paper, and think they are keeping the boss happy. In all these examples, central planning pulls one way and the market pulls another. There may even be some savings from central purchasing through ordering larger quantities at once. But the biggest "saving" for the corporation is to get around the market's controls and impose its own. Economists speak of market failure—cases where markets don't work the way they're supposed to and the results are not what some people want. Examples of market failure range from environmental rules and regulations to simpler things like making sure that the internal market in the corporation can be controlled the way management wants it to be.

The Communist nations of central Europe all collapsed under central planning. Far from burying the West, as their cold war leaders once promised, the Soviet Union and the rest of its political bloc collapsed in the late 1980s. They failed under the weight of crumbling economies that could not provide consumer goods, compete in world markets, or even cover their domestic or military needs. Yet this same central organization seems to be used internally by many modern corporations. What gives?

The answer is information. To replace a market with central controls requires a lot of information. What markets do is balance costs of production (supply) and people's willingness to pay (demand) to signal how much anything and everything is worth. If you know all the information, you don't need the market. In the Communist nations, the central planners never had enough information to really do their job. They didn't know how much it costs to produce a ton of steel. Since the steel factory didn't have to pay for the iron ore, coking coal, and labor it needed—it just got them from the planners—its managers didn't care either. Now, when you don't pay for stuff you get and don't get paid for stuff you produce, why bother to produce efficiently or sell at a profit? For the factories in a centrally planned economy, it is all orders and funny money. No wonder they do whatever is easiest or whatever they please.

In a corporation where information is gathered and distributed and where there are central goals, most of the information is usually available and the central controls can work fairly well. Also, in corporations the market signals may not always be the ones the corporation wants to follow. Suppose that the corporate decides it is important to have all its employees use the same computer software so that files can be easily shared and the computer department has to teach new workers only one set of programs. That makes sense from the corporate standpoint. But some small branch office might find a way to get a great deal on some other kind of software that it thinks is easier to use. The market signal—the great software deal—is different from the corporate need. If the corporation didn't have central planning, it might find itself spending extra time teaching people about more and more software. Moreover, if a big corporation centralizes its purchasing, it can throw its weight around and get better prices from vendors. If it lets everybody buy stuff at the corner stationery store, it won't get any quantity discounts.

Markets fail sometimes. They fail in free-enterprise economies like the United States, not just in places where they are outlawed, as in the Soviet Union. Sometimes the government tries to do something about market failure; other times it doesn't. Sometimes, too, the cure for market failure is worse than the disease, or the apparent failure is used as an excuse by politicians to take control away from the market. Just as learning how markets work can help us understand them, learning how they fail and what the supposed remedies are can help us get the best of them.

Once people realize that there is a labor market and that's where we all go to find jobs, some of them decide the market has failed because they can't find a job. This is not necessarily market failure. It's not easy to find a job paying $1 million a year for only 3 weeks of work with no qualifications. Nor is there an easy way to (legally) buy a fancy sports car for a mere $99. Of course, there are other kinds of unemployment that aren't so blatantly nonsensical. When able-bodied workers are laid off and can't find new work at the same wage, most will blame their difficulty on the market's failure. In a sense they are right—something has changed and there aren't enough buyers. A similar thing happens when home prices fall. Suppose you bought a house for $145,000 a few years ago. You kept it in good shape and now you decide to sell the home and buy a bigger one. The only thing is that the housing market is weak and no one will give you more than $100,000 for your house. The market didn't fail; conditions changed. And before you think this is terrible, switch roles and imagine you're a buyer, not a seller. Can you get a house worth $120,000 for a "mere" $100,000, or more than 15 percent off?

When there are no buyers or sellers left to make a deal with, economists say that the market cleared completely. If there are people left who want to do business at the current price and can't, the market didn't clear. This is what happens with unemployment. But remember that there are always buyers who would buy, but at less than the market price, and sellers who would sell at more than the market price.

MONOPOLIES

One kind of market failure worth noting, if for no other reason than that the government is always trying to do something about it, is a monopoly. Some monopolies have everything to do with taking over markets and nothing to do with market failure. One of the more infamous monopolies in recent decades is the Organization of Petroleum Exporting Countries (OPEC). The principal oil-exporting nations got together in the 1960s and decided to form a cartel—a kind of producers' club—to monopolize the oil business and raise prices. OPEC didn't do much until 1973 and again in 1979, when it created oil crises and forced oil prices up to $40 or more per barrel (pushing gasoline prices close to $2 per gallon). But the markets reasserted themselves and prices slid back to levels we are more used to, even if we may not like them.

Other monopolies really do have something to do with market failures. Suppose your city has two cable TV companies that refuse to work together. One sells only even-numbered channels and the other sells only odd-numbered channels. So, if you want all the major networks, you have to subscribe to both services! Even worse, both cable companies run their own cables under the street and through your house or apartment. You have two sets of cables and two companies digging up the streets all the time. Sounds pretty wasteful. But things aren't likely to work out quite that way. First, cable TV companies are sometimes called natural monopolies—the idea is that it may make sense to have only one in a community.

In the case of cable TV, it costs a lot to build the cable network and very little to add another customer. As each customer is added, the average cost per customer gets lower. Maybe it costs $20 million a year to maintain the cables and only $50 to install a new customer. When there are 1000 customers, the cost for each is $20 million divided by $1000, plus $50 for the installation. That's $20,050. But if there are 1 million customers, the cost is only $20 plus the $50 for installation. If there were two cable companies each serving 500,000 clients at a cost of $40 each (ignore the installation charge for a moment), they could merge into one company and combine their systems or scrap one of them. Before the merger, they might have been charging their clients $50 each and making a profit of $10 per client. Each company made $5 million profit ($10 per customer times 500,000 customers).

Now they merge and combine the systems. The new company, Super Cable, tells customers that they can now get all the channels for the same $50 instead of having to buy two subscriptions. Further, Super Cable promises to dig up the streets only half as often. Sound like a deal for the community? The new company now serves all 1 million clients at a lower cost of $20 each and charges $50. It makes $30 per customer on 1 million customers, or $30 million! Seems that the community isn't the only player to gain from the merger. And since Super Cable is the only company in town, there is nowhere else to buy cable TV when the service starts to go downhill or the price goes up to $54.95 from $50.

The cable TV story is a bit exaggerated, but there are some industries that do have such extreme economies of scale. The usual response is to regulate the business. This has long been done with electric power and local telephone service in the United States. But it was not always the case—in the early days of electric power there were often competing electric companies in the same city. The regulations usually try to set limits on how high prices can go and try to make sure services are kept at acceptable levels. (How the regulation works is a very involved issue, worth several books. See the Appendix for further reading.)

Regulation does not replace the market, but sometimes it offers an acceptable substitute. Both electric power and telephone service have been regulated as long as any consumer can remember. In the vast majority of cases, the results are reasonably satisfactory. Most complaints relate to customer service more than to price or basic delivery. Of course, over the last 60 or more years of regulation, technology has advanced and costs have dropped and dropped and dropped. The result is an almost miraculous world where prices have fallen and producers have prospered. A more problematic industry is the airlines. When regulations were done away with in the late 1970s, prices tumbled and air travel boomed. New airlines sprang up like wildflowers in spring, only to wilt and die a little while later. Today air fares are probably cheaper than they were under regulation 20 years ago, but there are fewer flights and fewer nonstop flights except between a handful of major cities. There are also fewer airlines, and some of those that remain are barely profitable.

EXTERNALITIES

Natural monopolies, scale economies, and falling costs represent one kind of market failure. Another is tied to two related economic concerns. Conservatives call them property rights; liberals call them externalities. Air pollution is the standard example. Supposing a power plant burns dirty coal directly across the street from a laundry. To save money, the power plant doesn't use scrubbers on its smokestacks and puts out a lot of soot. To save money, the laundry dries shirts on an outdoor clothesline instead of using electric clothes dryers. The soot from the power plant gets the shirts dirty, forcing the laundry to wash and rewash shirts.

If you owned the laundry, you would probably say, "There ought to be a law against air pollution and dirty smokestacks." That is the approach that has been taken in most environmental regulation. The power company's dumping of soot in the air is outside of the market for electric power and the market for laundering shirts. It is external to these markets and doesn't take them into account. The market system doesn't work because there is no market for clean air or for dumping soot. For a long time conditions like this existed and nothing much was done. Then about 25 years ago environmental legislation began to appear and regulations followed. There were laws.

Of course, the key question is how much should be spent to clean up the air. Suppose that the only costs of dirty air are the damages suffered by the shirt laundry, damages that work out to 2 cents per kilowatt-hour (kwh) of electricity generated. (That is, we know how much is spent each day rewashing sooty shirts and we divide this figure by how many kilowatt-hours of electricity are generated. Two cents may sound cheap, but the average cost per kilowatt hour in the United States is about 7 cents, so this is real money.) The economist's solution is to put a price on the soot—equal to the cost of the damage it causes. Tax the power plant 2 cents per kwh if it keeps on polluting. If the power plant can clean up its act at 1 cent per kwh, it will do so and avoid the tax. We all come out ahead, since we spent 1 cent per kwh (after all, we consumers will pay for it in our electric bills) and saved 2 cents of damages. If it costs 3 cents per kwh to clean up the power plant, let it be dirty and give the tax money to the laundry as compensation. This would be cheaper than the cleanup. No matter what, there are events outside the market, and government regulators can (in theory) step in and straighten them out.

Things are not this neat and simple in reality. For one thing, no one really knows the true damage costs of the pollution or the true costs of cleaning things up. For another, the real world is not just one power plant and one old-fashioned shirt laundry. It is tens, hundreds, or even thousands of consumers and companies all jockeying for position amid regulations and laws.

There are other ways to look at these issues. Earlier I noted that big corporations are organized from the top down in almost a socialist fashion. In our parable of the power plant and laundry, we could let the laundry and the power plant merge. Then the new company could decide either to buy electric clothes dryers and move the shirt drying inside or to put scrubbers on the stacks—whichever is cheaper. When the companies merge, what had been an economic problem with no market to resolve it in became an internal issue to the new company. This solution points to a different way to look at the whole question of pollution and market failure.

The problem in the original story was that the laundry and the power plant each wanted exclusive use of the air, something that neither of them owned. The laundry wanted to use clean air to dry shirts, while the power plant wanted to use the air to get rid of dirty soot. Suppose that the shirt laundry (because of better political connections) owned the air. Then it would have no problem. If the power plant's cost of cleaning up its stacks were less than what it would have to pay the laundry to buy the air, it would clean up its plant. If the costs of cleanup were higher than what the laundry wanted in a deal (2 cents per kwh for damages), the power plant would buy the air and the laundry would be compensated. This is the same as the tax solution we just saw.

Now, suppose that the property rights for the air are reversed—the power plant owns it and the laundry must buy air from the electric company. The results are still the same. If cleanup is cheap, it gets done; it it is expensive, the laundry buys clothes dryers. In fact, and equally surprising to many, if ownership of the air were simply given to someone, the problem would be solved—even if the air owner were neither the laundry nor the power plant. The air owner would run an auction and the power plant would bid the cost of cleanup while the laundry would bid the cost of its damages (or of buying clothes dryers if that is less). If it costs 2 cents per kwh for the laundry and 3 cents per kwh for the power plant, the power plant would get the air rights and the laundry would buy clothes dryers.

If things are so simple, why do we have pollution? The economics are almost that simple. But no one owns the air and the cost of getting all the buying and selling done—the transactions costs, in economic jargon—are very steep. The conservatives answer to pollution issues is property rights. If there were clear property rights to anything and everything, all these problems could be negotiated without any government intervention or regulation. That answer is no more right or transparent than the idea that simple regulations can solve it all.

One place where property rights don't really exist and where markets can fail is the "commons," where everyone owns something together. Clean air is one example. Others are things like parks, which everyone wants to use, but no one wants to pay for. If all the owners can agree on how to manage a commonly owned resource, things are easy. When they can't agree, things can get very difficult and often end up in court. Ask someone who lives in a condominium or co-op housing development about spending money to redecorate the elevators or the lobby entrances. We have all experienced getting a group of people together to go out to a restaurant, with all agreeing in advance to split the bill evenly. While most people wouldn't normally order only the most expensive thing on the menu, they all find it pays to spend with abandon if the bill is to be shared equally. Likewise, a fisherman may deplore overfishing, but as long as the fishery is owned jointly and in common, it pays to catch as much as possible as quickly as possible. For these kinds of market failure, single ownership or regulation may be the best answer.

One real-world problem of the commons today is the attempt to eliminate the production and use of chlorofluro-carbons (CFCs) such as freon, which is used in air conditioners. CFCs in the air increases the amount of ozone, a pollutant that destroys the upper atmosphere, thereby permitting more ultraviolet radiation from the sun to reach the earth's surface. This radiation contributes to the increase in skin cancer. The short scientific story is that the cheapest solution is to replace CFCs with other chemicals that are almost as effective as coolants. Regulations and international agreements have been put into place. But just as it pays fishermen to overfish, it pays some people to cheat on the CFC ban. In fact, smuggling CFCs may be second to smuggling drugs in some places.

The way society is organized has left certain actions (such as pollution) external to the market and has not vested ownership (property rights) in all the things that matter to people. The result is that markets don't always work as well as we might hope. But the vast majority of time markets do work. They remain the best way to establish values and communicate those values to people who need to know.

RONALD COASE AND THE NOBEL PRIZE IN ECONOMIC SCIENCE

A bit more than 20 years ago the Nobel prizes were expanded to include economics. The purists will quickly point out that the Bank of Norway put up the new funds and that the prize in economic science is handled separately from the other Nobels. Less pure than the purists, others may point out that economics is one of the few sciences in which two people can both receive the prize for saying exactly the opposite. Economics often leads to debates when it tries to deal with pollution and how to regulate industry to reduce pollution. After all, economists will argue that we should clean up pollution only as long as the benefits of less dirt cover the costs of cleaning up the dirt. (Not a discussion parents should have with a teenager about the state of the offspring's bedroom.)

Economist Ronald Coase received the Nobel prize in 1991 for essays he wrote in 1960 and in 1937. The 1960 article, "The Problem of Social Cost," discussed the economics of pollution control and the fact that, as long as the polluters and the pollutees (the power plant and the laundry in our example) can negotiate, they will reach a satisfactory solution.

Whereas much of modern economic prose is besieged by long equations in Greek letters alternating with short paragraphs of turgid English, Coase's writings avoid mathematics and are unusually well done. When we consider that he tackles some of the more subtle and stickier issues, this is quite an accomplishment. One other notable aspect of Coase is that, unlike many modern champions in the publish-or-perish world, he has written relatively little. In fact, the two articles cited by the Nobel committee represent a significant portion of his published work. For any economist, these two articles would represent a major contribution to the field. For the rest of us, such brevity can restore some faith in both English and economics.

(*Continued*)

MARKETS INSIDE FIRMS

Some of the more amusing cases of markets found, lost, and avoided seem to occur in firms made up of economists who try to practice what they preach. Several years ago I worked for a consulting firm that was made up largely of economists and that did work in economics. (This was a while back and the firm has certainly changed since then.) As in many offices, the flow of work was often uneven. Some weeks one group or department would be swamped while at other times there would be junior staffers sitting around with little to do. Roughly speaking, there were three kinds of employees: senior economists who directed projects, research assistants who worked on the projects, and secretaries who kept the whole place running. There were one or two overriding rules in the office. The firm charged its clients by how many hours people worked on each project. One key to success for a senior economist was to have as few idle research assistants as possible, since the firm paid the assistants whether they worked or not, but made money only when there was work to be paid for. Another key to success was to keep clients happy by getting the work done on time. Of course, to ensure that things were done on time, research assistants were needed. To solve the question of whether to keep a lot of research assistants and risk that some would occasionally be idle or have a few and miss client deadlines, an active market in trading research assistants arose.

Some people get upset when markets involve labor or people. Slave labor is illegal. But we all buy newspapers for the latest gossip about other labor markets—whether it is sports trades or movie stars under long-term contracts to studios.

The labor market at the consulting firm was very simple. If you were short of research assistants, you got on the phone about 9 a.m. and called around looking for a department with some excess labor. If you found some, a trade was made. The buyer agreed to cover the seller's costs by taking the temporarily excess researchers and charging their time to the buyer's client. The buyer got work done and could meet the deadline. The seller managed not to be seen by the boss with unemployed (and costly) idle resources. Both sides benefited—what economists call "gains from trade." There was a real price: Each trade carried an understanding that the favor would be returned sometime in the future. As a long time trader in this market, I know it worked quite well.

What made it most interesting was that in this firm of economists and fervent believers in free markets and free enterprise, the labor-trading market was an underground affair. Sometimes the office administrator—no occupant of the position seemed to last very long—would become convinced that the economists could not be left to themselves to reallocate labor resources by redistributing excess research assistants. Instead the administrator would try to assign extra research assistants on the basis of some unknown (and probably indescribable) system. The problem with any centrally planned system is that, unlike the real buyers and sellers, the central planners rarely know even a fraction of the true demands and supplies. In the consulting firm, the office administrator somehow never got the researchers with the right experience assigned to the right projects. The economists—who were looking out for their projects or for their own valued

(Continued)

researchers—did a much better job of correctly assigning the workers.

What happened to this firm and its internal black market in labor? It flourished and so did the black market. And the rules were gradually bent to accommodate the process. Labor market trading normally took place between 9:00 and 9:30 every morning. The office administrator decided that she needed to limit the time she spent on reassigning researchers and that there were more critical things to be done first thing in the morning. So she asked that all requests for extra researchers reach her by 10 a.m., when they would be promptly acted on. Of course, by 10 a.m. the trading for the day was over. To keep the system working, a few trades were usually reported to the central planning agency to make the planners feel needed. The market flourished and the firm prospered.

(Continued)

Now that we think we know a market if we stumble into one, it's time to consider some real markets instead of all this maybe-yes, maybe-no stuff. Markets are really everywhere. The following sections look at a number of them. Some we know are markets because of their name, like the stock market and the bond market, even if there is no physical location for them. Others we all participate in, like the labor market. Still others we talk about a lot, like real estate. Even food and clothing are part of a market— retail sales. Through it all, we will try to see what makes markets move and how we can understand what might happen next.

The order of discussion is:

- The stock market
- The money market
- The foreign exchange market
- The real estate market
- The retail market

As we tour these markets, there are some questions to keep in mind. Most of all, what will economics do for us? More specifically, how does the market set prices and what are the leading factors that determine prices? This leads to where we can look for a hint about what prices will do next. Of course, if we don't like the price, it would be nice to know where to get a bargain. Markets carry some risks, and the risks vary from market to market. As the tour continues, we should also understand the risks in each market and how to control or avoid them if possible.

THE STOCK MARKET

Of all the markets we are likely to confront, the stock market is probably the subject of more lore, theory, law, thought, ideas, folly, and sheer nonsense than any other. Perhaps Mark Twain pegged it best in Pudd'nhead Wilson's calendar for October: "October. This is one of the peculiarly dangerous months to speculate in stocks in. The others are July, January, September, April, November, May, March, June, December, August, and February." Twain may have been thinking about how little rhyme or reason stock prices sometimes have. It is not unusual for stock market averages to rise or fall 10 or 20 percent in a year. In fact, a movement of 0.5 to 1 percent on a single day is typical. This doesn't sound like much, but compounded over a year a 0.5 percent gain adds up to over 300 percent. That is, stock prices would quadruple. Before you run to your broker, realize that prices don't go in only one direction. In the words of one banker, allegedly J. P. Morgan, "they fluctuate." As to the individual stocks in some average, it is common for one or another stock to rise by 20 percent or more in the course of a few months.

People become upset with the stock market because they don't think prices should fluctuate as much as they do. People look at the price of a company's stock and don't believe that the company's real value—whatever that may be—can really fall or rise by 25 to 50 percent in a year. After all, when the price of an airline's stock tumbles it still owns as many planes and can fly as many routes, so why is it worth so much less?

Airline stock prices don't really depend on how many airplanes the airline owns. Rather, when you buy the stock you buy two things—a share in the company's future earnings and the chance to sell the stock to someone else. What the future earnings are worth is a matter of opinion, as is the price of the stock tomorrow when you try to sell it. What drives stock prices? People's opinions more than anything else. What happens if people think a particular company is headed for fantastic profits and they turn out to be wrong? In the beginning the price of its stock is likely to soar on stockholders' forecasts of future riches. But then one day the news may come out that things aren't what they hoped for and the stock could crumble. Of course, if you guessed correctly that the company wouldn't really strike it rich, you could have stayed away from the stock. Had you been daring, you might have bought shares anyway and then planned to sell them *before* the truth came out. Had you been very daring, you would have bought shares, sold them before the truth was revealed, and then sold short even more of the stock (by borrowing shares) to make hay on the fall. Sounds easy, but it isn't because you would need to (1) correctly forecast the company's true fortunes, (2) really understand how people would react, and (3) time it all right.

SHORT SALES, MARGIN, AND OTHER CURIOS

The stock market and Wall Street have various ways to trade stock that strike some people as strange or even a bit outrageous but are second nature to veteran stock traders. Among these are selling short, buying on margin, and trading options. All these techniques allow investors to act as if they own stock without paying for it in the beginning. Many also allow investors to take on large risks. These approaches are often profitable, completely legal, and certainly not immoral. But if you think buying stocks is the same thing as buying groceries, you might change your mind.

Selling short is selling what you don't own. Suppose you think a particular stock, Gravity, Inc., is about to fall. The stock is now selling for $20 per share and you think it is going to fall to $10. If you do own it, sell it. If you don't own it, you can make money on this forecast—sell it anyway. That is sell it short. In this transaction, your broker will arrange to borrow the stock from another investor so you can meet your obligation to deliver the stock 3 days after you sell it. Your broker will also ask you to keep the cash from selling the stock in your brokerage account and check your credit to make sure you can pay for the stock if the price goes up. If you're right and the price of Gravity, Inc. does fall, you can buy it back at $10 and realize the difference—$10 per share less brokerage fees—as profit. Buying the stock is called covering the short. Short selling can be risky. If you buy Gravity at $20 per share, the most you can lose is that $20. If you sell Gravity short at $20 per share, the sky's the limit on your possible losses. If the stock defies your prediction and hits $100, covering that short means buying the stock at $100 after you sold it short at $20—and losing $80 per share.

If short selling isn't for you, there is buying on margin. Here you can borrow some of the money to buy the stock. Suppose you want to buy 100 shares of Sure Thing, Inc. at $30 per share but you have only $2000. Open a *margin account* and your broker will lend you the last $1000. Currently regulations permit margins of 50 percent, so you can borrow up to half the money needed to buy a stock. Some brokers may be more restrictive in certain cases. If Sure Thing goes from $30 to $50, you just doubled your money. At $50 you sell out for $5000, pay off the $1000 loan, and have $4000—double the $2000 you started with. But if Sure Thing isn't a sure thing and it falls to $10, your broker will call up and tell you to pay off the $1000 loan. If you say no, the broker will sell the stock and use the money to repay the loan. Actually, if the stock falls, that *margin call* will come

(*Continued*)

sooner than $10. Margin magnifies both the gains and the losses and makes the investment riskier.

Another game is trading options. An option gives you the right to buy or sell a stock at a particular price. You might buy a *call option* to buy High-Flyer Corp. at $20 when the stock is selling at $18 per share. If High-Flyer climbs to $28, the option will let you buy the stock at $20 and turn around and sell it at $28. Options typically have time limits or expiration dates. If the options expire and the stock is still selling at $18, they are worthless. There are also *put options* which give you the right to sell the stock at a set price. If you own a put at $20 on High-Flyer and the stock stays at $18, you can make $2 by selling it (putting it) to the option writer. Yes, anyone (including you) can write an option. If you own a stock selling at $45 and you are sure it won't go to $50, you can sell someone the option to buy it from you at $50. You pocket the money and hope the stock doesn't jump to $55. If it does, you will probably be forced to sell at $50 and lose the amount between the call option price and the market price. Now if all that sounds simple, try naked calls. You can sell a call option—the right for someone to buy a stock from you at a given price—without owning the stock. Needless to say, options can get involved, profitable, and risky.

Margins, short selling, and options are all part of the stock market. More variations are possible when you are trading with money, paper, and promises than when you are just buying groceries.

(*Continued*)

Approaches to Market Analysis

It is probably harder to figure how other people will forecast a company's fortunes than to figure out what you
think those fortunes are. One economist who played the
market with success was John Maynard Keynes. Keynes
managed his own funds and the endowment for his college
at Cambridge University for a number of years. He
described the market as a peculiar beauty contest in which
the aim is to pick the winners by figuring out who (or
what) everyone else will pick to be a winner. If you think a
stock's earnings are about to soar and you buy the stock, it
will still languish if no one else has ever heard of it. Even if
you're right, it may still languish for a long, long time.

There are, broadly speaking, three ways people try to
beat the stock market. They go to fortune tellers and read
tea leaves, they try to figure out what the company's future
earnings will look like and bet that the market will come
around to their way of thinking, or they look at market
trends for some sign of what other people are thinking. The
first method is rather crackpot, but used. Nevertheless, we
will say little more about it here. The second is often called
fundamental analysis, and the third includes everything
from psychology to stock charts. Both the psychologists and
the chartists are urged to follow the fundamental approach
and read on before condemning the present analysis, which
lumps these two together.

Investors who believe in fundamental analysis plan to
beat the market by finding stocks that no one else has recognized for their true potential. This is not easy, but it can
be very rewarding. Warren Buffett, one of the most famous
and probably most successful investors around, is dedicated to fundamental analysis. He counsels investors not to

worry about the market's opinions and to stick to what they know about companies. Does his success—Buffett turned a modest nest egg into several billion dollars over a period of 30 years—mean that the stock market depends only on fundamental values and not on what people think? Not at all. Rather, Buffett tries to buy stocks before everyone else recognizes their true value. He succeeds more often than not, but there are many others who try to same thing and don't succeed at all. Buffett's real skills are in understanding the companies he pinpoints, having the courage of his convictions, and sticking with them until the rest of the world sees the light. Analyzing Warren Buffett has become a small industry of its own. (See the Appendix for books on Buffett and his investments.)

In direct contrast are the chartists. Rather than seeking stocks that are unrecognized gems, they hope to understand other investors' opinions and buy a stock before it becomes popular and enjoys a price run-up. Chartists literally pore over charts of stock prices in the hope of forecasting tomorrow's price. It may sound like reading tea leaves to those inexperienced in the ways of Wall Street. Yet most major brokerage firms have "technicians" who do exactly that, and most brokers will accept chart readings as sound reasons for buying stocks. On the other side, there are numerous tales of plotting things like flips of a coin on a stock chart and finding someone who will confidently forecast the "stock's" next move. If you really could tell which stocks would be popular tomorrow, you could make money by buying the stocks before everyone else rushed into buying them.

Psychologists too try to understand how the masses think and outsmart them. This approach may work for a few, but it is very few. After all, markets seem to be subject to huge swings in prices and opinions. The stock market surge and crash in 1987 is a recent and dramatic example. Still, the pattern is far from new. In a classic collection called *Extraordinary Popular Delusions and the Madness of Crowds* Donald McKay, a nineteenth-century journalist, recounts market manias that make today's stock market look more like a Sunday bake sale. For example, for a brief period in the 1630s ordinary Dutch tulip bulbs commanded prices worth a king's ransom—or at least several times the annual income of a middle-class merchant. There was futures trading in tulip bulbs as well. But the market crashed and sparked a recession. No matter whether an investor reads charts or tries to read minds, the game is the same—to guess what stocks will be popular before the populace starts buying them.

Information Is Money

There may be some kernels of truth in all these approaches that you can use to try to understand or predict stock prices. The difficulty lies in the fact that stock prices reflect the current consensus, so knowing what everyone else knows merely lets you agree with everyone else about what a stock might be worth now. If you, and everyone else, know that a stock will pay a dividend of $5 per share in each of the next several years and that the company will grow at the same rate as the general economy, chances are you can all agree on the stock's price. But this stock won't be a great buy. In fact, it will be a very average buy. Suppose for a moment that you study the stock and decide that it will really pay $10 per year, not $5, but that no one else understands your analysis. (Don't worry about where you got this great revelation for the moment.) You buy a lot of it at $100 per share. Then one morning the company announces some wonderful new product that you guessed would be introduced. Sales boom and shortly thereafter the dividend is doubled. Investors, seeing how much more valuable the stock is, rush in. When the buying frenzy stops, the price has been driven up to $200 a share and you have doubled your money. Not bad. What changed was both the dividend rate ($5 to $10) and the public perception of the stock. You got rich because you figured out the higher dividend *before* anyone else. If you had figured it out late, you wouldn't have made anything special. And since, after the price jump, the price again reflects the consensus, there are no extra profits left in owning the stock.

So how *do* you get rich in the market? Analyze stocks better than anyone else or anticipate how the rest will think. There are books on financial analysis. Likewise, there are books on crowd psychology and investor behavior. The key to either the financial or the psychological analysis is easier said than done. It is to go through the facts to find what someone else missed.

Nonetheless, there may be some bargains left on Wall Street, or at least some hints about where to look for them. Academic research suggests that some stocks tend to have better-than-average chances of rising and greater-than-average volatility or risk. The two characteristics are small-cap size and low price-to-book ratio. That all sounds like Wall Street jargon and it is. Small cap (capitalization) means that companies that are small in terms of their total market value (share price multiplied by number of shares outstanding) tend to do better than medium- or large-size companies over time. But they also bounce around a lot more. Price to book reflects the ratio between a company's market value and the value as shown on the company's books. Generally, companies with lower-than-average ratios will also do better than average. The comparison with the average may be the key. The idea is that these companies are currently thought to be less valuable relative to their accounts than is the average company. They may be unrecognized gems. But before you rush ahead with some get-rich-quick scheme, remember that these stocks also carry more risk and that you're not really getting something for nothing. (As a start on finding the research, look at the books by Malkiel and Siegel—for a different angle—in the Appendix. Beyond that, you need to wade through the academic literature in more depth.)

Getting something for nothing is, of course, what attracts many people to Wall Street. Two of the peculiar angles are some pricing anomalies and the inescapable penalty of transaction costs. Mark Twain's advice on investing in October never fails to bring chuckles from an audience, no matter what time of the year. But analysts will talk about the "January effect" with a straight face. This is simply the idea that the market does better in January than in any other month. It is even possible to hear this straight-faced comment about a market rally that began in November or December: "The January effect came in November this year."

If it were only so simple to buy stocks in December and sell them in February and get rich. Yes, the market does rise more often than not in January, and over the last 60 years the percentage of Januaries in which stocks rose was greater than the percentage of all months in which stocks rose. But it isn't a way to guarantee wealth. The problem is that once you figure in the costs of buying and selling stocks, you pretty much eliminate the profits. Moreover, this should not be much of a surprise. Recall that we talked about how markets create and spread information. Information is money and good information attracts money. If investors really could buy stocks in December, sell them in February, and make a sure profit, everyone would rush to do so. The rush to buy in December would boost prices while the rush to sell in February would knock prices down. All of a sudden these sure-thing investors would be buying at too-high prices and selling at too-low prices—just the reverse of what they want. The story of why the market would kill off the January effect if it worked is an example of arbitrage. Arbitrage used to be called the law of one price: The same thing can't sell for two different prices in two different markets if you can profitably buy in one and sell in the other. It is the underpinning of most modern financial economics.

THE EFFICIENT MARKET HYPOTHESIS

There is another theory of how the stock market works which is firmly grounded in the idea of arbitrage and the speed with which modern markets move. It is called the *efficient market hypothesis*—EMH, for those who like acronyms. The idea is that markets are so efficient at finding and using information and incorporating that information into prices, that the only way anyone ever beats the market is by dumb luck. There may be some truth to the idea. Consider a widely followed and heavily studied stock like IBM, AT&T, or Microsoft. There are up to 50 or more Wall Street analysts covering each of these companies, poring over every little bit of news that comes out. In addition, numerous investors, newspeople, market watchers, portfolio managers, and so forth study these widely followed stocks. At any moment all that is (legally) known about the company has been read, studied, analyzed, and digested by all investors in the market. The only thing that can move the stock is a new piece of news. When that piece is revealed, it spreads so fast that the price adjustment is almost instantaneous. The result is that practically no one ever studies the stock, correctly deduces the future, and invests accordingly.

One key factor is the speed at which information is distributed and incorporated into stock prices. For widely held stocks the story is reasonably accurate. On September 20, 1995, AT&T announced it would divide itself into three companies in the largest corporate breakup in modern history. The news broke at about 9:15 a.m. New York time, and was carried on major news services reaching Wall Street brokers and analysts. The stock jumped when trading began 15 minutes later. It opened 6 points higher than it had closed the night before. At the end of the day, after over 20 million shares of AT&T had changed hands, the stock closed within a point of where it opened. Essentially all the price change related to the most important announcement AT&T had made in over 10 years took place in a single trade 15 minutes after the first headlines hit the news wires. To say that prices adjust to news events almost instantly is not that much of an understatement. Markets can be, and usually are, that efficient.

One message of the EMH is that, if the analysts are any good, all the news about large companies is already in the price. Unless you are really convinced that you know something everyone else missed, your time might be better spent looking at stocks that are not followed by hoards of professional analysts and traders. You may realize better investment returns on your time and effort if you research some of the less widely followed companies on the Street. That is not asking too much—plenty of well-known companies are followed by 10 or fewer analysts. On the other hand, there are moments when widely followed companies turn in big gains. The past several years have seen some auto companies and even such fabled blue chips as IBM come back from near death.

The second message of the EMH is probably more important. It suggests that trying to pick the right stocks among those that are widely followed is a losing battle. Losing because your chances of picking the right ones are sheer chance, so your efforts at analysis are wasted, and because you probably are spending a lot on trading commissions and other transaction costs. If you're "lucky," you're also spending a lot on capital gains taxes every time you sell a seemingly well-chosen stock. This doesn't mean that stocks are a bad bet. In fact, over the 20 years ending September 1996, stocks returned about 15 percent per year, including reinvested dividends. Put another way, $1000 invested in the market in 1975 would have been worth $15,265 in 1996. Stocks are a very good long-haul bet and they beat inflation.

If you believe in the EMH and can't choose the right stocks, but still like the 14 percent per year compounded return, what can you do? Simply buy a piece of a lot of stocks. It's easier than it sounds. There are a number of indexes that gauge market action. The most widely used index among investors is the Standard & Poor's 500. This is not simply an average of 500 stock prices, since two companies can have similar stock prices but differ significantly in their size. Rather, it is an average of the market values of 500 companies. More important, when people say the market was up 14 percent last year, they mean the S&P 500 was up 14 percent last year. You could buy each of the 500 stocks in the right proportion. But it is easier and cheaper to buy an index mutual fund which buys the stocks. It's easier because mutual fund companies have gone to great lengths to make things easy. And it's cheaper because there are economies of scale, so your overall costs should come in at much less than 1 percent of the value of the stocks, annually.

The most common comment about buying index funds is that you just settled for the market average and you won't beat the average, ever. True, but you won't miss it by much either. Moreover, in a typical year two-thirds of the mutual funds and money managers don't beat the market. So, with the index, you're already beating two-thirds of the pros. Index fund investing has gotten a lot of interest lately. The readings listed in the Appendix should keep you as busy as you like.

Before leaving the stock market there are some closely related markets worth mentioning again. Options were introduced earlier in the chapter. If you own an option, you have the option of doing something under preset terms. The most common kind is a *call option,* which gives you the right to buy a stock at a preset price. Many corporations give their middle- and upper-level employees options good for several years with a "strike" price (the price in the option) close to the market when the options are given out. That way, if the stock price rises, the employees share in the riches. Of course, if the employees can boost the stock price, they will.

Other than corporations rewarding employees, do options make any sense? Yes. First, people buy, sell, and trade them and try to get rich in the process. It may be a game with as many losers as winners, but it is popular. Second, options can be useful in other ways—mainly, by transferring risk. Options are a form of insurance, just like insuring your car or your house. The simplest insurance example is a *put option,* which lets you sell stock at a preset price. Think about the IBM stock again. Maybe you think IBM management will be brilliant and the stock will soar to $150. But there is a chance the managers won't be so smart, or they might all quit and join the competition, or maybe (just maybe) your analysis is wrong. If IBM is selling at $100, buy some stock and buy a put at $90. The put is the insurance—if the stock craters, you can use the put to sell the stock at $90. You take a loss of $10 plus what you paid for the put.

The interesting thing is that the put is insurance; you paid someone else to carry some of your risks—to do your worrying for you. The person who sold you the put covers some of your risks in owning the stock. But don't think you got off easy with the put. After all, if the stock falls but doesn't go below $90, the put is worthless. And if the stock rises, the put is worthless as well. In the latter case, you bought insurance for little more than peace of mind—which is why most of us buy insurance anyhow. The point of all this is that markets can be used to buy and sell a lot of different things. Here we are buying and selling the risk in stocks. Why would anyone buy the risks? If you pay people enough, they might make money at it. Or they may buy an offsetting contract or need the opposite position.

THE MONEY MARKETS

The stock market is only one of many financial markets—a collection of related markets for different kinds of financial items. Once upon a time, the financial markets talked about "paper" because stocks, bonds, Treasury notes, and so forth were all printed on paper. Nowadays these exist mostly as electronic specs in a computer memory, not as printed documents. In fact, the paper has literally become a collector's item in many cases. The money markets have always traded promises to pay certain amounts of money in certain circumstances—what's changed is the way those promises are recorded. While prices are still set by bargaining and arguing, in some cases the mechanics have changed as well. Once upon a time, prices were set by face-to-face bargaining. In many markets this is still the case. Stock options are traded by "open outcry," meaning one trader announces what is for sale and the others shout their offers. If they don't shout loud enough, they miss the sale. Today most stock trades are made by "upstairs brokers" on the phone or by traders communicating by computer or even computer to computer. But even in the modern electronic age, business is still done face to face on the exchange floor.

The biggest financial markets don't exist in a single place. They are called "over the counter" markets and consist of traders using telephones or computers to communicate. While the most famous over-the-counter market, NASDAQ, trades stocks, the biggest ones trade U. S. Treasury securities and foreign exchange. Traders talk to one another and agree on sales and prices. Their trades are recorded on computers in their offices, and the prices are reported by various computer-based quote services. In some cases, it is faster to connect two computers over a specialized network than to make a phone call, and the transaction is done by typing messages on computer screens. Recently, computer-based order systems have come into play. When the stock exchange opens in the morning, the computers sort out all the orders filed overnight and match buyers with seller—in effect, executing the trade at the opening price in the market for many of these transactions.

The computerization of modern financial markets is both total and fascinating. The computer power brought to bear on the financial markets exceeds almost any other computerized undertaking. A modern trading room has more screens per person than anything the Defense Department, NASA, or some Hollywood sci-fi movie director ever dreamed up. While the first place a new desktop supercomputer may be used is in the engineering firm that designed it, the first paying customers are usually on a trading floor. Almost every financial instrument is traded electronically. Some kinds couldn't exist without computers.

Our interest is more in what is being traded in the market and how the price is being set than in the modern computerized pyrotechnics. While stocks may be the corner of the financial markets that garner the most ink in the morning papers or that make headlines on the 6 o'clock news, there are other important markets as well. Among these are the markets for bonds; for short-term borrowing done through such instruments as Treasury bills, commercial paper, and certificates of deposit; and for foreign exchange. These are all interrelated. Tradition is to begin with the "money market," where borrowings are for less than a year. Then we turn to foreign exchange. (Bonds and other long-term instruments are discussed in Chapter 3.) After that we will escape from the financial markets to what some economists like to call the "real" side of the economy—although they are not suggesting that there is anything unreal or fake about the financial side.

The money market probably got its name because the instruments traded are very close to money. They consist of short-term borrowing in which the borrower's ability to pay back the loans is considered to be above reproach. That's not to say that defaults don't occur occasionally. They do, and they can be real dillies. History is littered with financial crises brought on by the failure or near failure of a short term borrower thought to be above reproach. A recent example is Orange County, California. Older, but equally infamous examples include Franklin National Bank in 1974, Penn Square Bank in 1982, and the Penn Central Railroad in 1970. Rather than dwell upon the failures, let's look at what happens in the vast majority of cases when the market works.

As with most markets, we can look at what is being sold in the money market, how the price is set, what can upset it, what risks must be considered, and what an understanding of the market might do for us. The money market is pretty much the domain of professionals trading with other people's money. *Round lots* in these instruments—meaning the typical size of the deal (something like buying eggs by the dozen) are either $100,000 or $1 million. The instruments take a few basic forms. There are Treasury bills, certificates of deposit (CDs), and commercial paper. All of these are short-term loans to some big borrower. In the case of Treasury bills, the borrower is the federal government.

Each Monday the Federal Reserve sells about $20 billion of 3- and 6-month Treasury bills for the federal government. Treasury bills are called *discount securities* because of the way interest is calculated and paid. The name indicates that you buy at a discount and then get back the full face amount when the bill matures. The system is fairly simple. You give the government about $9700 and 6 months later you get back $10,000. The difference—$300—is the interest you earned. Specifically, you earned $300 on $9700, or 3.1 percent over 6 months. (This is roughly 6.2 percent annually.) The mathematics—which won't concern us here—are a little different from the math for a home mortgage, but the idea of lending and borrowing at interest is the same.

The federal government is not the only borrower in the money market. A second large group is banks, which borrow money by accepting deposits from people like you and me. When the deposits are big—at least $100,000—they are called jumbo CDs and they are traded in the markets. You might deposit your money in the bank by buying a jumbo CD. If you need the money suddenly, you don't go to the bank and withdraw it early. Instead, you sell the CD in the money market. Of course, banks aren't the only borrowers. Others include large corporations. In many ways they are little different from banks, except that their borrowing is called commercial paper. Both commercial paper and certificates of deposit are similar short-term loans to creditworthy (or supposedly creditworthy) borrowers.

This is a market for the pros. A round lot is $100,000 as a minimum. If you want to trade, don't go to the local bank branch or ATM machine. You need a contact in a trading room or at least a preferred account at your bank. And you probably have to pay with something called Fed funds, which are readier than ready cash because they're on deposit at the Federal Reserve, not at your local bank. Despite all these trappings of high finance and mystery, the money market matters more than most for the average person. If you have invested in a money market fund—at last count the public had about $0.5 trillion in money market accounts—you have a big stake in this market.

A money market fund is a mutual fund that buys only money market instruments. These funds began in the late 1960s and early 1970s. At that time regulations limited the interest that banks and savings and loans could pay on savings accounts. When money market interest rates rose in the late 1960s, and again in the early 1970s, people shifted money from bank accounts to money market funds to take advantage of the higher interest rates. Some large mutual fund companies that knew a good business when they saw it promoted money market funds. The money flowed out of the banks and the savings and loans and into the money markets. Things have never been the same since, despite various celebrated bank failures, recessions, recent difficulties in a few money market funds, and other disruptions. If you keep some extra cash in a money market fund, this market is your market.

In most markets there are two key factors—supply and demand. In this one there are three. The third is the Federal Reserve. Without the Fed, prices are set by the balance of borrowers and lenders. Suppose some companies are enjoying stronger business and need to buy more raw materials. They may start borrowing in the money market. Or if they had been lending money in the market, they may put the cash to work buying materials for their business instead. Either way, the demand for cash rises and the supply falls. That means that the price of money—interest rates—will climb. If the reverse is true—if business is slow and companies decide to hold onto their cash rather than stock up on raw materials—then the price of money, the interest rate, will fall.

The Fed can play in this game too. In particular, the Fed can draw money out of the money market or pump money into the financial system through its dealing with banks. If the Fed wants to raise interest rates, it draws money out of the banking system by selling Treasury securities to banks. When banks pay for the securities, money is removed from the banking system and interest rates rise. You can also think of the Fed as selling securities and pushing the price of the security lower. Since a lower price means higher interest rates, selling securities raises interest rates. When the Fed wants to lower interest rates, it will buy securities. When the Fed pays banks for securities, it is adding money to the banking system. The first interest rate affected is the Fed funds rate. Fed funds are money that banks lend to one another overnight to make sure they have enough cash on hand to comply with federal banking regulations. The Fed funds rate is the linchpin for most short-term rates. If the Fed funds rate climbs, investors and traders presume the Fed is trying to raise rates and they push up short-term interest rates in response. Occasionally the markets will misread the Fed, but most of the time the signals are correctly understood.

The result is that prices are set in the money market by supply, demand, *and* the Fed. Following the Fed is a combination of economics and psychology. Fed-watching is a game everyone can play. For the money market, supply and demand is mostly a reflection of other things in the economy. If overall activity is slowing down and people or businesses have excess cash on hand, they may invest it for the short term in the money market. This supply of cash will push interest rates down as the economy slows. The reverse can also happen. In boom times when business begins borrowing to build inventory and add new jobs, the demand for loans rises and so do interest rates.

When we are looking at interest rates as the price of money, there is still another wrinkle to consider—inflation. Suppose that prices are generally rising and the inflation rate (the speed at which prices rise) is 5 percent per year. If you loan someone money for a year, it is worth 5 percent less when you get it back. So you would like the borrower to cover that 5 percent loss. In effect, if you would loan money at 3 percent in an economy with no inflation, you would want 8 percent (5 percent inflation plus 3 percent lending) in an economy with 5 percent inflation. The idea which comes from Irving Fisher, an American economist of the first half of the century, is the basis for comparing market interest rates with inflation-adjusted or "real" interest rates. What it means is that when inflation rises, so do interest rates.

An important issue in any financial market is how to protect yourself from price swings. Earlier we discussed options in the stock market. Options and futures are also available on various money market instruments. But there is a seemingly simpler way to protect your position against rate changes. Instead of lending money for a short time like 90 or 180 days, you can buy a bond and lend the money for a long time—5, 10, or 20 years. Sometimes long, or very long periods of time are considered. But tying up your money for 20 years is riskier than lending it for 6 months. Usually, you get paid a higher interest rate for longer periods of time. There is no sharp split between short term and long term and the bond and money markets follow each other closely. In effect, they are almost one market together.

THE FOREIGN EXCHANGE MARKET

Before leaving the financial markets, there is one other variant of the money market worthy of some comments. It is a market in which money is bought and sold for other money—the foreign exchange market. All those who travel outside their home country participate in it, albeit in a very small way. The total size of the foreign exchange, or "forex" market is several billion dollars bought and sold *each day*. That's right, each day. One factor in its overall size is Europe. In the European Community travel and trade between countries is almost as common as travel and trade from one state to another in the United States. One of the differences is that currencies change from country to country, while all 50 states use the U.S. dollar.

The politicians and economists are always trying new ideas and theories in the forex markets. Over the last 100 or more years, numerous systems or regimes have been touted. One of the most fabled, and least understood, is the gold standard. We have not had one in any form for over 50 years and haven't had one that is even close to what some gold bugs dream about since before World War I. From the end of World War II until about 1971 we did have an extended period of fixed exchange rates. Currently we have floating rates, with currency values depending on a market. However, there is a serious effort under way in Europe to establish a system of fixed exchange rates and create a single currency for Europe by 1999. This effort is called the European Monetary Union (EMU), and the currency has been named the Euro. Debates over the benefits and costs of EMU continue to rage in numerous European nations, and it is far from clear (as of early 1997) if these efforts will succeed in establishing fixed exchange rates. Even if Europe does establish a single currency, there will be forex questions for the rest of the world to deal with in the markets.

Forex markets pose many interesting problems. For economists, a leading one is to find a theory that really does give reliable predictions of future exchange rates. The most widely accepted and easiest understood theory is called *purchasing power parity* (PPP). The idea of PPP is that you can't get something for nothing—an old and revered thought most of us try to beat every time we go shopping. The PPP variant depends on inflation rates. The idea is that if two currencies start off with a given exchange rate and have different inflation rates, the exchange rate should adjust to offset the different inflation rates. If the U.S. inflation rate is 5 percent, then the dollar is losing 5 percent of its value each year against a currency with a 0 percent inflation rate. Of course, if the U.S. dollar loses 5 percent per year to inflation and the Mexican peso loses 20 percent per year to inflation, then the dollar, relative to the peso, is gaining 15 percent.

An example might help. Suppose that in the beginning the dollar is worth 200 yen. Suppose further that inflation is 5 percent per year in the United States and 0 percent in Japan. After a year, 200 yen should buy you $1.05, not $1.00, because the greenback is worth 5 percent less. (We could flip everything over and argue that a dollar which used to buy 200 yen now costs only 195 yen—the numbers are the same to one or two decimal places.)

As an idea this sounds neat and plausible. In fact, it is a classic case of an economic theory in search of some real data. The only time the theory even comes close to working is when a country's currency suffers incredible inflation—like 100 to 500 percent—and the central bank simply resets the exchange rate once a week. At times in the 1970s and 1980s, Brazil followed this practice. To help keep things straight, Brazil periodically changed the name of the currency and announced that its economy had turned over a new leaf. Eventually things were straightened out after several governments. Repegging the currency exchange by using PPP to offset inflation is scarcely an enlightened monetary policy. After all, the same central bank that is doing it is also running inflation at triple-digit rates!

Now that we have settled one of the theories that does not work, let's look at what does. One thing special about PPP is its apparent simplicity—there are numerous other theories of forex prices and none of them seem to give reliable forecasts. That may not be all that bad, since it is possible to hedge currency positions at reasonable costs for most major currencies.

At the risk of sounding too simplistic, the question of the exchange rate—that is, the price of, say, the dollar in terms of English pounds—starts with supply and demand. Suppose for a moment that the supply of dollars is fixed and that the demand by foreigners for dollars rises. It might rise because oil prices surge and oil is almost always priced, bought, and sold in dollars. So when oil prices climb, more dollars are demanded to grease the wheels of the oil trade. Alternatively, investors might decide to switch out of German marks and into dollars if they believe that U.S. dollar investments offer better returns. Or a strong U.S. economy might boost the demand for dollars, push U.S. interest rates up, and increase the demand to hold dollars. If the supply of dollars is fixed, the value of the dollar will rise. Looked at one way, a dollar will be worth *more* yen or marks. The dollar will rise from 100 yen to 110 yen or from 1.5 marks to 1.65 marks. Looked at the other way, a pound sterling will cost fewer dollars. The pound will drop from $1.60 to $1.45. Of course, if the demand for dollars falls, the reverse will be the case.

HOW FOREX RATES ARE QUOTED

There are some odd traditions, worth noting, to the way foreign exchange rates are usually reported in the newspaper. Typically, all currencies except the British pound are quoted as units of that currency per U.S. dollar. For instance, the Japanese yen is quoted as 107.50 yen per U.S. dollar, or simply "the yen is at 107.5 or ¥ 107.5."

Likewise, the German mark is reported as 1.55, meaning 1.55 marks per dollar. It would be equally accurate to report the rate as dollars per mark. In that case, the number would be the reciprocal: 1 divided by 1.55, or 0.645. The British pound is quoted as dollars per pound. A typical quote for the pound is $1.55.

Another quirk is that trading in currency options uses quotes of dollars per foreign currency—the British pound approach—for all currencies. The reasons seem to be as much historic accident as anything else. Under the Bretton Woods system created at the end of World War II, all currencies were technically stated in terms of the U.S. dollar and it made sense to quote them as so many units per U.S. dollar. The previous centerpiece of the currency markets had been the British pound. Out of either respect or historic accident, the pound was left the way it had always been.

Forex traders often talk of *cross rates*. These are rates between two currencies, neither of which is the dollar. If the yen is 107.5 and the mark is 1.55, then the yen/mark cross rate is 107.5 divided by 1.55, or 69.35 yen per mark.

(*Continued*)

So if the demand for dollars rises, the value of the dollar will go up. Right? It's not that simple. First, predicting when the demand for dollars will climb isn't easy. Second, if the demand for dollars rises but the demand for yen rises more, the dollar will go down relative to the yen. Third, and maybe most of all, the supply won't be fixed for any of these currencies. The supply can be shifted in two general ways.

First, the supply of a currency might rise from shifts in the domestic economy. As long as there aren't regulations that separate the domestic economy from the rest of the world, this will increase the overall supply of the currency. Second, and more likely, flows of investment capital and trade between countries will affect the supply of the currency.

In the United States we save less than we invest. Each year the total investment in the economy—building homes, offices, schools, roads, new machinery for factories, computers for business, and so forth—exceeds what we save. In round numbers, savings represent almost 16 percent of U.S. output, and production (GDP) and investment represents close to 18 percent. A difference of 2 percent, or an estimated $140 billion in 1995. Since this amount is for the entire American economy, we don't just go down to the neighborhood bank and borrow the difference. After all, the neighborhood bank is part of the economy. Rather, we borrow the money from the rest of the world. In exchange, we offer various investments—bonds, stocks, and U.S. money. That raises the supply of dollars and investment denominated in dollars available around the world. For the currency markets, it means a gradual and continuing rise in the supply of dollars. Unless the demand for dollars is rising at least as fast as the supply, the dollar will lose value in terms of other currencies.

There is another aspect of saving less than we invest. Our overseas debts are mounting. There was a time when we did not draw in investment capital from overseas. From World War I until about 1980 the United States was a net creditor—everyone else owed us more than we owed them. But since the late 1950s or early 1960s we have been saving less than we invest and drawing money in from abroad. Our debts have built up so that we have been a net debtor since about 1980. Don't get worried that the United States is suddenly in hock to everyone else.

The investment flows—*capital flows,* in economists' jargon—are also reflected in the more familiar reports about imports and exports. Each month when the trade report comes out that shows how much we imported from abroad and exported overseas, politicians collectively groan because we have a trade deficit of $10 billion per month. It's been that way for a long time. Moreover, as some people have pointed out, it's not a bad trick. In effect, we are buying everything from cars to computer chips and giving back pieces of paper with George Washington's portrait on them. Doesn't sound that bad, does it? In the late 1980s, there was a wave of Japanese investment in American real estate. Japanese real estate investment firms bought, among other buildings, the Exxon office tower and Rockefeller Center in New York City. Of course, they didn't take the buildings apart and send them home to Tokyo. They are all still there in midtown Manhattan (Exxon later moved its headquarters from New York City to Texas and the building was renamed.) Moreover, it wasn't even a very good investment. The new owners of Rockefeller Center discovered that the rents weren't high enough to cover the mortgage payments and later were forced into bankruptcy. The point of the story is twofold. First, the trade numbers must be examined with some care before any conclusions are reached about what they mean. Second, the trade figures do say something about currency values. In this case, they mean there is long-term downward pressure on the dollar.

Before we leave the foreign exchange market, one more item, or theory is worth mentioning: The *macho theory* of currencies. Somehow, politicians are convinced that countries should have "strong" currencies. There is an idea that all deficits are bad, all surpluses are good, a country is better if its currency is worth more, and all citizens should sacrifice to boost the currency higher and higher. It is largely nonsense. Under some circumstances, it would be helpful to have the dollar worth more in terms of the yen. In other cases, it works out better to have it worth less. In either case, we would do well to keep moralizing out of it as much as possible.

THE REAL ESTATE MARKET

It's time to move from the financial markets—stocks, bonds, money, and foreign exchange—to some other markets. The others may not move as fast, but they are no less interesting or potentially profitable. We start with one that many of us participate in from time to time—real estate. Two traditions have guided the real estate market. One is that buying a home is the largest single purchase most Americans ever make. The median new-home price of $145,000 in 1995 was 3.6 times the median family income. The other tradition relates to the three most important factors in the price of a home: location, location, location. Maybe, but not quite.

Like any other market, real estate depends on supply and demand, on how many willing sellers are seeking anxious buyers, or vice versa. When we look at the market for homes, the number of potential buyers can change significantly. There are almost always a lot of people who want to buy homes. However, the portion of these families that can qualify for a mortgage and then actually buy a home can vary with interest rates and the health of the economy. When interest rates climb, the size of a monthly mortgage payment climbs as well. A larger portion of the people applying for a mortgage find that the bank won't approve them—because the monthly payment is too high compared with their monthly income to meet the bank's guidelines for a "safe" loan. ("Safe" means that the bank believes the borrower will pay back the loan on time.) As a result, when interest rates are high or rising, the number of buyers in the market for a new house gets smaller and smaller. On top of that, rising interest rates usually lead to a weaker economy or a recession. If buyers know this, they may get pessimistic about the economy and decide that it's not a good time to buy a home. Even if the buyers aren't pushed out of the market by high borrowing costs and scared off by recession mongers, they might look at those high interest rates and decide to buy bonds instead. In any event, fewer buyers make for desperate sellers, who tend to cut prices. So rising interest rates make for falling home prices.

The reverse also holds: Falling interest rates tend to boost home prices. Buyers flood into the market because more and more are bankable, because the falling rates portend good times for the economy, and because when bond yields are low, buyers decide that real estate might be a better investment. Interest rates aren't the only thing that makes a difference, though. Inflation can be a big factor as well. Houses are sometimes called "real" assets—they represent something real, not paper denominated in dollars like stocks and bonds. When inflation is high and prices are rising, real assets maintain their value while paper assets denominated in dollars don't rise with inflation. During the 1970s and early 1980s, when inflation in the United States was running at double-digit rates, home values soared. But in the late 1980s and early 1990s, a recession, rising interest rates, and falling inflation buried home prices.

Once you get past interest rates and inflation, location-location-location does make a difference for home prices. But don't shrug, because there may be some hidden advantages here. Your needs and desires about location are different from those of the next buyer and that could be your salvation. Some neighborhoods are known for their good schools (and usually for their high school taxes). If you have school-age children, finding a home in a school district that you like is important and certainly worth paying a premium for. But suppose you don't have school-age children. Why would you pay a premium to live in a neighborhood with good schools? Unless the demand for schools is going to rise during the time you own your house, forget about buying in that area because it is a better investment. In fact, in many areas the number of school-age youngsters is dropping, and "good schools" is no longer a drawing card for future home buyers.

A good school system isn't the only thing that gets rolled into the price of the home. In fact, anything that can't be easily moved or changed becomes part of the price. Taxes are another example. The wealthier suburbs outside of New York City include sections of New Jersey and Connecticut as well as communities in New York State. Both New Jersey and Connecticut have lower income taxes than New York. Until a few years ago there was no state income tax in Connecticut, while New York State had one of the highest income tax rates in the nation. Sellers of Connecticut homes made sure that any potential buyer from New York knew all about taxes. And, try as they could, New York house sellers couldn't completely disguise the tax issues. The benefit of the lower taxes becomes part of the higher price of Connecticut homes. Whose taxes? Roughly speaking, the taxes of the marginal buyer attracted to Connecticut from New York by the cheap taxes. Moreover, what figures in the house price is the present value of future tax payments. It is not exact, but it sure is there in the price.

Suppose you are buying a second home for weekend use within an hour or two of New York City. Since it is a weekend house, it can't be your legal residence for tax purposes. So why pay a premium for a "tax haven" you can't use? Let's go to the other extreme. Suppose you are buying a primary residence that will determine where you pay taxes. Unlike some wealthy folks with tax-free municipal bonds, trust funds, and fancy shelters, you earn fully taxable income. The state tax break will make a much bigger difference to you than to your uncle living off his tax-exempt bonds. For you, the house in Connecticut is cheap, especially with the tax benefits for a typical buyer (not you) rolled into the price. Maybe the moral to this lesson of real estate economics is that location matters, but so does what location you're in.

While timing, interest rates, and a crafty sense of location can get you a leg up in the real estate market, hedging that position is very difficult. In stocks and bonds it is easy to buy a little insurance and protect today's market value for your assets by using options. That is very difficult in real estate. Because each house is different or almost unique, it is hard to figure out some financial instrument to hedge it with. The closest answer may be to diversify your investments after you buy that dream house. Don't find a great income-producing investment in the form of another house a block away. If you lose the value of one— in a falling market, an earthquake, or a hurricane—your chances of losing the value of the other at the same time are very very large. But, lest you despair, remember that you probably have a partner in your home investment called, "The Bank." No one ever wants to walk away from a loan, but for the first few years you "own" your house, your friendly banker owns a lot more of it.

THE RETAIL MARKET

"I can get it for you wholesale!" is music to every shopper's ears. Behind it is the thought that while economics works in markets that we all know are markets—stocks, bonds, real estate—it somehow fails to make much sense when we walk into a department store or a supermarket. The difficulty many people find in taking the economics they remember (or didn't manage to forget) from their college course and applying it to their everyday experiences is that what they see in the supermarket or the mall doesn't look a lot like the theory of supply and demand they read about in a textbook. If anything, the mall was a dream hatched in the marketing and business psychology courses with nothing to do with economics. When we try to see what drives prices and how we can use a little economics to our advantage, we come up dry at first.

But economics didn't take a vacation when the first suburban shopping mall was opened. Time and time again economics talks about demand and supply and how the price is determined by where these two infamous lines cross. "Demand" is a list or a chart that shows how much of something will be bought at different prices. If the local music store sold CDs for $15.99, you might buy one a month, or 12 a year. If the price were higher, say $19.95, you would buy only one every other month. If it were lower, say $9.99, you would buy one every 3 weeks, or about 18 a year. If the price plummeted to $4.99, you would binge and buy one a week, or over 50 CDs per year. Those combinations of prices and quantities is your demand curve for CDs. The only thing that changes in all those combinations is the price of a CD, and all the prices are on the demand curve. At each price, some economist can look at your demand curve and tell how many CDs you'll buy this year.

The reason this system doesn't work at the mall is that most of what marketing and advertising tries to do is to *change* your demand curve. Throw away the numbers—an example or two will help. Your portable tape player breaks and you replace it with a portable CD player. You now have two CD players (one at home) and twice as much time to listen to CDs, but no reason to buy tapes. Your demand for tapes plummets and your demand for CDs rises. Instead of buying 12 CDs a year when the price is $15.99, you now buy 15. Factors other than a broken tape player will also make a difference. Your income might rise and you feel rich enough to afford more CDs. You might read a lot of articles in stereo magazines that convince you CDs are much better than tapes and you resolve to buy only CDs, no matter how cheap tapes are. You might see a series of advertisements that convince you CDs are better. Or you might watch a popular new movie in which the heroine is always listening to some really cool CDs. Congratulations. The Great American Marketing Machine is playing with your demand curve.

Advertising, promotions, and pushing products used by the good guys in popular movies are all ways that sellers try to make you want to buy more of their stuff. They are trying to whet your appetite and pique your curiosity—and raise your demand curve. It's not that economics doesn't work at the mall; rather, it works very well in ways we often don't expect. The same is true at the local supermarket.

In most of the markets we readily recognize as markets, price changes a lot. In stocks, constantly. In real estate, every transaction is about setting the price. The mall is different. Here the sellers set the price and see how much they sell. If they put a $15.99 ticket on a new CD and it sells out overnight, they probably could have done better with a $19.99 price and a week before it sold out. For many companies, changing prices is expensive and they are better off setting the price and hoping they sell out their stock. Seasonal goods, like fall clothes, are an example. When the new colors and styles come in, department and specialty stores set the prices. If the prices aren't too high, all the goods sell out before the end-of-season sales. If the prices are too low, every item sells out right away, customers who didn't get there in time become irate, and stores lose money because they could have charged higher prices. At the mall, things are reversed: The sellers set the price and the market determines the quantity sold. In stocks, bonds, real estate, and most of the other markets, the sellers set quantities and the market sets the price. But remember, not even an absolute monopolist sets both price and quantity.

If the seller does a really bad job of setting the price, the price won't hold. If styles and fashion don't follow one another, some sellers may be stuck with a lot of unwanted goods and they have no choice but to unload them at any price. Sometimes they sell the goods to a discounter rather than sully their own good name. Then again, if prices are set too low, demand may overpower the sellers and prices are forced to rise. A scalper who sells tickets to a rock concert for five or ten times the "ticket price" is profiting from a price that was set too low given the market demand and the available supply.

Back to the mall, still looking for that bargain. Obviously you're alert to those "sale" signs, but you also should look for inventory levels. If you see a store with a lot of air conditioners available in October, bargain hard. The store is stuck with them and the manufacturer has probably been demanding payment for a month or two. If fall clothes appear in late August for the back-to-school specials, they should be sold out of the store by Thanksgiving to make room for Christmas goods. So start looking for bargains around Halloween. On the other hand, wonder about special sales on goods that have just arrived. It sounds like hype as much as anything else. If the goods are reduced, the reduction is from a price no one really took very seriously. The secret to bargain hunting is to look for spots where there will be pressure to lower the price. Too much on the shelves is the best kind of pressure a consumer can find.

We could go on touring markets almost endlessly. While we certainly haven't run out of possibilities, it is time to move on to other aspects of how economics can help. Be warned, though, that there are very few spots that economists don't think are really markets, albeit in disguise. Illegal activities, from drugs to prostitution to underground immigration, have all been subjected to economic analysis. Sports activities and professional sports leagues are another popular item with economists. Most political issues, and even love and marriage, have been put under the economic microscope at one point or another.

HOW THINGS CHANGE

Plus ça change, plus c'est la même chose.

FRENCH PROVERB

In the economy, as in many things, change may be the only constant. True, there are patterns that repeat and sequences of events that happen over and over, but in the end the economy is always changing and evolving. Sometimes, in some places, people find change very difficult to deal with. In other places, including in the economy and economics, change represents opportunity. You can buy a bond and clip the coupons every 6 months. But this is a slow way to get rich—and one that may not always work. Or you can buy a stock and hope that the price rises and you get rich faster. The stock approach is both more exciting and potentially more rewarding.

If the economy never changed, we could look at it once and know all the answers. Of course, it is always changing, and the change is where the challenges, and opportunities, lie. But changes in the economy are not random events like the roll of the dice. Much of what we have discussed above— how markets work, how we measure economic variables, and what happens in the economy—are the tools that will let us recognize and maybe predict changes in the economy.

This chapter is devoted to understanding the different ways the economy changes. To start, different kinds of changes, shifts, adjustments and developments are identified. Some move very quickly while others evolve at an almost glacial pace. Some changes affect only a small corner of a small market while others ripple through the entire economy. In all these, there are some patterns that can be anticipated. The patterns and anticipations are not as accurate as a stock market chart watcher would wish. But they are not totally random either. In the absence of complete randomness and the presence of some patterns lies the opportunity to make money.

CYCLES AND STRAIGHT LINES

Fortune telling, predictions of the future, and dream interpretation have been around as long as men and women could talk, argue, and imagine. Most economic books cite the Bible and the story of Joseph's dream as the first business cycle. The 7 fat years, followed by 7 lean years may be the first recorded or reported boom-bust cycle. But it was only one expansion and one recession, and it lacks the hidden attraction of studying business cycles: that the past will be prologue to the future and the cycle will repeat itself. The idea that something that happened before will happen again, or knowing what will happen before it happens, seems to touch a hidden desire in all of us. "If I only knew then what I know now, I would have bought stocks in_____, sold bonds when_____." Even more hidden or interesting desires than market killings can emerge.

Changes in economics is either cyclical or secular. Cyclical things tend to repeat. *Business cycles*—periods of expansion or contraction when most sectors of the economy are synchronized—are the most famous. Most stock market watchers believe in market cycles and talk about bull markets (prices rise and fortunes are made) and bear markets (prices fall and fortunes are lost). Some cycles are blamed on events outside the economy. Every 4 years, during a presidential election, there is a flood of discussion of election-year cycles in the financial markets and the overall economy. The hallmark of cycles in the economy are regular patterns with some degree of predictability. While the precise timing and details vary a lot from boom to boom or bust to bust, there are some similarities that can be identified.

Some cycles are so common that we may not even think of them as repeating changes in the economy. Most consumer-related businesses have a boom in November and December followed by a lull in January. The boom is called Christmas shopping; it comes every year. Yet this is a regular cycle that repeats and drives a lot of what happens in the economy. There are other seasonal cycles as well. The new-model year for cars starts in the fall; boats sell better in the spring. Clothing sales run through numerous seasons. Even these simple cycles can prove very useful to ordinary people, and not just for buying clothing at the end-of-season sales that seem to come more and more often.

Few people worry about the season of the year when selling a house, yet it can make a big difference. If you are buying, or selling, a home that is likely to attract families with school-age children, recognize that most families don't like switching schools in the middle of the school year. This means that people would like to be able to move into a new house and get a little settled before schools open in September. Count backward, allow for moving during the summer when snowstorms won't cause delays, and you can figure that the prime time for buyers to be searching for a house is probably March through May or June. If you're a buyer and you can be independent of these seasonal patterns—it's a local move and no school changes will be involved—you might start looking in October or November. These are slower months and sellers may be anxious to make a deal before the market shuts down for the Thanksgiving–Christmas–New Year's holiday period. Of course, the seasonal patterns are different for summer homes, ski chalets, houses that are too small for families with children, and so forth. Most important, prices rise when demands are heavy and sink when demands are seasonally lighter. Timing can add (or subtract) something significant from the price of a home.

We tend to think of cycles and repeating patterns that have a period of a few months to a few years. We have just seen that some cycles last only a year before repeating. Some are even shorter—there are intraweek cycles within the stock market, although they may not be clear enough or reliable enough to profit from. At the other extreme, some cycles are quite long and merge into secular shifts. A *secular shift* is a gradual, long-running change in the economy that affects how things work and what they cost. What distinguishes a cycle change that takes several years before repeating from a one-way secular shift is often open to question. Two recent, and ongoing, secular shifts are cuts in defense spending and the baby boom.

Beginning in the late 1980s with the end of the cold war and the collapse of the Soviet Union and its various satellite states, the U.S. government began to reduce defense spending. This reduction is continuing nearly a decade later. The Gulf War in 1991 did not interrupt these cutbacks. In fact, the Gulf War was largely fought out of a vast inventory of munitions. This movement toward less defense spending has had widespread impact. Defense-related jobs are declining and some regions of the country, including New England and Southern California, found themselves in long-term slumps as a result. The nation's expenditures on research and development, especially basic research, were also affected by the defense cutbacks.

Of all the long-term shifts in the economy, the baby boom may be the best known. In the period 1946 to 1964, births surged and a generation far larger than the one before it, or after it, appeared in the U.S. population and the U.S. economy. In the early days of the baby boom, the 1950s and 1960s, all these growing children contributed to the demand for suburban homes, automobiles, and schools. In the 1960s and early 1970s they fueled an expansion of America's colleges, universities, and centers of higher education. In the late 1960s and into the 1970s, as they entered the labor force, the average level of experience and the average growth of labor productivity fell. Now, we are beginning to look toward the point where the baby boomers will start retiring. The first of them will be 65 in 2011. However, because of the stress the boomers will place on social security funds, retirement benefits are likely to be delayed until they reach 68 in the year 2014.

One common consumer-oriented business strategy is to hitch a ride on the baby boomers and follow them through their life cycle. Sell sporty cars in the 1960s, family cars in the 1970s and 1980s, and sporty-looking two-seaters early next century for the recently retired whose children have moved out. Simpler versions of the same idea are increasingly heard as targeting the leading edge of the boom— everything from reading eyeglasses to dental care to the resurgence of golf and the decline of tennis as popular participation sports. In the 1980s there were attempts to identify, and profit from, a baby boom echo when the baby boomers were expected to be starting families. The echo turned out to be fuzzier than many marketers hoped.

For investors or for the rest of us seeking an edge in the economy, understanding these kinds of shifts can be helpful. Knowing that the baby boomers are getting older doesn't make every hospital management company, nursing home, or funeral services corporation an instant buy in the stock market. But realizing that defense spending is shrinking may lead us to expect some changes in the aerospace and defense industries and some opportunities to make money.

SPEED AND DURATION

How fast things change makes a big difference as well. Seasonal patterns, like Christmas sales or the prime time for buying a house, are easy to take advantage of. Of course, these patterns are slow enough for a lot of people to spot them and learn about them, so some of the advantage may be lost in the markets. There are shorter cycles as well. Some stock market watchers talk about weekly cycles. In the bond markets, releases of new economic reports at 8:30 a.m. (Eastern time) often set off cycles during the same day. If the report is unexpectedly good, bond prices will rise sharply between 8:30 and 9:00 a.m. and then slip back during the rest of the day. At the other extreme, some cycles are measured in terms of years. Some cycles are over in a day, others in a few months, still others in a year, and some in several years. The length of the cycle and the speed of the changes in the economy can vary over a large range, depending on what we're looking at.

The most famous of the year-or-longer cycles is the business cycle. Modern capitalist economies experience periodic booms and busts. In booms, most everything grows—stock prices rise, incomes gain, and just about everyone is smiling. In busts, stocks fall, incomes shrink, business weakens, and long faces predominate. Since World War II the average business cycle has been about 4 years—3 up years and 1 down year. But business cycles, like many cycles, are not all that regular or routine. Expansions have been as short as 11 months and as long as over 100 months.

Cycles that are longer than a few years can be hard to spot because they take so long to repeat and be noticed. Yet hope or imagination may spring eternal. People have written about various-length cycles, including the Kondratieff wave, a 50-year-long cycle. Kondratieff, an early-twentieth-century Russian economist, proposed the long cycle in the 1920s. At that time the longest data series available was about 100 to 150 years. From a scientific perspective, a sample of only three cycles is pretty thin. Kondratieff's story had a sad ending. His writings predicted the Great Depression in the United States and Western Europe. When the depressions hit, the Communist Soviet regime hailed his forecasts as being in the tradition of Marx's predictions of the demise of capitalism. Unfortunately, Kondratieff was a better economist than politician. He responded by predicting recovery in the West as the up cycle followed the down cycle. The Kremlin responded by sending him to Siberia, where he died.

While 50-year cycles may seem excessive, there are some long-term movements in the economy that are very much worth watching. Demographic shifts, such as the baby boom, give rise to predictable trends. Everyone who will be in the labor force in the year 2011—less than 15 years from now—is already alive. By comparing the schooling and education of future workers with those of earlier generations, we can make some educated guesses about how the labor force will be changing into the next century.

EXTENT AND REACH

The third important aspect of cycles is their reach. Some cycles sweep through the economy—recessions and the Christmas season are common examples. Others can be limited to a single market or a geographic region. Seasonal cycles are often restricted to a few markets and a region of the country. Snow shovel and snow blower sales have their own seasonal cycles in the North, but never sell well in Florida. Other cycles with limited impacts include seasonal travel and clothing fashions. These cycles make a difference to the people in the middle of them, but little difference to anyone else. If you run a hardware store in New Hampshire, the snow shovel cycle may be a big part of your business. If you merely want to buy a snow shovel, and usually the old one lasts for several years, it is not worth waiting for a spring lull and hoping that the hardware store ordered too many last fall.

The most interesting cycles extend beyond the markets they originate in or extend to longer periods than one season or one year. Stock market cycles are one example. (See Figs. 5-1 and 5-2.) One of the more colorful, but less useful or likely theories of the stock market is that it follows women's hemlines. If hemlines rise, stock prices rise; if hems fall, so do stocks. One market watcher pointed that the ultimate folly of this theory is that hemlines have a

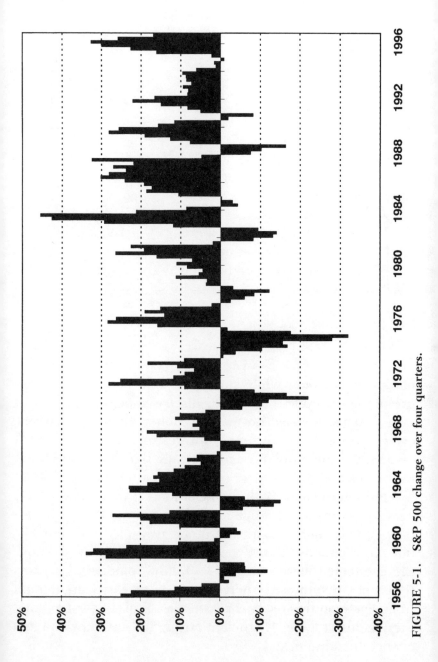

FIGURE 5-1. S&P 500 change over four quarters.

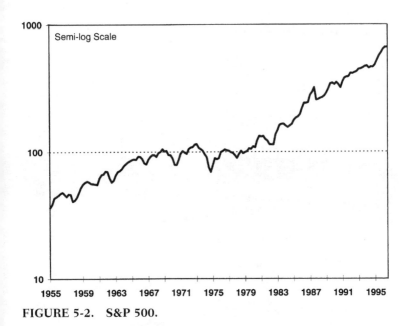

FIGURE 5-2.   S&P 500.

natural upper limit while stock prices do not. Some more useful market cycle theories are discussed below.

For those focused on making money, financial market cycles are probably the most interesting. For those concerned with doing better economically than mere survival, recessions and the business cycle may matter the most. The two are interrelated. Both financial market cycles and business cycles extend throughout the economy. Often a business cycle is defined as a pattern of expansions and contractions in economic activity that extends across many parts of the economy. These changes do follow some regular patterns, but they are not perfectly or even easily predicted from simply averaging over past cycles. Still, understanding these kinds of cycles is crucial to using the economy and its changes to advantage.

SPECIFIC CYCLES, SHIFTS, AND CHANGES

The best way to look at cycles, shifts, and changes is with some examples. We begin with the most commonly debated shifts in the economy—the business cycle, made up of recessions and expansions. Next is a cycle that may be as much appearance as reality—the political cycle tied to election years. Then we shift slightly to changes in which the cycles are far less evident and longer or more variable. We look at inflation, corporate mergers, and oil prices.

BUSINESS CYCLES

One of the most used, abused, and feared words in modern economics is *recession*. One of the few (almost) immutable economic facts of life is the business cycle. An economy like ours tends to have periods when everything seems to grow and prosper and other periods when everything seems to shrink, collapse, and slump. "Slump" is often used in Britain to describe a recession. Certainly not everything in the economy is synchronized with everything else. And virtually nothing in the economy works like clockwork. But there are some regular patterns when most everything tends to rise together or fall together. These are business cycles.

In the United States business cycles have been watched and studied for decades. The first systematic American studies of the overall economy were in the nineteenth century. Various researchers have traced a pattern of business cycles back to the 1830s in the United States. The responsibility for monitoring these dates is now placed with a private nonprofit research group called the National Bureau of Economic Research (NBER). The NBER got this role as a leading source of research funding in economics and as the sponsor of much of the original work, including a series of studies led by economist Wesley Clair Mitchell. Mitchell pioneered modern business cycle analyses, developed the dating system used today, and also helped lay the foundations for much of the current economic data used to monitor cycles. The NBER cycle dates are widely (but not universally) accepted in economics. It is amusing that in a profession where the joke is that if all the economists in the world were laid end to end they still wouldn't reach a conclusion, there is widespread agreement on the basic outline of recent economic history.

Because cycles, and the idea of forecasting the next move, are perennially exciting, there are almost as many theories of business cycles as there are would-be cycle theorists. From this plethora of untested ideas, we will try to extract a few items that are worth keeping in mind if you want to guess (predict would be overstating things) the cycle's next move or want to judge the validity of someone else's predictions. There are some regular patterns to business cycles and the order of events should be roughly repeated each time. The most important bit of order and sequence that will repeat is the cycle itself. In the pit of each recession, remember there will be a recovery and expansion. So far, there have been some long, deep, dreary, and fearsome recessions—but they have all ended. Unfortunately, the same thing can be said of expansions. As good as times may get, there is always another recession. Remembering that there is up as well as down is important to both one's mental and financial health in the bottom of a recession.

Other than what goes up comes down and what goes down comes up, there are additional sequences that are likely to repeat. Suppose we start the story with an economy that is growing rapidly and expanding nicely. First, interest rates begin to rise. They rise because with a general expansion everyone is upbeat and optimistic, and more people and more businesses borrow money. The demand for credit increases. Second, in many expansions increases in business lead to increases in prices and inflation. Rising inflation means rising interest rates. Third, after a while, the Federal Reserve will begin worrying about inflation and will push interest rates higher. Rising interest rates are typical of an aging business expansion. Interest rates affect some parts of the economy more than others. Higher loan costs will weaken housing. Rising interest rates mean lower bond prices and—unless corporate earnings are very strong—rising rates may mean a softening stock market. Sooner or later, the economy will peak. A while later, interest rates will peak and come down. This sets the stage for some reversals—housing, which suffered from high rates, will perk up. Stock prices, which probably began to tumble as interest rates rose, will also perk up. Interest rates have a predictable pattern, and the sequences are likely to repeat.

It would be nice if everything related to business cycles repeated itself in neat patterns. It doesn't. The biggest missing item is timing. While the sequence may be (somewhat) reliable, how long things take to rise or fall is not. Look at expansions and recessions. Since World War II we have experienced expansions as long as 100-plus months and as short as 11 months. We have had recessions as short as 6 months and as long as 16. Before World War II the variations were even larger. Business cycles have their own clocks, which can run very fast or very slow for little apparent reason. The timing of sequences is difficult to predict. You may think you're at the bottom, but you can only guess how long you're likely to stay there.

Part of the problem is that everyone wants to draw nice neat sine curves to show what the business cycle looks like. Figure 5-3*a* and *b* is a very crude example—a little like comparing a child's drawing of a valentine heart with a cardiologist's review. But it may be useful for at least one item. Look at how the recession and the expansion are marked. Most people want to make the top half or upper bump of the cycle the expansion and the bottom or lower bump the recession. That's not what is meant. The recession is when things move down and the expansion is when they move up. This has one important result: Things are at their absolute rottenest worst when the recession ends and the *expansion begins.* It is in the dark before the dawn that hope returns, stocks rise, and fortunes are made. Whether it is better to place your bets too early or too late is an open question.

A number of economists have filled up entire books on the business cycle, and some of these are mentioned in the

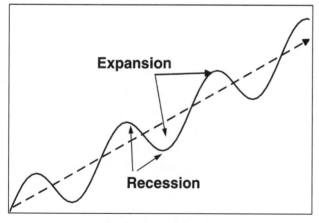

FIGURE 5-3a.   The business cycle.

Appendix. For our purposes we can turn to Table 5-1, which shows some of the sequences that go with the valentine chart in Fig. 5-3.

Economics isn't the only thing that moves in cycles. So do emotions. For economy watchers, the two principal emotions are fear and greed. (Love might be nicer, but economics isn't always nice either.) Combined, these two seem to create an ever-present wish to be able to forecast the future. When things are improving and the economy is gaining, we tend to get greedy or jealous of others, and we look at recent trends and forecast growth forever. (Recall the sine curve in Fig. 5-3.) If things are headed up, we all think—and want to believe—that they will go up forever. So we act accordingly. We rush out and invest more in stocks or buy a bigger house. In business, we hire lots of people, plan to double our sales in 6 months, and buy lots of inventory. In the world of greed there is no reason to fear that the goods in the warehouse won't be sold in

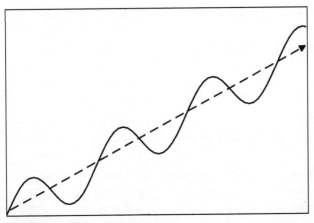

FIGURE 5-3b.

Table 5-1 Business Cycles at a Glance

	Trough	Expansion	Peak	Recession
Interest rates	Falling	Turn up late in the expansion	Climbing	Peak early and then slide
Stock prices	Starting to rise	Rising—bull market	May rise further until profits collapse	Falling—bear market
Consumer confidence	Bottom	Rises after slow start	"Sky's the limit"	Tumbles
Corporate profits	Falling	Begin to climb after expansion starts	Close to a top, but usually hold on for one more quarter	Peak after economy, then collapse
Consumer spending	Bottom	Spending, especially on interest-sensitive big tickers, leads the way	Looks like it will rise forever; it won't	Falls
Industrial production	Bottom	Rises	Peaks	Falls
Housing construction	Turns up shortly after economic trough	Helped by falling interest rates, leads the economy	Peaks when interest rates begin to climb	Falls as interest rates rise
Business investment	Bottom	Rises, but lags overall economy	Still climbing	May gain as recession begins
Typical times (months)	Moment when the outlook is darkest	36–60 months, or more	The most optimistic, and misleading, time in the cycle	10–12 months

record time and every reason to worry that if the shelves are bare we will lose sales. We also raise prices in expectation of good business. The boom is on.

How long will it last? It is something like a cartoon character who runs off the edge of the cliff and progresses across open space with no difficulty until he looks down and sees thin air below. Then he falls. In many markets the same thing is true. All of a sudden, the customers are not beating down the doors and there is excess inventory on the shelves. Suddenly the stock market seers pause to wonder whether a stock that was priced at $35 per share 6 months ago should really be worth $100 today. Thin air looks frightening and the collapse is upon us.

The same story can be told on the downside. In the bottom of a recession, fear dominates all and greed has vanished. No one is willing to try to put money to work. Businesses don't want to hire people, build factories, or even buy inventory. If anything, thin air looked at from below is even more frightening than looked at from above.

Fear and greed are not the only part of the story. Time lags as well as inventories and investments that last for some time are also crucial. Inventories are surprisingly important to the business cycle. If we remove inventories from the numbers, business cycles shrink to half their size or less. In a business that sells things (not services) it is usually necessary to build extra things to meet unexpected demands rather than turn away irate customers. Moreover, it may be cheaper to build a lot of one kind of product and then switch to another product. The extra units that are waiting to be sold are inventory. If times are good and greed is the rule, sales expectations rise and inventories are built up. Suppose this week's business is twice as good as last week's and we want to keep a 2-week supply on hand.

If we sold 100 widgets last week, we need a 200-widget inventory. Now business is running at 200 widgets a week so we need a 400-widget inventory level (2 weeks' supply). Look at what the inventory levels and increase in sales do to the production schedule: Last week we sold 100 per week and built 100 per week. This week we sold 200. So now the inventory is down to 100 from 200 last week. But it should be 400, not 200. So we need to make 300 widgets for inventory (boosting it to the 400-unit target) and another 200 to sell this week. We need to *quintuple* output! Meeting the new production schedule could mean a lot of overtime. That's where the boom comes from.

The bust is the same story, in reverse. After a few 200-widget weeks, sales fall to 100 per week. Now we cut production from 200 to 100. But we have 400 in inventory, not the 200 we need to keep a 2-week supply in reserve. So we cut back production by shutting down the factory for a week. That's the bust.

What is behind all this is plans made today for next week, next month, or next year. The time lags between now and then combine with the greed and fear to be our undoing. Until we can eliminate time lags, greed, and fear, we are likely to have business cycles.

The time lags can generate cycles in some unexpected spots as well. One case that often surprises people is in the supply of specially trained people such as lawyers and doctors. (We will politely exempt economists from this discussion.) It takes 3 to 5 years between deciding to go to law school and beginning a practice, plus passing the bar exam. For doctors the time lag is longer—4 years for med school plus internships and residencies. If something comes along to boost the demand for lawyers—a wave of corporate mergers or a new set of regulations and laws—

law firms will start hiring junior attorneys. All this hiring will drive up wages and make law look more attractive. But even as college graduates switch from business (or music or art history) to law, it will take 3 years before any of the new lawyers reach the market. In these 3 years, demand for new lawyers keeps climbing and wages are pushed up. In many such cases, the demand pushes wages far above the level needed to attract enough new students into the legal market. Four or five years into the process, the flood of new attorneys hits the market. There is an oversupply, and salaries for starting lawyers fall (so do the chances of becoming a partner in a prestigious law firm). Soon students abandon the law for greener pastures. But the stage is set for a shortage and another cycle. In this case, the villain is the 3-year lag created by going to law school.

Political Business Cycles

Ideas in economics, somewhat like economics itself, have cycles. One idea that has a reliable 4-year cycle is that patterns in the economy can be tied to political cycles. The most interesting political cycle is the 4-year presidential term. Attempts have been made to explain movements in both the stock market and the economy by the presidential election cycle. A closely related idea is to use economic figures to forecast the outcome of presidential elections.

The economic election cycle is based on three simple ideas. First, a President (or the incumbent's party if the President has completed two terms and cannot stand for reelection) will do his best to spruce up the economy in an election year. Second, the President will try to push unpopular and unpleasant policy through in the first year of his term so that voters will forget the pain by the time the next election comes around. Third, Congress generates a political minicycle tied to the 2-year terms in the House of Representatives. Specifically, it is difficult to pass controversial legislation in even-numbered years, when elections are looming. But it may be easier to pass landmark bills that have some support in the second (or even-numbered) year of a Congress that has a do-nothing reputation.

For the economy, these ideas mean that there is a higher than normal chance of recession in the first year of a President's term, a lower than normal chance of recession in the last year of the term, and little chance of a tax increase (but a larger chance of a tax cut) in any even-numbered year. Politics being even less predictable and consistent than economics, we might be well advised to remember the advice given Caesar about trying to predict political changes with timing studies: "Beware of the Ides of March."

INFLATION

When the economic history of the second half of the twentieth century is written (which could be quite soon), the analysis is likely to note that the major economic issue was inflation rather than unemployment. (See Fig. 5-4.) Presuming that there are no colossal crises before the end of the century, the peak unemployment for the last 50 years will be less than 11 percent (10.7 percent to be exact, reached in the 1981–1982 recession). In sharp contrast, the inflation rate reached levels not seen since the Civil War, and the price level rose substantially in the 50 years. Unlike the trend in most previous long periods, there was a consistent net increase in the price level. Before we examine the whys, it is worth looking at what happened, since the pattern shows an interesting mixture of cycles and secular changes.

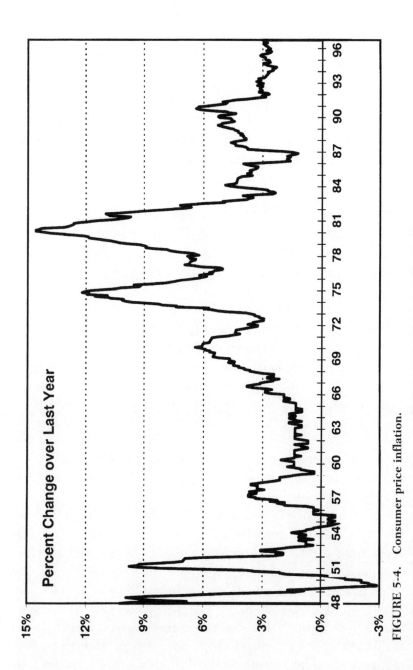

FIGURE 5-4. Consumer price inflation.

205

In the period from 1960 to 1979 inflation climbed through a series of cycles with each peak higher than the previous peak and each trough higher than the previous trough. Then inflation turned around in 1979–1982 and began to decline in the same kind of cyclical pattern. On both the way up and the way down, many economy watchers failed to recognize what was happening and missed out on various opportunities. Until the second half of the 1970s, few people realized that the economy was experiencing a steady increase in inflation. Investors knew that real assets—especially real estate—did well in inflations. Yet it wasn't until the recovery from the deep 1973–1975 recession that homes were recognized as superior inflation-hedge investments. Even more dramatic was the refusal of many investors, including a lot of pension fund managers, to abandon bonds even though interest rates were rising, bond prices were falling, and bond coupons consistently lagged behind inflation.

When the tide turned in 1979–1982, it took a while for investors to realize that the economy was headed the other way. In fact, right through the mid-1990s, inflation forecasts have been higher than reality. On the way toward lower inflation, few investors realized the bonanza available in bonds or the poor prospects in real estate. The 1980s were the best decade since World War I for bondholders; they were one of the worst for homeowners.

This kind of economic myopia can be difficult to correct. Even in the mid-1990s, with interest rates in moderate single digits (6 percent yield on 30-year Treasuries) compared with double digits at the start of the 1980s, the rates are seen as rare or astoundingly low. In 1993 some smart bond investors made out very well simply because they knew enough history to understand that both bond yields and inflation could drop to 6 percent and 3 percent, respectively. The lesson of the inflation story is to look at the past and remember that if it happened once, it can happen again. Mark Twain once remarked that truth is stranger than fiction because fiction sticks to possibilities in life. To this we might add that a truth that has happened once, at least in economics, might happen again.

As long as policymakers fear inflation, they are likely to try to prevent it. As long as the Fed sees inflation as the chief villain, it will be willing to slow the economy down to keep inflation at bay. But if the Fed stops worrying about inflation—as it did in the 1960s—price increases are likely to creep up on us and gradually become ingrained in the economy. Once that happens, it can take a substantial shock and severe downturn to wring inflation out. The last such shock was in 1979–1982, with two back-to-back recessions and the highest unemployment rate since the Great Depression. The current generation of policymakers remembers the pain felt in tackling inflation. But sometime in the next few decades we will get some policymakers who no longer remember how hard it is to fight inflation or how rising prices begin to warp business planning and judgment. When that happens, buying a home will be a great investment again.

CORPORATE MERGERS

Inflation has both a cyclical and a long-term component. Other shifts also seem to move in long waves. In the twentieth century, the economy experienced four periods of large-scale corporate mergers, interspersed with periods when corporate marriages, or divorces, were relatively uncommon. In the early 1900s a number of horizontal mergers took place between competitors. These ended in 1911 when the U.S. Supreme Court ordered the breakup of the Standard Oil Trust. Exxon Corporation, formerly Standard Oil Company of New Jersey, is the lineal descendent of the trust. But Chevron (Standard of California), Mobil (former-ly Socony Mobil or Standard Oil of New York), and Sohio (Standard of Ohio, now part of British Petroleum) were all part of the original oil trust. From 1910 to 1920, a series of vertical mergers picked up where the horizontal mergers left off. If a company couldn't buy up its competitors, it did the next best thing by buying its suppliers and its customers. This effort also ended in the courts with the U.S. Steel case in 1921. The decision kept things quiet for some time. Through the Depression of the 1930s and World War II, merger activity was rather modest.

Mergers reawakened in the 1960s—this time, with conglomerates. If a company couldn't buy its competitors, suppliers, or customers, why not buy something complete-ly different? Conglomerates were combinations of dis-parate companies linked under one roof. The impetus for conglomerates was the stock market. A company with a high and rising stock price could use its stock to buy out a less popular company with solid earnings. Mergers paid for with stock were nice—the acquiring firm could print more stock, like printing money. Moreover, when the earnings of the recent acquisition were added to the parent's earnings, the stock price would rise further. This magical multiplier came to an end in the market slump of 1973–1975.

The last merger wave of the century was in the 1980s. Again the financial markets were the catalyst. In the 1980s, junk bonds—low-quality debt—blossomed as a way for almost anyone to raise money for almost anything. It seemed possible to sell junk bonds, buy a company with the bond proceeds, and then use the company to pay off the debt. Sometimes things worked out. Other times, even though the acquired company was chopped up and sold in pieces, the proceeds didn't yield enough money to pay off the bond debt. The bonds defaulted.

Nevertheless, with all that money floating around some-one had to spend it. While some of the early deals were attractive, the later ones were more suspect. Suppose sever-al investors tell you that they can take a company whose stock is worth $1 billion, use it as collateral for loans total-ing $1.2 billion, buy the company with the loans (a lever-aged buyout, or LBO), then take the company apart and sell the pieces for $1.4 billion—and do it all in a matter of months. You might suggest that instead of buying compa-nies of Wall Street, these investors take a look at the Brooklyn Bridge. Yet this is what people tried, and in some cases succeeded in doing.

Of course, when each of these merger waves started, the deals made a lot of sense. But mergers are simply buy-ing companies in a market, like any other "goods" in the economy. As the action heats up in a market, the hype rises and so do the prices. What was a steal at $30 per share and a reasonable deal at $35 becomes a stretch at $40 and doomsday at $50. If the market for stocks, old-master paintings, or homes can see prices run up, why not the market for buying companies for mergers? In the merger case there are two distinct phases in the run-up that pro-vide some clue to what is going on. Earlier, in talking about stocks, we discussed how a stock is worth the pre-sent value of the firm's future earnings. Sometimes, the present value of the future returns and the current market value of the company get out of sync. If today's price is too low, the company is a buy; if it is too high, the stock is a sell. When a merger is done and the buyer (the acquiring company) keeps the purchase and runs the business, we are in phase 1, with cheap companies and attractive deals. But when the buyer decides to sell the pieces of the com-pany as fast as possible, you can bet it's damaged goods at a fire sale. The fire sale is phase 2.

For investors tracking mergers, there are two lessons. First, it's OK to own stock in the acquiring company in the early days, but not in the later days of a merger boom. Second, play it safe and own stock in the company that loses the battle and is purchased, not the one that wins the battle and buys the loser for an inflated price. In fact, academic studies have shown quite clearly that stockholders in companies that win merger wars rarely win much at all. Stockholders in companies that get bought out and taken over smile all the way to the bank.

OIL PRICES

While inflation and mergers may be the dominant factors in twentieth-century economics, one of the most dramatic issues has been oil prices. (See Fig. 5-5.) Oil prices soared

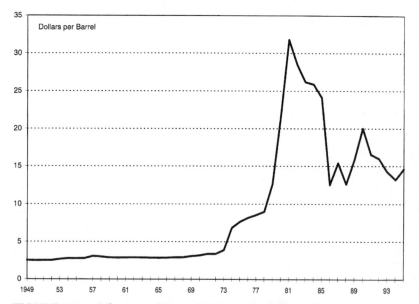

FIGURE 5-5.   Oil prices. (*Source:* U.S. Dept. of Energy.)

twice in the 1970s, ending the decade ten times higher. But by the mid-1980s they had fallen to twice where they were before the first run-up. In inflation-adjusted terms, oil was cheaper in 1986 than in 1976 and about the same in 1966. Yet both investors and consumers constantly believed that whichever direction oil prices moved last month was a sure sign that they would move in the same direction for the next several years or decades.

Once oil climbed from $8 per barrel to $18 and then to $28, investments that would pay off only with oil at $38, $48, or $58 per barrel were being made by otherwise very intelligent people. It is difficult for observers to see prices moving upward and confidently predict that they will fall. For instance, there was shale. Oil shale—the idea that certain kinds of rock (yes, rock) could be mined and refined to produce oil—was one hot prospect. The economics of oil shale are quite simple: Whatever the current price of oil is today, shale will be economic at $8 *more* per barrel. If oil is $12 today, shale is a shoo-in when oil hits $20. If oil is $26, shale is a sure bet the moment oil prices break through $34. If this sounds like something like *Alice in Wonderland* and "Jam tomorrow, jam yesterday, but never jam today," it's no accident.

Many economic changes seem to underscore a version of Newton's law that every action has a reaction. Prices often overshoot and then slide back toward their starting point. Markets develop a bandwagon effect as everyone rushes from one extreme to another. In the case of rising oil prices, it was easy to forget that there are some substitutes for oil and even for energy. The substitutes aren't perfect or costless, but if the price of oil triples, burning coal or turning down the thermostat doesn't seem quite so silly after all. Moreover, market shifts begat their own reactions. When oil prices tripled, supplies appeared from places where few expected them. In the beginning of the 1970s, the only people who talked about the Mexican oil industry were historians. A few years later, Mexico almost single-handedly defeated the pricing power of the supposedly invincible OPEC. Finally, the oil crises taught everyone some important lessons about cartels.

A cartel is a group of sellers or producers that band together and cut back production to push prices higher. OPEC and oil is the most infamous recent case. Others of recent decades have included coffee producers and cocoa producers and various natural resources such as copper. For a cartel to work, the producers have to be limited in number and it has to be hard to become a producer. That makes natural resources a likely place to start a cartel—you can't start an oil industry if you aren't sitting on the right kind of land. At OPEC's peak of power and influence, cartels were widely feared.

But cartels hold the seeds of their own destruction. If you are a producer and you join a cartel, you can get quite rich. But if you join the cartel and cheat on the cartel price a little, you soon discover that you can get even richer. At the high cartel price there are plenty of consumers looking for bargains on a no-questions-asked basis. Suppose the free-market price of oil is $10 per barrel while the cartel, through production cutbacks, pushes the price to $25. A producer that joins the cartel will get the higher price but will have to cut production to help keep the price high. Suppose the producer cuts production 40 percent to get a price 250 percent higher. The producer is richer, with revenues up 50 percent. But now there is 40 percent of unused, idle capacity. The producer quietly sells a few extra barrels at $22 each, for extra profits (remember the barrels once sold at $10 apiece), and no one needs to know. So by cheating, the new cartel member gets very rich, not just rich.

At times greed can be very helpful. As the cheating spreads and production rises, prices will fall. Once a tanker is loaded and at sea, it is difficult to tell exactly where it goes or who might be buying the oil. An interesting tactic for a wealthy oil-importing nation to consider when facing a world of cartels is to encourage cheating. Such a deep-pocketed buyer could indicate that it was willing to buy large quantities of oil at 10 percent under the cartel price on a no-questions-asked basis, with payment made through a convenient numbered Swiss bank account. Some sellers would surface. Of course, once the business begins to percolate, reselling the "hot" oil to further depress the market would also be attractive. Such an approach is certainly an attempt to manipulate the market. But the difference between market manipulation and market stabilization may be more a question of who's doing it than what is being done.

Market Madness

Almost any contemporary discussion about investing will sooner or later get to Warren Buffett. Buffett has reached almost legendary status as a plain-speaking midwesterner who became a billionaire through wise, skillful, and patient investing. Even when the myths are stripped away, Buffett is clearly a successful investor. Although he is a legend on both Wall Street and Main Street, he is not the first to reach such status. One of his predecessors in the legendary column was Bernard Baruch. If Buffett is the man for the last 50 years of the twentieth century, Baruch was the investor for the first 50 years. Baruch's claim to fame was selling out before the crash of 1929. Just as Buffett cites Benjamin

Graham, a Columbia University professor as his investing mentor, Baruch cited a then-obscure British author, Charles Mackay, who wrote a tome called *Extraordinary Popular Delusions and the Madness of Crowds* in 1841. Mackay's descriptions of the madness of market fads are well worth reading, as are more recent debates of the accuracy of some of Mackay's sources. For example, in seventeenth-century Holland, the cost of tulip bulbs rose by several thousand percent over a period of 2 to 3 years. Prices did not hold and came crashing down. The collapse destroyed fortunes built on flowers and the over-the-counter futures market which had developed to support tulip bulb speculation.

Bernard Baruch loved Mackay's book, because Baruch recognized the signs of market madness and made millions from his understanding of the crowds. Mackay's description of tulip bulbs could easily have been a chronicle of the stock market in the 1920s or in 1987. It is a classic example of what happens when greed and madness descend upon an otherwise reasonable asset market. Rapid market shifts leading to wild booms and even wilder busts are more common than most believe. There are certainly a number of stock market manias in any investor's lifetime. Recent years have seen the 1987 boom and crash, the energy and oil stocks of the late 1970s, and the nifty-fifty craze and subsequent bear market of the early 1970s.* I have left out the 1990s, not because they were placid, but because proximity makes reasonable perspective more difficult. However, the bond mar-

---

*In the late 1960s and very early 1970s about 50 leading companies became the darlings of Wall Street. This group, nicknamed the "nifty-fifty," saw their stock prices soar. In the 1973–1975 recession, investors realized that these 50 companies were no less vulnerable to hard times than the rest of the firms on the exchange. Twenty-five years later some of the nifty-fifty still hadn't regained their all-time high (late 60s–early 70s) stock prices.

ket in 1993 and 1994 may be worth noting. Bonds scored their best and worst years of the last 30 years back to back. Currencies also provide recent examples, including the Mexican peso and the yen/dollar rate, which ran up (and down) by 25 percent in less than a year in 1995.

There are a couple of things to watch for in the movements within asset markets as they rise and fall. The first, and most difficult, is loss of sanity. Mackay's stories sound outrageous—paying a sum exceeding a full year's wages for a single flower bulb. Yet most any year on Wall Street offers examples of a stock that appreciated by two, three, or even five times its value. Anyone who has lived through a market boom can recall otherwise reasonable people making logical arguments to support seemingly impossible events. Baruch's skills, aided by Mackay and Baruch's own experience at losing a fortune or two, was to keep his sanity in the midst of chaos.

Keeping one's sanity is most important when a market makes a transition in how it values things. Stocks should be valued by the dividends and earnings the company is expected to return. This is fine for sane markets. But, at times these assets are valued, not by their returns, but by what someone else will pay for them. When this shift in valuation is made, we are moving toward the greater-fool theory of valuation—pricing the stock (or the tulip bulb) at what a greater fool than the current owner will pay. Unless the supply of ever-greater fools is growing faster and faster, the sighting of the first should be a sign to bail out. Of all the kinds of shifts, changes, and cycles that characterize the economy, the market dynamics as the greater, and greater fools arrive are among the most exciting, potentially most rewarding, and certainly most dangerous.

These kinds of shifts are not limited to tulip bulbs or

stocks. In fact, the patterns can be seen in many places. Along with Mackay's tale, a more modern and more carefully assembled analysis is Charles Kindleberger's *Manias, Panics, and Crashes,* (1989). Kindleberger is an excellent economic historian who provides both some history and some theory for fast-moving economic changes and shifts.

KEY PLAYERS
IN THE GAME

*But apart from this contemporary mood, the ideas of econo-
mists and political philosophers, both when they are right and
when they are wrong, are more powerful than is commonly
understood. Indeed the world is ruled by little else. Practical
men, who believe themselves exempt from any intellectual
influences, are usually the slaves of some defunct economist.
Madmen in authority, who hear voices in the air, are distilling
their frenzy from some academic scribbler of a few years back.*

JOHN MAYNARD KEYNES

The General Theory of Employment, Interest, and Money, Chap. 24.

Economics matters, and so do the people in the economy:
the mad authoritarians, the practical thinkers, the defunct
academic scribblers. The most important characters in the
economy are the people. They all matter. Without us—
consumers, investors, businesspeople, policymakers,
traders, and everyone else—there wouldn't be any economy. Moreover, without us, there wouldn't be any reason for
an economy. Since we are it, who are we? Who plays in
this game? This chapter is about us, the players in the
game. We will start with the few and advance to the many.
The few are those who make policy and sometimes determine the direction of the economy. The many, or the rest
of us, are the ones who suffer or enjoy the policy and, by

responding to policy, really determine where the economy goes.

The policymakers are largely at the government level and fall into a few discrete groups. After these select few, we look at businesses, consumers, and even clubs.

POLICYMAKERS

Although we begin with the policymakers and the government, they are not always the players that matter the most. The policymakers do things to the economy; the government agencies talk about the economy. But neither of them are as deeply in and part of the economy as are consumers and business.

In some almost forgotten high school class, where students had to read the Constitution, there were a lot of talks about the three branches of government and checks and balances. For economic matters there are also three branches—two in the government and one in a strange halfway house between the government and the financial markets. Together, these form the official leadership of the economy. They are the President, the Congress, and the Federal Reserve. Of these three, the most important on a day-to-day basis is the Fed, followed by the President and then the Congress. The Supreme Court, representing the judicial branch, is very important in the government but does not play a leadership role in the economy.

The Federal Reserve, or the Fed, is America's central bank. It is also half government, half not. And it is far younger than the nation. The Fed was founded in 1913 by Congress. Its start ended a hiatus of about 80 years when the nation had no central bank. Before the Fed, way before the Fed, there were the First and Second Banks of the United States. Before that there was the Congress and the Continental Congress. Without a central bank, the economy supported business and the government was able to borrow money. But the rising level of economic complexity, industrialization, and development of financial markets set the stage for the founding of the Fed. In the end, it was the child of efforts by various financiers to wrest financial market transactions from London, combined with populist fears that if the government didn't provide a central bank the East Coast financiers would form and control the banking system. In the years leading up to the Fed's founding, there were a number of market crashes (called "panics" in those days) and deep recessions. In the panic of 1907 and the ensuing depression, J. P. Morgan (at that time the man and the bank were essentially one and the same) did fulfill the role of a central bank by providing loans to prevent bank runs and containing spreading financial collapse.

The Fed is partly a government agency and partly a creature of the banking system. Its current status is similar to its original structure in 1913, though there have been some notable changes over time. The Fed consists of a central Board of Governors in Washington, DC and 12 regional Federal Reserve banks in various cities around the country. The 12 banks divide the nation into Federal Reserve districts, with each regional bank responsible for various supervisory roles in its district. According to some observers, the districts are outdated and should be redrawn. Don't hold your breath, since there is a lot of political power at stake and any change will be difficult to accomplish.

The Fed's Board of Governors has seven members. They are appointed by the President with the consent of the Senate (as are the justices of the Supreme Court), and they serve for 14 years. While the justices of the Court serve for life, 14 years can seem like a lifetime as well. No two Fed governors can come from the same Federal Reserve district unless Congress agrees to an exception. From the seven governors, the President selects one to be the chairman and one to be the vice chairman. These appointees serve for 4 years. This rather complicated system means that the Fed's governors are somewhat protected from politics by their long terms and the strong chance that, at any given moment, some governors are holdovers from an earlier President. On the other hand, the chairman's term in the top spot is not so long that he (so far there haven't been any Fed chair*women*) can afford to ignore politics. If he did, the Congress would remind him of it quite soon.

Although the Fed's top brass are appointed by the President, technically the Fed is owned by its member banks, not by the federal government. Nonetheless, any profits the Fed makes are given to the U.S. Treasury. The district Federal Reserve banks are run by boards of directors drawn from their own regions and selected by the district banks. The president of each district Federal Reserve bank is appointed with the approval of the Fed's Board of Governors. If all this isn't confusing enough, there are two groups at the top of the Fed that matter for the economy. One is the Fed's Board of Governors, which runs the show. The other is a group called the Federal Open Market Committee (FOMC), which is the real key to the Fed.

The voting members of the FOMC are the seven governors of the Fed and five of the 12 presidents of the district Federal Reserve banks. All 12 presidents go to all the meetings, but not all vote at any meeting. The president of the New York Fed always votes and is the vice chairman of the FOMC (not of the Fed itself). The other 11 district bank presidents share the remaining four votes. At the start of each year, those four votes rotate among the 11 district presidents. By now you may be wondering whether any of this bureaucracy really matters at all and what, if anything, this group could do. It calls to mind the description of a camel as a horse designed by a committee. Not quite. The FOMC meets eight times a year, for either 1 or 2 days at a time and usually beginning on a Tuesday; the schedule is announced early in the year. The FOMC may be complicated, but what it does is simple: *It sets interest rates.* In particular, it decides what level of short-term interest rates it would like to see and orders the Fed to run the banking system to achieve that number.

To be fair to any reader who has suffered through a college course in banking or monetary theory, the background is much more involved and is steeped in even more arcane procedures and policies. But when the day is done, the FOMC sets the Fed funds rate. This is the rate of interest banks pay when they lend money to one another on an instant-delivery, guaranteed-cash basis. Fed funds are literally "money in the bank" where the bank is the Federal reserve. The Fed can affect the amount of cash available to banks by buying or selling government bonds. If the Fed buys bonds, it pays for them by putting money into the banking system; if it sells bonds, it pulls money out of the banking system. When it changes the supply of money in the system, the Fed changes the balance between supply and demand and the price of money. That price is the interest rate. Since money can flow from one use to another and from one place to another, the price of a loan between two banks affects the price of a loan from a bank to a business or from a consumer to a bank (that's a deposit). Setting the Fed funds rate establishes the key number in a complex structure of interest rates.

While the Fed can set the Fed funds rate closely (usually to within one-eighth of a percentage point), it cannot set all interest rates. Most important, it cannot set the rate paid on much longer loans, such as those for 10 years or 30 years.

If being able to set one interest rate for loans among big banks seems like not too much, consider the impact that action can have. In 1979–1980 the inflation rate was around 15 percent and the Fed, under Paul Volcker's leadership, decided that inflation had to be brought down even if that meant putting the economy into a deep recession. Over the next 3 years interest rates rose as high as 20 percent, unemployment climbed to a postwar high of 10.7 percent, and inflation began to decline. By the mid-1980s inflation was under 5 percent. The Fed can have an impact on a much shorter time scale as well. On the morning after the 1987 stock market crash, the Fed put out a one-sentence press release that sufficient liquidity would be available to prevent any spreading financial collapses. That cryptic message expressed to the financial markets the Fed's commitment to make sure that the market crash did not lead to a severe recession or any major bank failures. The Fed's efforts were successful.

The Fed is even more mysterious than it is powerful. At times the governors seem to be convinced that the only way for the Fed to retain its power is to shroud itself in mystery. That is not the case. Moreover, with some diligence there need not be so much mystery. While it sometimes seems that you need to be the member of a special club to understand the Fed, the central bank does publish a lot of information and reveal a good deal about its thinking. For economy watchers there are two key publications. In true Fed tradition, they come out on their own quirky schedule about eight times a year. A few weeks before each FOMC meeting, the Fed releases a review of the economy compiled from reports from each regional Federal Reserve bank. The report is called the *Tan Book* or the *Beige Book*, supposedly from the color of its cover. Until the late 1980s this report was considered confidential and restricted to members of the FOMC. Over time it began to leak into the press and the Fed responded by making it public. The *Beige Book* provides a good review of what is happening in the economy and what issues the FOMC may be facing. Any comments about inflation or recession are certainly worth noting.

The Fed's other release is the minutes of the FOMC meeting. These are made public with a one-meeting delay. In other words, if the FOMC meets in early February and again in late March, the minutes from the February meeting will be published on the Friday afternoon following the March meeting. The minutes are both the worst-written and most reliable contemporary comments on the economy and the financial markets to be found. They describe the economic conditions and thinking of the FOMC at the time of the meeting. With some skillful reading between the lines, you can usually reconstruct the details of the economic forecast—including inflation, interest rates, and possibly even stock prices—offered by the Fed's professional staff at the FOMC meeting. At the same time, simply for a fine example of obscure, dense, and distracting economic prose that would make most textbooks look transparent, go no further than the FOMC minutes. If nothing else, the price charged by the inflation fighters is right—the minutes are free for the asking from a local Federal Reserve bank or from the Board of Governors in Washington, DC. They are also on the Internet.

Because of both its power and its mystery, the Fed is a never-ending source of interest to economists and market players. The major investment banks and brokers often have economists—Fed watchers—devoted to monitoring and guessing (or outguessing) the Fed's every move.

THE PRESIDENT'S PEOPLE

The administration—that is, the President and his various aides and appointees—plays a part in the economy as well. The administration's role is less direct and less clearly defined than the Fed's. To begin with, the President proposes the budget, various federal spending programs, and laws and often suggests changes in the tax code. But he only proposes all these and sometimes the final result is very different from what was proposed. Second, the President through his speeches and his press dealings often has a large impact on what people think about the economy. Third, but most important over the long haul, the President sets the tone and the agenda for economic policy. Lyndon Johnson introduced the Great Society programs and set the tone for the next 30 years of government policy. Before him Franklin D. Roosevelt had set the tone for both government spending and regulation with his New Deal policies during the Great Depression. A generation before, Theodore Roosevelt established antitrust as a government tool of policy. Ronald Reagan introduced an era of less government and less regulation of markets.

In terms of the long-running changes and shifts discussed in the last chapter, the rise of regulation from 1900 to about 1975 or 1980 and the subsequent decline of regulation and its replacement with markets marked a major change brought on, and encouraged, by Presidents and their appointees. Lest one political party or the other claim all the credit, recall that the first efforts at deregulation were in the airline industry when an economist named Alfred Kahn was appointed to chair the Civil Aeronautics Board (CAB). Kahn proceeded to do what bureaucrats felt was the unspeakable—to take apart his own bureaucracy. The demise of the CAB marked the end of price regulation in airfares and the beginning of a period of deregulation that has spread to long-distance and local telephone calling, trucking, electricity, cable TV, and many other formerly regulated industries.

So who are all these men and women who fiddle with the economy? The various government agencies, bureaus, and so forth fall into two general groups: those that make policy and are in the White House and those that have responsibility for certain rules, laws, and programs and are in other parts of the government. A complete catalog would fill a book, so I will mention only a few and give some comments about which ones are worth watching if you want to know what the economy might do to you.

One of the more august-sounding groups is the Council of Economic Advisers. This is part of the Executive Office of the President, meaning that the advisers talk to and more often than not are appointed by the President. It also means that when the President changes, so does the council. The council consists of three members and a staff of about 50 people. The members advise the President on various policy matters such as whether to lower taxes or allow regulators to raise prices or fight Congress about the deficit or other questions. Early in the year the council publishes a book called *The Economic Report of the President*. Actually, only the first 20 pages is the President's report, and that is written by the council anyway. The rest of the book is the council's report to the President. It is usually the longest (and longest-winded) discussion of the President's economic policy to be found anywhere. Some years the *Economic Report* is very good and full of new insights. Other years it is old politics warmed over. But it is always worth at least a quick look. Moreover, the back of the report is one of the best compilations of data about the economy in circulation. Everything from the stock market to farmers and livestock is covered. The tables alone are worth the price of the book.

The other key group in the Executive Office of the President is the Office of Management and Budget (OMB). These are the government's chief bean counters, the ones who watch the budget. Yes, the budget has been in the red since 1969, but OMB really does watch the budget numbers with some care. OMB writes the budget that the President submits to Congress early in the year. If all goes well—which it rarely does—OMB manages the budget process for the White House, and a budget is in place, or close to in place, by the following October 1. The government's fiscal year runs from October 1 to September 30. The year used to extend from July 1 to June 30 but the budget never got passed in time, so the rules were changed to gain an extra 3 months. Given the experience in 1995–1996 when the budget wasn't passed until late February, another adjustment might be in order so that the government's fiscal year is actually next year.

For economy watchers, investors, and the otherwise curious, OMB does publish the budget. The budget now consists of several volumes and the price for all of them is beginning to look like the national debt itself. I would not recommend reading the budget, or even the abridged version called the *Budget in Brief,* unless you are an insomniac. You can be satisfied with wading through the special three-page spread that either *The Wall Street Journal* or *The New York Times* offers.

The third key economic agency is the Treasury Department. If OMB is where they count the money, the Treasury is where they collect taxes. The Internal Revenue Service is part of the Treasury. So are the mints and the folks who print money at the Bureau of Engraving and Printing. But the Treasury shows up in some unexpected spots on the economic scene. If there is a foreign currency crisis and someone has to say something about the dollar, the yen, the pound, or the peso (almost anyone's peso), the job falls to the Secretary of the Treasury. The Treasury Secretary is often the one called upon to sell something to Congress, discuss sensitive issues with the Federal Reserve, and otherwise keep the wheels of government well lubricated and rolling. The Treasury's mandate is far broader than that of either OMB or the Council of Economic Advisers. Its impact depends a lot on who is the Treasury Secretary at any particular moment. For economy watchers, the Treasury can be either a disappointing quagmire or, occasionally, a gold mine of information. The former may be the more typical case.

In Clinton's White House there is another economic player, the Chair of the National Economic Council. Currently it is Gene Sperling; he acts as the President's chief economic policy adviser and mediates among the Secretary of the Treasury, the Council of Economic Advisers, and the Office of Management and Budget. The post is known as the chairman of the Economic Policy Council. When Clinton took office, this job was given to Robert Rubin, a key adviser with extensive Wall Street experience. He was not sent to the Council of Economic Advisers, because he isn't a professional or an academic economist. He wasn't sent to OMB, because he isn't a Washington politician. Nor was he sent to the Treasury, because he isn't an elder statesman expected to sway Congress to support the President's program. What Rubin is, is very smart and quite valuable to the President. When Clinton's first Treasury Secretary, Lloyd Benson, retired, Rubin was appointed to the Treasury. He has made the Treasury a key player in the administration's economic and political policy. Clinton created the Economic Policy Council to meet his staffing needs; it is not likely to survive in future administrations.

There are a long list of other federal agencies that make a difference to the economy. However, most of these have narrow focuses, in accordance with the legislation that created them. One example is the Securities and Exchange Commission, created to regulate the securities industry. The SEC is very important, but for most investors it matters most when they have a fight with their broker. The SEC is not the place to find hints about how the market will do next quarter. There are many others in the alphabet soup of the government. One of these is the Federal Trade Commission, which enforces various laws about antitrust and regulation. Another is the Federal Communications Commission (FCC), which covers radio, TV, and telephone. The FCC is the spotlight with changing rules for the telecommunications industry.

CONGRESS

The President's people aren't the only ones in Washington. Congress is also chock full of people trying to make the economy bigger, smaller, fatter, or thinner. Most of Congress's work is done in committees. Ironically, the committee that sounds like it is the key to the economy is one of the least important to actually getting things done. It is the Joint Economic Committee. It holds hearings, publishes a lot of useful stuff, and generally keeps a lot of people busy. But it does not have any direct role in writing legislation or setting economic policy. In both the Senate and the House of Representatives, there are a few key economic players. Both Houses have a banking committee that watches over the Fed. Both have a budget committee that leads the budget battles in each house, and both have various committees that oversee taxes and spending.

In Congress, maybe because there is a generous supply of politicians, the people who really matter are the ones who take strong stands and get noticed. In recent years the Speaker of the House has often taken a leading role in economic policy. Newt Gingrich in the 1995–1996 congressional years played a major role in the House. But it need not be the Speaker. For a number of years the Democratic head of the House Banking Committee was a populist congressman from Texas named Henry Gonzalez. He took a strong stance about Fed policy and probably had more impact on the Fed's policy and operations than most of the rest of Congress put together. For those of us watching the economy, it is the vocal member of Congress with a strong stance on economics who can make a difference in how the markets behave or the economy does.

Beyond the committees in the congress, two congressional agencies are often sources of interesting economic information. These are the General Accounting Office (GAO) and the Congressional Budget Office (CBO). The GAO does studies on just about anything that some member of Congress thinks is worth studying. While there is often little obvious rhyme or reason to the topics chosen, the GAO's work is always well done. It is unlikely that you will be able to find a recent GAO study that precisely answers some burning economic question. But if you stumble across some of the GAO's work, take a moment to look at it.

The CBO, on the other hand, is in the thick of most worthwhile policy arguments. It is the congressional counterpoint to all those Executive Branch agencies (OMB, the Council of Economic Advisers, the Treasury, and so on) when Congress wants its own economic gunslingers to shoot down administration policies. The CBO's work is well done and often easier to follow and understand than some of the White House political stuff. The CBO is a good source of information about the budget and about what can be done to cut spending. One of its larger, but more worthwhile, publications is an annual tome the size of the Manhattan phone book that chronicles where cuts can be made in different programs and how much will be saved. With this, no one in Congress can be at a loss for ideas on saving money. Yet at least some members of Congress don't read it, since a lot of the good ideas appear year after year.

BUSINESS

Probably the most maligned, least understood, most honored, and certainly most talked or written about player in the economy is business. It seeps into our language: "The business of America is business." "What's good for General Motors is good for America." We talk about the bottom line, we tell jokes about salespeople, and we wonder if being in business is a profession, an avocation, a bonanza, or a tragic mistake. Big business often has a bad image or connotation, while small business may be seen as almost virtuous.

As we look at how business acts in the economy and

what it does, it is helpful to try to put some of the politics, philosophy, and arguments aside. To most people, business is different because it is out to make a profit. Profit should not be all that mysterious an idea. Simply put, at the end of the year after everything is paid for, what's left over (positive or negative) is the profit or loss. Everything means everything, though with some occasional adjustments. Labor gets paid wages, materials and equipment are paid for, rent is paid on real estate, interest is paid on borrowed money or debts, and taxes are paid on income and sales. What's left—if anything—are profits. Economists sometimes call this *accounting profit*. It really is more than the true profit. When investors or stockholders put money into a company, they expect some kind of return. That normal return must be covered first. If there is something left beyond the normal return a stockholder ought to expect on the basis of business risk, it is a true profit. In all these calculations, there are always some adjustments. For instance, some expenses may be rearranged to reflect long-lived equipment. Any business that buys a building that will last 20 years doesn't count the entire expenditure as occurring in 1 year and then imagine it uses the building for free for the next 19 years.

What is left for business after everything is paid? What's left is the profit—the extra return that a business earns for doing its business better, faster, smarter, and more skillfully than the competition. While some businesses get along with barely anything more than a minimum return on capital, they are not likely to grow or attract new investors. Other businesses surge forward, make generous profits, attract a lot of investors, and get their pick of the best and the brightest workers. On one level the differences may be obvious; on another they are very subtle. At the obvious level, the successful, fast-growing, and profitable business is the one that brings out new products, meets its customers' needs, and doesn't rest on its laurels. The staid, but not very profitable business is the reverse. The legendary success stories of business in the last two or three decades are all about computer companies that proved to be incredibly successful, at least for a time. Apple Computer was started by two tinkerers in a garage who figured out how to build truly useful one-user computers. ("PC" was a name coined by IBM, and before the Apple II there weren't many computers small enough or cheap enough to be used by only one person.) Microsoft began when two programmers managed to write a version of the basic computer language for machines even more primitive than the Apple II.

The stories go on and on, but one that hints at the unique role of business and profits in the economy is Intel. Today Intel is one of the largest makers of computer chips. Its chips power most of the PCs people use, as in the "Intel Inside" labels pasted on them. Early on one of the founders of Intel, Gordon Moore, realized that technology was developing so fast that computing power would double every 18 months. In simple terms, in about a year and a half, the brand-new, state-of-the-art PC you just bought will be eclipsed by one twice as fast, twice as powerful, and cheaper besides. What Intel realized was that making profits—real profits, not just rent on the capital—means being always first on the cutting edge. Business, in pursuing profits, invests in research, development, building, construction, and doing.

Intel doesn't keep on introducing faster, smarter chips to be nice or well liked. It does so to make a profit. If it doesn't, someone else will gain the edge and make the profit—and after a while Intel may not be around. The economy is littered with companies that didn't make it. In technology alone there is a long long list. Software techies may recall Visicalc, WordStar, CP/M operating systems, and other dusty names. Neither PCs nor Apple IIs were really the first PCs—there are other forgotten names like Altair, Radio Shack TRS-80, and Osborne.

Another example from the computer industry is Hewlett Packard laser printers. HP showed both American and Japanese companies how to compete in the printer business by always taking the lead to build the next great printer and make the next big profit. Time after time, HP introduced a new-model laser jet printer that had a solid competitive edge and could make true economic profits from its temporary position as the best performer at the best price. What set HP apart was what it did after each new printer was on the market. Instead of sitting back to enjoy a temporary monopoly before its competitors caught up, HP went back to work building a better, faster, cheaper printer. Each time, it replaced its own product with a new product that was better. A business that thinks it should sit back and smell the roses after a new product is launched might look at HP. It rarely smells the roses, even though no one else has made any successful inroads in the laser printer market.

In the pursuit of profits, businesses do research, attract investment funds, take risks, and create new ways of doing things in the economy and the world. Profit is usually measured in money and rewards. Why do we seek profits? Polite analysts label it the profit motive, others say it is how we keep score, and still others call it greed. When the system works—it usually does, but not all the time—the profits are rewards for creating products that people want and delivering the products to customers. Those who do it well earn profits and attract more investors for their next effort. Those who don't, don't earn profits or attract investors and often end up working for those who prospered. In industries where companies can enter businesses easily and quickly, where consumers know what they want, and where there is free competition, the system works very well. In the last two decades, technology has been one of those places. Wall Street and finance represent another area where firms compete by developing new ways for companies to raise capital and for individuals to invest.

In industries where entry is difficult, change is slow, and the leading companies seem to have been born into their positions by regal birthrights, not by profitable results, the system doesn't work too well. Air travel before deregulation was one such industry. Prices were high, and few efforts were made to try new routes or new ways of serving passengers. It was a closed club in which admission was granted by a government agency, the CAB, rather than by going to market and doing a better job of serving customers. When the air travel regulations were scrapped, several years of turmoil resulted. As the dust now settles, things are not entirely resolved and profits are rather scarce.

Out of these battles does come a clear and unique role for business. Sometimes business fills it, sometimes business fails. For the economy to grow and advance, someone somewhere must do research, risk doing things differently, try new ideas, and offer the results to the market. Businesses do this. When the system works, they do it for the rewards of profits and earn profits as their rewards.

Whether the system truly works in America is a topic of some debate. However, the technological developments in our nation, the growth of our economy, and the productivity of our workers are a direct result of the willingness of business to take risks to bring products and services to market. Without business, it might not work at all. Indeed, some would argue that the history of Eastern Europe in the second half of the twentieth century is a clear demonstration that growth does not work without business.

A more interesting example from the past is Thomas Edison. He is celebrated as the preeminent American inventor, with over 1000 patents to his name. That is true, but he was a businessman as well. Edison didn't just invent the light bulb—he developed the idea and the process of generating, distributing, and selling electricity to provide light. He offered a new source and made a profit doing it. But his biggest contribution to business and to the economy may have been the idea of establishing a large-scale industrial research lab so that new ideas could be things business invested in instead of praying for. Edison was not a lone inventor in a garage; he was an organizer and developer seeking rewards for his hard work. The rest of us happened along and got electric lights, motion pictures, and phonograph records, to name but a few of his profitable results.

ECONOMIC RENT AND CAPITALIZING RENTS, OR HOW THE PROFITS OFTEN SEEM TO VANISH FOR NEW OWNERS

Most businesses are worth more than the purchase price of their obvious components. A retail store is worth more than the combination of its storefront, its employees' wages, and its inventory. There is something extra—customers who know the store and are regulars, its reputation for service and quality, its well-known spot on the corner. This isn't unique to retailers. After all, what is it that makes a well-known brand like Coca-Cola different from some other soft drink? What is it that makes fashionable jeans a hot commodity? Accountants call this extra something the "going concern" value to remind us that the whole is really greater than the sum of the parts. Sometimes this extra value is created by skilled managers; sometimes it is just a matter of luck. For instance, in real estate location counts for a lot whether you get it by being skillful or being lucky.

In the early nineteenth century, British economist David Ricardo discussed the notion of rent in describing English agriculture. (See the account of Ricardo in the Appendix.) Today, *economic rent* has become the economist's term for the extra value that a business has because it is unique, different, or special or owns a popular brand name. As Ricardo explained in the case of English farming, payments for rent are payments for that something extra. The payments are based on the value of what the business sells, not on the wages its employees should earn or the costs of any inputs. Serving Coca-Cola may cost more because it is Coke, not because the employees are paid more or it costs more to make Coke, or green glass bottles, than it costs to make some other soft drink.

But a funny thing happens to rent once it is created by some clever business manager. Suppose a business is started and a new product is created that catches on and builds a brand. Snapple fruit drinks is one recent

(*Continued*)

example. It was a new idea that became a hot item. After a while Snapple was more than just a business of novel-flavored fruit drinks in glass bottles. It had some extra added value because it was Snapple. The Snapple owners sold the business. Snapple's owners were paid for the regular replaceable things in the business like inventory, offices, equipment, and machinery. They were also paid a lot extra because Snapple was something special. They were paid the value of all the future returns from the economic rent of being Snapple—all the future times when being Snapple would mean selling more bottles of juice and higher prices. In fancier terms, this is the capitalized value of the future economic rents.

For the sellers—the ones who created or discovered or fell upon the economic rent in Snapple—it was a nice deal because they got paid for the special value in the business. For the buyers, it wasn't all that wonderful. When they bought Snapple they paid a price that would cover their costs and would pay for buying Snapple and its economic rents. The buyers wouldn't get anything extra unless they managed to do what the sellers had done: create something special that earns more just for being special. This process turns economic rent, the true value of a going concern, into an accounting cost to be paid. There is some justice to it. The first person to recognize the rent gets paid for it and those who come after merely earn an ordinary return on their money, not something extra.

(*Continued*)

CONSUMERS

If the last shall be first, it is appropriate to talk about consumers last. In recent years it has become fashionable for businesses to claim they strive to understand their customers, to be customer-friendly, customer-oriented, customer-intimate. Consumers may not be kings or queens, but business wants us to believe we are. Royal or not, consumers are the major part of the economic game. Consumer spending accounts for over 60 percent of gross domestic product. Consumers also represent the largest savers and the largest taxpayers in the economy. Almost anything business does is designed to earn a profit by serving customers and consumers. Consumers are also among the most studied, most watched, most worried-about, and most feared groups in the economy. We are analyzed, segmented, reviewed, portioned, reanalyzed, and observed. Is it any wonder that consumers are often fickle, unreliable, and unpredictable?

For economy watchers, consumers are important, since how much consumers spend or save, buy or don't buy, can make a big difference in how things go in the economy. "Consumers" represent all 250-plus million Americans in the U.S. economy. Collectively we spent some $5.1 trillion in 1996, based on the GDP accounts. This represents about 68 percent of GDP for the year. We bought more than half the cars and trucks manufactured, most of the homes sold, and most of the goods and services produced in the economy. We also paid most of the taxes and did more than all of the savings. So how can you tell what we (you!) might do next in the economy? To start, we look at some of the more common surveys, turn to three or four major spending categories, examine savings, and review some of the ways marketers divide consumers into groups. Finally, we examine what computers might do for consumer mass marketing.

Surveying consumer sentiment is a popular game. There are innumerable surveys of how happy, or sad, consumers are. Two of the most widely followed are done by the Conference Board and the University of Michigan Survey Research Center. Both are nongovernment, nonprofit research groups. The two groups use similar questionnaires and techniques, though some of the details differ. Each month they survey consumers to see how people feel about the economy, their jobs, future inflation, and if this is a good time to buy a car or a house. The Conference Board releases a summary of its findings to the press and sells the details. The Survey Research Center does not release any summary, but most of the information quickly leaks out from Wall Street customers of the Survey Center.

The surveys give a general picture of how people feel about the economy as it affects their lives. If consumers are gloomy, don't expect booming Christmas sales or a rush to invest in the market. Likewise, if consumers are upbeat and the local discount store files for bankruptcy, don't believe the owners when they blame all their woes on the economy. But if you want to know how fast you can sell your home, don't look at the national measures of consumer confidence; look at local trends in real estate sales and prices.

Most economic studies of consumers break spending into three major categories: services, durable goods, and nondurable goods. Spending on services is very steady and shows little volatility in total, though some of the details will bounce around a lot. Purchasing nondurable goods also is relatively stable and less exciting. Both of these will do better in good economic times when income gains are strong, but both are fairly stable in most economic environments. They include some goods and services which stock market watchers assume are necessities that are never cut out—so the stocks are good to own in bad times. Included are food, drink, tobacco (selling addictive products has a certain perverse investment appeal), and services such as medical care. But beware that, in the extreme, little is every truly immune from the forces of supply and demand. Dental care, no matter how much our parents admonished us to brush our teeth or see the dentist, is often seen as optional in economically difficult moments.

We are, after all, more than consumers. For us there is another side that we often find more important than consumption and how we spend our money. That other side is income—how much we earn. Income is certainly important, because without it we wouldn't be able to get food, clothing, shelter, or much else. Moreover, income is often the way we "keep score." For most people most of the time, knowing how much they earn—or how much more they earn than the next person—is how they keep score.

Lately there has been a lot of discussion about income, wages, wage gains after inflation, income growth, income distribution, and the general fear that we are not doing as well as we used to. Moreover, if economic statistics are confusing, misleading, or relatively easy to lie with, income statistics are the worst of the lot. Rather than wade through reams of numbers and risk getting lost in the fog, let's analyze how the 1980s and 1990s compare with other periods in the recent, and not so recent, past. Most of the data support the analysis, but I would not be surprised to hear some vigorous arguments from any of the many other sides.

Are we better off than we were in the 1970s? For the average American, the answer is yes, but not by a whole lot. Our incomes are equal or higher, the things we buy are better, more desirable, and more reliable, and we are living longer.

Are our jobs more secure than in the 1970s or before? Compared with the period since World War II, maybe not. Since 1980, the economy has spent less time in recession than on average for the entire period. But employment is, by some measures, less secure than in the 1960s and 1970s. The answer probably depends largely on the kind of job involved. An auto worker today is more secure than in 1983 or maybe than in 1973. A white-collar middle manager may be less secure; he or she certainly feels less secure. This sense, or lack of sense, of job security is one of the key issues in how consumers feel about their income, their spending, and their economic lives. But before you conclude that we are sliding backward into some deep economic abyss, realize that the 1950–1980 period was quite unusual. The economy and productivity grew far faster than in any other comparable period. The United States, as the only industrial nation that emerged from World War II with its industrial base intact (not in tatters and bomb craters), ruled the economic world. Moreover, with the memory of the Great Depression fresh in their minds and the promise of scientific economic management dancing before them, policymakers sought to ensure strong economic growth. Inflation was a concern, but deeply embedded inflation—as seen in the 1970s—was neither a fear nor memory for policymakers of the 1950s and 1960s. They sought, and got, strong economic growth.

Will our children be better off economically than we are? The best way to convince pollsters or politicians that you are a real pessimist is to tell them your kids won't do as well in the world as you have. (Even if you don't have kids, this statement works.) That much pessimism is overdone.

Technology and knowledge are growing at a fantastic pace and will keep growing. It is not possible to prevent curious scientists from making discoveries, some of which will be useful. While predicting cures for AIDs, cancer, the common cold, political terrorism, or the business cycle is for charlatans, things will get better in the future. If there are any doubts, wander through a store and consider what you couldn't have found (because it wasn't there) 10 or 20 years ago. In terms of technology, computers, medical care, travel, and communications, the past—and future—advances are impressive. Certainly we can't expect all our children to be in the top 10 percent of the income distribution or as rich as if they were, but the material opportunities for the good life aren't about to vanish from the economy.

So why do we feel so glum and did this ever happen before? Two things may be contributing to the current malaise. First, as hinted at a few paragraphs above, the 1950–1980 period was unusually successful for the American economy and the American people. We have a hard act to follow in the 1980s and the 1990s. Second, it did happen before to some extent. When the industrial revolution swept through Europe and America, people were pushed off farms and out of their farming life and livelihoods into cities and factories. People's lives were disrupted. They felt like they were losing control. Computers and information are doing some of the same thing today.

Computers are rapidly changing people's lives. First, tasks that some people used to do for a living as specialists can now be done by anyone with the aid of a computer. We used to have secretaries to type, accountants to do taxes, telephone operators to find phone numbers, statisticians to provide numerical reports, and even schoolteachers to teach spelling. Almost all these tasks are now done by computers. The machines may be wonderful, but there are few, if any, of us who are not affected by them. Second, when information is added to the mix, the impact is multiplied many times. Until recently, most "middle managers" in large corporations were conduits for information. They translated some senior executive's needs into tasks for junior staffers to perform and then reported back to the senior executive on the results. The organization man of the 1950s was an information messenger. Now computers and e-mail can do it all.

The computer revolution has a peculiarly economic aspect to it that should not be ignored. Much of what computers do today they did 20 or 30 years ago. Few calculations or scientific analyses that are run today on a PC or a super workstation couldn't have been run on a 1970s-era IBM 360 series computer. Of course, the 1970s machine took up an entire room and cost several hundred thousand dollars. The same is true of most other operations done with computers and related technology. Car phones were around 30 years ago but they were too expensive for most people to afford. Cellular changed all that. The Internet is about 30 years old, but it was limited to a few Defense Department researchers in the early days. Cheap PCs and deregulated phone service is changing that. The list goes on and on. The essence of the computer revolution is not what the technology can do, but how cheaply it can do it. Why are computers invading every sector of our lives? Because they're so cheap that they can do almost anything cheaper than we can without them. In the end, it is not computer technology that makes the difference; it is computer economics.

GROUPS AND CLUBS

Groups and clubs may sound like a strange thing to discuss in a book on economics. Groucho Marx commented that he would never join a club that would have him as a member. But in the economy, people often find it useful and economically profitable to join a club or a group. Further, the economics and politics of some key issues such as trade and protection often depend on groups such as political pressure groups.

The economics of a club are fairly simple—the costs are shared among the members. For some kinds of benefits, this means the club makes a lot of economic sense. Few of us can afford to build a golf course for our private use. Few of us have the free time to play golf all the time, either. (Though some of us might like to.) By joining together to form a club, golfers can share the costs of building and maintaining the course and share its use. Since no member can realistically use the course 7 days a week for all the daylight hours, the sharing can be worked out. Clearly, a golf club has many other attributes and advantages that figure in membership decisions and costs. Some of these relate to the idea that clubs may exclude some members—a noneconomic but socially significant issue that we leave aside. Clubs or groups tend to be formed when individual members receive more in benefits by joining than it costs them. At times, the benefits are multiplied by increases in membership. While a club may not be worthwhile for a few, it will work for many. One silly example is a very small golf club which can afford to build and maintain only a three-hole course. A more realistic example is a labor union that reaches a critical mass, at which point the membership can afford to be well organized and is large enough to wield some significant power.

It is important to note that the costs of joining a group and the benefits of membership may rise faster, or slower, as the number of members increases. Typically, once a modest number of members join, the benefits of belonging climb faster than the individual costs of joining. This means that the club enjoys increasing returns to scale and will grow. It also means that being a member becomes valuable. Being on a growing computer network in which more and more people can be contacted by e-mail or can provide help with computers is one example. The costs of joining depend on phone lines and modems and tend to remain the same as the membership rises. But the rising membership means more people to talk to and increased benefits of being a member.

Unions are a prime example of economic groups that form in the economy. Their goals are to boost members' wages or enhance members' job security. Unions aim to take care of their members, not all working people. Since the members put in the time, money, and effort, this makes sense. Anyone who doubts it should look at the various wage deals made in the last 10 to 15 years. Typically, wage levels for existing employees with some seniority are maintained while wages for entry-level workers are cut back very sharply. This protects the incumbent workers while giving management some benefits of lower wage costs.

The idea of groups also has some powerful implications for the interaction of economics and politics. Trade and protectionism—raising taxes on imports to keep them out in order to "protect" American industry—is a perennial argument among both economists and politicians. Raising tariffs will often raise the costs of imported goods while increasing profits and/or wages in the domestic industries that compete with the imports. How much of the tax or tariff results in higher wages and how much in higher profits depends on the labor-management conditions in each industry. These higher wages or profits are not created by spreading the tax revenues among the protected industries. Rather, the higher taxes push up the prices of competing imports. When this happens, the domestic producers raise their prices and the rest of us—domestic customers—pay higher prices.

There is an interesting dynamic at work here. The benefits of protectionist laws tend to be concentrated on a small group: workers, owners, managers, and shareholders in the protected industry. The costs—the higher prices—are dispersed among a much larger group. Some people may not even realize they're paying the price. One recent example was the quota placed on importing cars from Japan in the early 1980s. These were limits on how many cars the Japanese auto makers could sell in the United States. The limits worked in the sense that they created a shortage of Japanese cars and let Japanese car manufacturers raise prices on the cars they did sell in the United States. (The Japanese auto companies would have preferred to sell more cars at lower prices. Probably they felt that more cars would have meant larger total revenues and larger total profits.) When the prices of Japanese cars rose, U.S. car companies could raise their prices as well. The benefits were jobs and salaries for the auto workers. The costs were higher prices for cars for the rest of us.

Now the small-group phenomenon comes into play. For the average auto worker, the quotas were a good thing. Whatever little more he or she paid for a car (either American or Japanese) was far less than the benefits of keeping a job. Moreover, the benefits were large enough to encourage auto workers to help lobby the government for more quotas. For the rest of us, the added cost of a new car was hard to identify and mattered only when, or if, we were in the market for buying a car. Protectionism often works this way: The benefits are concentrated and it pays a small group very well to fight for tariffs, taxes, or quotas. The costs are spread among a lot of people, many of whom barely notice. It doesn't pay for any of those bearing the costs to make a big fuss. But the unfortunate result is protectionist trade policy making everyone worse off. How can we tell? Because we can do a thought experiment to decide if we could tax the people an amount equal to the tariffs and be able to compensate the ones who would benefit from it (the auto workers in this example) and have money left over. Often, we would have funds left over.

One last point about trade protection. The goal of trade is *not* to create jobs in export industries. Rather, it is to provide imported goods that are either cheaper than domestic supplies or unavailable domestically. We export so we can import. Trade is about expanding our choices for purchasing and consuming through imports, not about exporting to create jobs.

USING THE ECONOMY TO YOUR ADVANTAGE AS AN INVESTOR

Flying with a Tailwind

Learning about and understanding the economy can be rewarding in its own right, but it may also be profitable financially. This chapter and the next look at putting economics to use in the market. In this chapter we look at some general approaches drawn from the discussions of the economy, markets, prices, data, and people. In the next chapter we examine some more formal approaches to forecasting. None of this discussion will make you an overnight Nobel laureate in economics. Some of it may be useful at cocktail parties, especially if talking about professional sports is not your avocation.

Most of the discussion in this chapter focuses on investing in stocks, bonds, and mutual funds. Maybe it should be called one of the shortest investment guides you've ever seen. The chapter examines two general approaches to investing: passive and active. Active investing requires a more detailed analysis and greater effort, but for most of us passive investing may be more successful. The next chapter takes using economics further, with more details and some applications beyond investing.

PASSIVE INVESTING

Over the long haul, owning common stocks can be quite rewarding. An investor who in 1975 put $100 into common stocks, as measured by the S&P 500, and then reinvested all the dividends in the same fund would have amassed a tidy sum of about $1500 by the end of 1995. Before you decide to disown your grandparents for not investing and saving enough, recognize that the calculation ignores paying any taxes, paying investment management fees, and trading expenses. Even with all this added back in, the results are attractive.

This whole thing may sound almost too easy, but it really isn't. There are a number of mutual funds which buy and own the stocks in one or another major stock market index. The most widely used index is the Standard & Poor's 500. It covers 500 leading stocks and is designed to reflect what happens in the economy and the stock market. The S&P 500 is the most widely used index to track the stock market. It is also a very difficult target to beat. In a typical year about two-thirds of all equity mutual funds don't beat the S&P 500. Moreover, its long-term performance has been quite good. There is certainly no assurance or guarantee that the stock market or the S&P 500 will go up in value. As the advertisements always point out, past performance is no guarantee of future results. If this kind of laid-back armchair investing is appealing, there are a number of different mutual funds to choose from. The details, fees, and restrictions may vary a little bit from one fund to the next. Although funds are based on various stock indexes, the S&P 500 is the one most widely used.

There are also bond indexes and bond index funds. However, because bonds tend to be more alike than stocks, index funds are less developed in the bond arena. Even if an investor chooses the passive index route, there are a few decisions to be made. The biggest one is how much money to put in stocks and how much to put in bonds. For this, there are all kinds of rules of thumb and more and more sources of worksheets, guidelines, tests, and similar tools to help with the decision. In general, the longer the time until the investments will be spent, the more you should put in stocks rather than bonds. The idea is that if you have a lot of time, you can afford to hit a bad year in stocks, because you'll get it back over the long haul. Maybe the simplest version of this approach is that if you are saving for retirement, the percentage of your portfolio that is in bonds should equal your age: If you're 40, have 40 percent in bonds and 60 percent in stocks; if you're 55, make it 55 percent bonds, 35 percent stocks. Since people are living longer and possibly retiring, you might want to boost the stock proportion a bit for these numbers.

Financial history suggests that this kind of approach to stocks and bonds should work. While we may worry about getting caught in stocks in a bad year, in most cases bonds also do poorly when stocks do poorly, so stocks aren't such a bad choice after all. The notion of good years and bad years brings up the other key to passive investing: rebalancing. Many brokers' favorite piece of advice is buy low, sell high—not that anyone can really do so all the time. But you can get close to this ideal. Suppose you start the year with a portfolio worth $100,000: 60 percent, or $60,000, in stocks and 40 percent, or $40,000, in bonds. It is a typical year and at the end stocks are up about 11 percent to $66,000 and bonds are up about 5 percent to $42,000, for a total portfolio of $108,000. Now get back to the 60-40 split by selling $1200 worth of stocks and putting it in bonds. This puts you at $64,800 in stocks and $43,200 in bonds. Next year, things switch around— there's a recession and bonds rise on falling interest rates while stocks move very little. At year end you have a 10 percent bond gain for $47,520 in bonds and a slight gain in stocks of about 0.3 percent to $65,000. Your portfolio is now at $112,250 and you again rebalance to 60-40. What you have done is sell some of what did the best and put the money into what did the worst. Since there are ups and downs and what was last is sometimes first, the rebalancing is almost like buy low, sell high.

But suppose you get a string of strong stock years. Have you missed the action? Not quite. If 60-40 was the right number, you stuck with it. Suppose for 3 years going stocks return a nice 15 percent per year and bonds return 5 percent. Your $60,000 in stocks is now $91,250, and your $40,000 in bonds is now $46,305. And your portfolio is now over 66 percent in stocks. You are richer, but riskier than you wanted to be. Rebalancing is almost as boring as using index funds, and equally rewarding in the long run.

Almost every investment book talks about the magic of compound interest and includes examples of why people should start saving early as well as keep it up. While finance and economics often take credit for compound interest, it is really just simple mathematics. Beyond one or two very simple examples, we leave compound interest to others. Suppose two people start savings $100 per month at the age of 25 and investing it in some conservative stocks that return 7 percent per year with reinvested dividends. The first saver is very diligent and keeps saving until he retires. His nest egg at retirement is worth $240,000. The second saver stops saving at age 40 but leaves the nest egg in place to keep growing from reinvested dividends. She does almost as well and has $164,000 at age 65. Enter a third saver who starts off as a free spender, but at age 40 gets religion and starts putting away $200 per month. He comes out worst of all, with a retirement nest egg of $152,000. The moral is start early and, if at all possible, keep it up.

ACTIVE INVESTING

If the get-rich-slowly route described above is too slow, or too boring, you might want to consider a more active approach. For many investors, the rewards are part entertainment and stories to tell and part financial. Of course, every investor hopes there are some positive financial rewards so that the entertainment isn't too expensive.

So what can economics do for investing? For most investors, the biggest factor in how well they do is whether their money is in stocks, in bonds, or in cash. The pros call this *asset allocation*. While the day-to-day or week-to-week movements of stocks and bonds are seemingly due to random luck, the weather, and news reports, longer-term movements depend on the economy. For bonds, the key issue is interest rates. Inflation is also important, as is Fed policy.

For stocks, the two key factors are interest rates and corporate profits. There are times when stocks and bonds move together, and other times when they move in opposite directions. No matter which way things are headed, it is the economy that makes a major difference in what's rising or falling.

To start, let's quickly review what it is about earnings, interest rates, or inflation that drives stocks and bonds. Then, we'll see how the economy can tell us which is rising or falling.

INTEREST RATES, PROFITS, AND INFLATION

Stocks represent future earnings from the company. If corporate earnings are rising, stock prices will rise as well. If corporate earnings are falling, stocks won't be far behind. Interest rates matter too, because they determine how much $100 of earnings next year is worth today. If the interest rate is 10 percent (a high but round number), that $100 next year is worth about $91 today. If the interest rate is half as large, at 5 percent, the $100 next year is worth about $95 today. So if interest rates fall from 10 percent to 5 percent, stock prices will rise.

Bonds are similar. A bond pays a fixed coupon each year. When interest rates fall, the value today of next year's coupon rises, just the way falling interest rates make next year's earnings more valuable today. So falling interest rates are good for bonds. Inflation is not good for bonds. For one thing, bonds are fixed-income investments—the coupon is fixed when the bond is issued. If you have a bond with an 8 percent coupon, it pays 8 percent of its $10,000 face value each year—$800 per year until it matures. But if prices rise and inflation strikes, that $800 won't be worth as much in years to come. Moreover, infla-

TABLE 7-1 **Key Economic Variables**

	STOCKS	BONDS	REAL ESTATE	GOLD
Rising interest rates	Down	Down	Down	Down
Rising corporate profits	Up	Up	Up	?
Higher inflation	Down	Down	Up	Up

tion pushes interest rates up, because investors demand higher returns as inflation eats into their coupon income. Rising interest rates push bond prices down. Table 7-1 shows how certain key economic variables affect different kinds of investments. In addition to stocks and bonds, two others have been added to the list.

Real estate is a popular investment. First, owning a home is part of the American dream—successful Americans usually own some real estate. Second, real estate is usually a good inflation hedge. Somehow gold is an ever popular topic of conversation and a widely discussed investment, if investment is indeed the right word. Gold has not proved to be a very good investment; it pays no interest and it is harder to trade than stocks or bonds. Gold-bug investors are probably better off playing gold-mining stocks. Those who want to buy gold to have money for the next Armageddon should consult some other guide—the economy after the Armageddon may be different from ours. But ours is likely to be around for a long long time.

If we knew what interest rates, corporate profits, and inflation were going to do, we could figure out where to put our money. (As a colleague of mine once said, "If my grandmother had wheels, she'd be a wheelbarrow! So what does this do for me?") The trick is to use what we've been learning about the economy to see where these things are going. There are no perfect answers. If so, I would be investing instead of writing this book. But there are some good hints.

First, we must decide if the economy is in a recession or an expansion. This will tell us a lot about interest rates, profits, and maybe even inflation. How can we tell where the economy is now? Newspaper commentators, politicians, and others often claim to know, and sometimes they may even be right. In general, if the economy is expanding, here is what we should see in the economic numbers:

- Unemployment is declining.
- New jobs are spreading.
- Industrial production is rising.
- Retail sales are strong, with fewer markdowns and sales than last year.
- Auto sales are strong and dealers aren't offering everyone a rebate.
- People are more upbeat about their jobs.
- Airlines are crowded and cheap plane tickets are hard to get.
- Politicians are talking about social goals and morality, not a chicken in every pot.

If these same numbers are all headed the other way, take cover—you're in a recession. But don't lose your head, because sometimes the best investments are made when the economy looks the worst.

Finally, there is an official way of seeing whether the economy is in a recession or an expansion. The National Bureau of Economic Research—which is not a government agency, despite its name—announces when recessions and booms "end." You could call up the NBER and ask. Or you could look in one or another government or Wall Street publication for the current status of affairs. Knowing where you stand is the first step, as can be seen in Table 7-2, which splits recessions and expansions into a beginning and an end. These relate to what's happening in the economy, not to some clock or calendar. And they are averages, so any given event may be a bit different.

So now you've dug through 3 weeks of newspapers to find all those economic numbers, talked to Wall Street, and finally decided whether the economy is in recession. You still don't have the foggiest idea about what this all means for investments. If interest rates are climbing,

TABLE 7-2 **The Business Cycle**

BUSINESS CYCLE STAGE	INTEREST RATES	PROFITS	INFLATION	COMMENTS
Recession starts	Almost ready to start falling	Fall	Stable to rising	Stocks fall on disappointing earnings; bonds rally
Recession ends	Falling	Fall	Falls	Stocks rise on hopes for next boom
Early expansion	Falling	Start to rise	Falls	Stocks boom
Late expansion	Rising	On a roll	Worries people	Stocks climb until fear of a fall sets in

chances are the economy is in an expansion and past the beginning. This is not the time to buy bonds with long maturities. Bonds are likely to be hurt the most by rising interest rates and rising inflation—both common problems at the end of an expansion. If you want to avoid risks, you can buy shorter-term securities of 5 to 7 years' maturity or less. If interest rates are relatively high compared with inflation—more than 3 percentage points difference—you might be just as comfortable with even shorter maturities. In the last stages of an expansion stocks are rising, but when the economy peaks and turns down, stocks will drop as well. Buy stocks, but don't jump into some "sure thing that just needs 18 to 36 months to pay off." Chances are the economic expansion won't last that long.

If interest rates aren't rising, where are you? Either in a recession or just out of it. Now may be a time to seriously think about buying stocks. If you look around and all you see is doom and gloom and reports of layoffs, call your broker. If the brokerage firm is still in business, see what's around. When the economy plunges into recession, everything starts to slide. Part way down the hill either no one wants to borrow any money or the Fed gets worried and floods the economy with money. Either way, interest rates start to fall and the stage is set for the cycle to turn. This is the time when things look bad, often very bad, and the idea of buying stocks seems strange. After all, profits are falling so why would anyone buy stocks? Mostly because stocks rise on lower interest rates and rising hopes. Interest rates are already falling. And unless you think the recession will turn into another Great Depression, hope will begin to rise.

If you think it may be too soon to buy stocks, look at inflation as well. In the beginning of a recession, businesses think (hope?) that the downturn is only a blip and they hold the line on prices. When things get worse, they stop raising prices. So if inflation is slowing, chances are that the recession is closer to being over.

One half-serious suggestion is to buy stocks the moment the economists at the NBER announce that there is a recession. The NBER economists aren't the fastest to react—they strive for, and achieve, reliability and accuracy rather than speed. If you had used that strategy in the 1990–1991 recession, you would have missed the market bottom by about 3 weeks.

To move to some more details, focus on interest rates. They are important for both stocks and bonds. If you get interest rates right, you don't have to worry about too much else anyhow.

One place to start with interest rates is the Fed. The central bank is held up as the epitome of mystery, obscurity, and tradition. It is also a major publisher. The Fed operates through its policy group, the Federal Open Market Committee, as discussed earlier. It meets eight times a year, and the Friday after each meeting the Fed publishes the minutes from the previous meeting. (For instance, the Friday after the meeting of March 26, 1996, the FOMC will release the minutes from its meeting of January 31, 1996.) As stated elsewhere, the minutes are the least read, most valuable, and worst-written investment newsletter in the land. The price is right—they're free for the asking. It takes a few readings to get through it all and understand a small amount of the discussion. But if you persevere, there are rewards. The Fed will tell you where it thinks the economy is going, whether it is worried about inflation or recession, and what it might do. At the end, in terms that only the Fed can understand for sure, is a single-spaced section called "The Directive." It details the instructions sent from the Fed to the trading room at the New York Federal Reserve bank, telling the bank what to do about monetary policy and interest rates. It may be written in code, but the code isn't all that bad. (For suggestions on where to get information about the Fed as well as a copy of the FOMC minutes, see the Appendix.)

Now, before you run down to the neighborhood Federal Reserve bank to get a copy of the minutes, keep the publication schedule in mind. You, and I, always get the minutes one meeting too late—by then the Fed has already done what the minutes say it will be doing! But they are not totally useless. The Fed doesn't often turn on a dime or completely change its ways. More often it shifts slowly and gradually. If you really do read the FOMC minutes—they may be a mystery, but they don't read like a suspense novel—and a few other bits of commentary on interest rates and the money markets, you should have a good idea of the general direction of interest rates. You will also have some sense of whether the bond and stock markets think rates are rising or falling. The commentary may not make you an expert bond trader ready to risk millions on a phone call. It won't get you in the market precisely at the bottom. But the minutes do help.

The last thing to do about interest rates is to look at a few numbers. Most financial papers report rates for Treasury bills, notes, and bonds and even plot a yield curve. Check to see if the numbers match the story in the FOMC minutes or the tales being told by some pundit on TV or in the newspaper. Add this to what you read in the FOMC minutes, and you should have a better-than-average idea of what's happening. Also, if a neighbor tells you to buy a bond fund because interest rates are falling, you might be able to tell whether that is good advice.

Trends and Expectations

Now that we have interest rates covered, how about stocks and earnings? Unfortunately, there is no entity like the Fed and the FOMC on the stock side of the game. In fact, there is not even someone who decides when the good times—the bull markets—or the bad times—the bear markets—begin and end. There is a lot of herd instinct in the stock market, and when stocks are rising "on average" most of them are actually rising. This is especially true in a time frame of weeks or months rather than single days. So a place to start with the market is whether it is rising or falling. Look at the newspaper chart of the S&P 500 or the Dow Jones Industrials. If it's climbing, chances are it will still be climbing next month. Likewise, if it's falling, it will probably still be falling next month.

Of course, the market does change direction some times. But the changes are not usually all that sudden. Even in October 1987, when the market crashed and lost about 20 percent of its value in one day, it had been falling for the previous 3 months. Indeed, the turn was in August 1987, not October. The problem was that no one believed it until October! In simple terms, stocks tend to follow trends and knowing the trend can help.

Beyond trends and interest rates, corporate earnings also make a big difference. Here what counts is not only where earnings are going, but where the market thinks they're going. Suppose everyone expects earnings for Ajax Betasonic Computers (ABC) to rise 20 percent a year. The price of ABC stock is premised on an earnings gain of 20 percent per year. Another firm which makes musical candy bars, Xylophonic Yellow Zingers (XYZ), is seen as a dud and widely expected to report a drop in earnings of 10 percent. XYZ's stock price is based on a drop in earnings. Now comes the ironic part to many investors: If ABC reports that earnings rose 15 percent, its stock will tumble. If XYZ reports that earnings fell *only* 5 percent, its stock will soar.

There are various places to look for information about earnings expectations of stocks. In most commentaries on a company's stock in the paper or on television, the analysts will mention what they expect in the way of company profits. Various services compile analysts' estimates and publish them for use by investors and brokers. If you are considering an investment, you should look for a review of the company. Most of the time, the review will include some discussions of past, and future, earnings.

The same is true of the overall market. Suppose that analysts expect the earnings of the companies in the S&P 500 to rise 15 percent this year, but the results come in a little low, at 12 percent. All the pundits will advise selling stocks, because earnings are weak. Never mind that the economy is growing at only 6 percent, interest rates are also around 6 percent, and inflation is a mere 3 percent. The 12 percent earnings gain is too small—because the market was expecting 15 percent. So what we need to know to judge stocks and the economy is where corporate earnings are headed and where the economy is likely to push them next.

For stocks, we have seen that what matters is interest rates, market trends, and corporate earnings as compared with their expectations. All this applies to the market overall and to individual stocks. Of course, at the level of individual stocks, there are a host of company-specific matters that count as well. New products, new managers, new patents, takeovers, liability lawsuits—the list is almost endless.

For the market overall, there is one other issue very much worth mentioning. It is not the economy, although the economy may be able to offer some guides. From time to time, the stock market is bitten by euphoria. Stocks rise, rise some more, and rise some more. Just when sensible people should be expecting stocks to fall, they find a lot of reasons to believe the market will keep rising. In 1987— before the market crashed—everyone thought a system that used derivatives called *portfolio insurance* would ensure that no one would get hurt when the market fell. Sounds silly now, but a lot of real money was bet on it in 1987. Portfolio insurance didn't work. The market fell and a lot of people got hit. Hard.

When it seems that euphoria is striking, look at the economics and see if it still makes sense. If stocks are rising and rising and rising, interest rates are falling little, if at all, and corporate profits aren't rising much either, you should start to wonder what's happening. That's the time to begin looking at the direction and trends in stock prices and wonder when the turn will come, or when it came.

FORECASTING
THE NEXT MOVE

SPOTTING THE NEXT TAILWIND

Rules of thumb, hunches, feelings, and stories from your rich Aunt Maisie may all be good ways to try to anticipate what the economy will do next. But sooner or later some of us like to take a more scientific or rational approach to anticipating the future. Because soothsaying and oracles have had a bad name since Greek myths, economists prefer the word *forecasting*. Make no mistake. Neither economists nor anyone else can tell what the future holds. The objective in the game of forecasting is to have a better batting average than random choices, dumb luck, or your rich aunt's hunches. After all, you can always assume that tomorrow's economy—interest rates, stock prices, inflation, unemployment, and so forth—will be the same as today's. That is a forecast. Furthermore, it is free and it is almost certainly not 100 percent correct. But if a "scientific" prediction can't beat that simple no-change forecast, it may be time to try reading a different set of tea leaves.

FORECASTING MODELS

Economic forecasting has gone in and out of fashion a number of times in recent decades. Indeed, the whole idea of being able to forecast, or control, the economy has moved from sure thing to impossible to maybe it works. In the golden age of modern American economics—the 1960s—everything came up smelling like a rose. A month after John Kennedy took office in 1961, the economy emerged from recession and began an expansion that ultimately lasted for most of the decade. As the economy grew, unemployment dropped to under 4 percent and inflation was even lower. Jobs were plentiful and the promises of the 1950s seemed to be realized. Government economists were among the heroes of the day. These followers of an Americanized version of the theories of British economist John Maynard Keynes—theories offered as a way to escape the Depression—turned to modern computers to build elaborate mathematical models. The idea was that a good forecasting model gave policymakers a laboratory to test policies like changes in tax laws, government spending, or interest rates. With the lab work guiding them, policymakers would erase recessions before they happened, and growth would go on and on. The idea worked—for a while.

But two things came along which were outside the experience of the models or the model builders. Lyndon Johnson's attempt to finance both the Great Society and the Vietnam War put unexpected strains on the economy. Then, in 1973, the first OPEC oil shock sent oil prices skyrocketing to levels never even thought of. The economy came tumbling down. One of the centerpieces of 1960s ideology was the notion that a balance could be struck between unemployment and inflation. In other words, you could control inflation if you were willing to let unemployment rise, or you could create jobs if you simply accepted a bit more inflation. There were no free lunches, but the policymakers could order any one dish on the menu. In the 1970s the menu changed drastically and both inflation and unemployment climbed: 1960s-style American Keynesian economics didn't seem to work. Ironically, the plunge into the darkness created even more interest in economic forecasts. A number of commercial economic forecasting firms appeared during the 1970s even as the academics and the policymakers were looking for a different answer to their problems.

The disarray of the 1970s gave way to the old-time religion of no free lunch and no-pain, no gain. Beginning in 1979 the Fed, led by newly appointed chairman Paul Volcker, set out to cut inflation rates of 12 to 15 percent down to acceptable levels. The cure consisted of two recessions—in 1980 and again in 1981–1982. The second pushed unemployment to the highest levels since the 1930s. The cure was painful, but it worked. Inflation dropped to less than 5 percent in the mid-1980s and continued to fall in subsequent years. The Volcker Fed showed that in a more extreme and painful form, some of the old economic ideas about trade-offs between inflation and unemployment certainly worked.

The policymakers who arrived with Ronald Reagan's administration were a different breed. More driven by philosophy and more dedicated to shrinking the government than to using it to manage the economy, they tended to leave formal forecasting models aside. Strangely the policies that emerged from this mix—especially the tax cuts in 1982—were more reminiscent of Kennedy's Keynesian economics than of anything seen in the intervening years. Whatever the policy, the economy prospered in the 1980s.

Unemployment gradually fell, as did inflation. Slowly, almost without anyone realizing it, the idea that the economy could be managed crept back into the discussions. Forecasting was again something worth doing.

The crowning of the sense that the economy could be managed, especially through difficult decisions like raising interest rates to nip inflation in the bud, grew with the arrival of Alan Greenspan at the Fed in 1987. Greenspan was an old hand at the game. He had been chairman of the Council of Economic Advisers under President Gerald Ford. More important, Greenspan spent most of his career before the Fed appointment as an economic forecaster running a highly successful commercial forecasting firm. The forecasters were back and were in the driver's seat at the Fed, where it counted the most. In fact, as the debates over the budget deficit heated up in the late 1980s and the 1990s, Congress was paralyzed and unable to use fiscal policy. The Fed was the only game in town.

So welcome to the brave old world of economic forecasting. Today no one wants to admit to believing we really know how to forecast or control the economy. But everyone points to the past decade of economic performance as a tribute to the forecaster running the Fed.

For investors, the ultimate goal of understanding the economy is to forecast what it will do next to their investments. How can investors or any interested participants (in the economy) try their hand at forecasting? Economic forecasting depends on a mix of economic understanding, statistical computer models, and common sense. While statistical models are beyond the scope of the book, the understanding developed here can be used to forecast some economic developments and help put investors in the right place at the right time.

We will look at two or three key issues. First, we'll review some forecasts by others that are readily available. These can be used as starting points for thinking about the economy's future. Second, we will examine some easy-to-apply rules about different aspects of the economy that, taken together, can help build a picture of what is happening. Third, we will briefly touch on some places to find good economic data. The last topic continues in the Appendix— under books and the World Wide Web.

OTHER PEOPLE'S FORECASTS

My impression from doing forecasts and watching forecasts is that some people are better at them than others. Unfortunately, some of the less reliable seers seem to survive and keep on publishing. Nevertheless, it is useful to see what others are expecting. If you disagree with them, they may give you a chance to test your ideas and theories. If you agree with their outlooks, you can take refuge in numbers.

One reason that less reliable forecasters may prosper as much as the more accurate ones is that some forecast users aren't interested in accuracy. Most of the time a forecaster doesn't know exactly what will happen. Good forecasters realize how little they really know and will caution forecast users about the biggest areas of doubt. Other forecasters will sound as precise and as emphatic about their forecasts as they can. If a forecast user wants to buy certainty more than accuracy, the "seldom right but never in doubt" forecasting school is a good choice. For the rest of us, the "warts and all" forecast may be more useful.

The rounds of available forecasts fall into three general groups. First, commercial forecasting services generate complex computer models for their own use and for professionals, often at Wall Street firms. These are expensive, fun to work with, and often quite valuable. But unless an investor wants to spend as much time and money as a full-time Wall Street prognosticator, these kinds of models make very expensive hobbies.

Second, the government publishes its own forecasts. The Fed's FOMC minutes, discussed above, contain a forecast of the economy for the next 6 to 12 months. True, the Fed's discussion is clear as mud and you need to read between the lines more often than not. Third, numerous other forecasts can be found in business magazines like *Business Week, Fortune, Forbes,* and *Barron's.* Most of the large brokerage houses and banks also produce economic forecasts. Many of these are even free for the asking. All can be very useful, but for investors a little bit of work is required.

Two questions need to be answered before the investor can put a forecast to work:

1. Should I believe the forecast?
2. What does it mean for my investments?

Believing the forecast is a matter of comparing your ideas and your logic to the forecaster's and maybe giving the forecaster some extra credit for his or her track record. Once you absorb some of the ideas described below, you will be able to compare your forecast with someone else's. Figuring out what it means for your investments means putting to use some of the stuff in this book. Forecasting may be easiest to understand by imagining the kinds of analyses you as an investor might go through.

You are thinking about putting some money in bonds or in a bond mutual fund and you want to know if this is a good idea given the outlook for the economy. The two key economic factors to look at are inflation and interest rates. If interest rates rise, bond prices fall and bonds bought next year (after rates rise) are a much better deal than bonds bought today. If inflation rises, interest rates are likely to follow. Further, the dollars you get back as a bond owner will be worth less because they won't rise with inflation. So the would-be bond investor should be looking for forecasts of interest rates and inflation. A forecast of rising unemployment might be of interest, since it suggests a slowing economy and falling interest rates, but it is useful only as a guide to interest rates. If you are looking at bonds and someone offers you a detailed forecast of the semiconductor industry, don't bother unless you happen to be in the computer business as well.

Maybe bonds aren't to your liking. You prefer stocks. In particular, you like auto stocks. (That is not a recommendation, just a straightforward example.) In most stocks, the economic issues that matter are earnings and interest rates. In some cases there may be only high hopes for earnings, and psychology is a more useful guide than economics. Recent examples include stocks of "Internet companies," which serve the cyberspace community. We will stick to auto stocks for the moment. As you look at your collection of economic forecasts, you want to see what they say about interest rates and what economic factors might affect an auto company's earnings. Rising interest rates generally depress stock prices. Rising interest rates also make it more expensive to borrow money for a car or even to lease a car. Rising interest rates don't look very bullish for auto stocks.

What economic factors might hit auto company earnings? Start with how many cars the company sells and company revenues. A lot of economists forecast auto sales. A typical number is 13 million cars and light trucks annually. Light trucks—pickups and vans—account for about half of all the vehicles sold. Tractor-trailers are not included here. If this number is expected to rise from last quarter or last year, auto companies will be selling more cars and trucks, a plus. If you can't find an auto sales forecast don't despair. There are plenty of other economic factors that are worth looking at. Consumer sentiment, which we discussed earlier, is a key issue in car buying. Most people are buying a new car to replace one they have. Unless the current jalopy is completely done for, the purchase can be put off for a few weeks, months, or even years.

Two factors that drive consumer sentiment and attitudes toward buying cars are unemployment and inflation. If your neighbor is out of a job, or you are, buying a new car is likely to be delayed. Rising unemployment is not a good thing for the car business. Rising inflation is a mixed signal these days. In the last few years the Federal Reserve has become aggressive about controlling inflation with higher interest rates. A jump in inflation might goad the Fed to raise interest rates, hurting car sales as well as a lot of other things. But a small rise in inflation could convince people to buy quickly before prices rise later on. On balance, we would see higher inflation as a negative.

Of course, you shouldn't simply guess whether higher inflation is good or bad for cars. You can collect some real numbers and look at the past. You might get data on inflation and auto sales over the last 10 years and see if there is any pattern. One warning before you believe the first chart your computer draws. Since the economy is growing over time, most everything we measure tends to grow as well. This means that most graphs climb from right to left and look a lot like one another—a lot more alike than causation or economics would suggest. Second, despite this tendency, it is very easy to collect a lot of data, do a lot of statistical analysis, and have nothing to show for it. Don't get frustrated—the rise, or fall, of Rome wasn't forecast in a day! You might also look through other people's forecasts to see if they discuss the reaction of auto sales to different economic factors.

Sometimes applying forecasts depends on other kinds of issues. If you are thinking of buying a house rather than stocks or bonds, you should also look at some forecasts. Most home buyers are also borrowers via a mortgage, so look at interest rate trends and forecasts carefully. The choice between a fixed-rate and variable-rate mortgage can be important down the road. Also, look at inflation—not to second-guess interest rates but because without rising inflation, house prices may not rise too much either. If inflation is low and there is no local boom, don't buy a huge house or pay cash because you expect to trade up in a few years by selling this one for a lot more. That worked in the double-digit inflation days of the 1970s. It rarely works in the 1990s.

Buying a home raises another forecasting issue. Get a forecast about the right economy. Sound obvious? In home buying the economic strength of the community, the town, and the region matters far more than the state or the country as a whole. In recent years the national economy grew while Southern California suffered from cuts in defense spending and saw home prices nosedive. National unemployment, even national inflation rates, did nothing for California homeowners.

Among all the forecasts, analyses, prognostications, and diatribes available to look at, there are one or two that deserve mention. A few services collect forecasts from many sources and compile and publish them. In the United States the most famous is the *Blue Chip Economic Indicators*. These services are often called consensus forecasts because they try to find the consensus among many economists— often a thankless task. *Blue Chip* has been around a long time and is often cited by politicians who want an independent forecast. The longest-running such service was the *Livingston Forecasts,* published by a writer for the *Philadelphia Bulletin.* That survey has been combined with other surveys and is now published by the Philadelphia Federal Reserve. Services like *Blue Chip* offer an easy way to see a wide range of ideas about the economy. Some people also argue that the results of using the average of a large number of forecasts is much better than using only one or two services. This may be true much of the time. But when the economy takes a sudden run, a consensus service like *Blue Chip* will bury the one or two brilliant forecasters who foresaw the sudden turn in a sea of mediocre numbers.

There is another reason that surveys and consensus forecasts are very much worth watching. The financial markets tend to react to unexpected news much more than to expected news. If the bond market expects unemployment to rise sharply in the next monthly report, it won't move if that expectation is proved true. But if it expects a higher unemployment rate and there is no change, bond traders will rush to adjust their opinion of the economy and their bond holdings. "Rush" is no exaggeration—the entire rush may last only 15 minutes but create or destroy several billion dollars' worth of bond market value.

When you do your own forecast, you should compare it with consensus to get an idea of how the markets might react when your forecast proves true and the consensus turns out to be wrong.

YOUR FORECASTS

OK, get out the calculator, turn on the computer, download some data, and get ready to see what happens next in the economy. We will look at seven different economic sectors and examine a mix of ideas and rules of thumb. When we're all done we won't *know* the future, but we will have, hopefully, a number of profitable insights into tomorrow's economy. We will tackle interest rates, inflation, overall economic growth, unemployment, corporate earnings and profits, the stock market, and exports.

Interest Rates

There are a myriad of interest rates around, so we best start by deciding what to look at. We will take one short-term (overnight to 3 months) rate and one long-term (usually 10 years) rate. This will be enough to give us a framework for looking at interest rates and at the overall economy. The short-term rate is either the Fed funds rate or the rate on 3-month T-bills. Recall that Fed funds represent money loaned from one bank to another through the Federal Reserve, usually on an overnight basis. The Fed funds rate is the key short-term rate that all other short-term interest rates depend on. The funds rate can also be precisely targeted by the Fed if it chooses to do so. "Precisely" means within one-eighth of a percentage point on almost any day. The long-term rate is the yield on 10-year Treasury notes. These notes are widely traded and highly liquid, with a large floating supply. The yield on 10-year T-notes is often used to determine the yields for many other loans, including both fixed-rate and floating-rate mortgages.

With the funds rate, the key issue is the Fed. If the Fed wants to stimulate the economy, it will lower the funds rate. If it wants to restrain the economy to dampen inflation, it will raise the funds rate. If you know where the Fed is, you can figure out the funds rate. But how do you know where the Fed is?

- The Fed seldom switches back and forth from month to month. Rather, once it starts raising rates, it is likely to continue to do so for several months. Likewise with lowering rates. So look at the recent pattern in the Fed funds rate.

- Read the Federal Open Market Committee minutes to see what worries the Fed right now. Find out when the next FOMC meeting is. More often than not, the Fed adjusts policy at the meeting, not just any old time.

- Compare the Fed funds rate against inflation. It is rarely as low as inflation and will be pushed 3 to 5 percentage points over inflation if the Fed wants to slow the economy.

- Look at a few indicators that the Fed seems to watch. If capacity utilization is over 85 percent, the Fed is probably worrying about inflation. If real GDP is rising at much more than 2.5 percent over the last four quarters, the Fed is probably raising interest rates unless unemployment is high (greater than 8 percent) or the economy is coming out of a recession.

Now be daring and write down when you think the Fed funds rate will change and what the new rate will be. OK, short rates are the easy part, so let's turn to long rates. When we look at long-term interest rates, the Fed is important but is not the overriding factor. In fact, by looking at short rates we have already taken care of the Fed. The long-term rate is merely the result of a long list of consecutive short-term interest rates. There are some other factors that matter for the long-term rate: inflationary expectations, how much money people and businesses want to borrow, and how much money people think will be available for borrowing. In these discussions the money that people want to borrow is usually called the demand for credit, and the money available is the supply of credit. Far more time is spent on credit demand than credit supply, mostly because demand is more volatile. Note that all these factors are forward-looking—interest rates depend on what will happen next, not what happened yesterday. Let's work through these items one by one.

If inflation is expected to rise, interest rates will rise. One way to decide if inflation is expected to rise is to forecast inflation and then decide that everyone else agrees with the forecast. But since we really want to know what the financial markets think about inflation, not what it will actually do, there is an easier way. The simplest way is to look at the average inflation rate over the last 3 to 5 years and the trend over the same period of time. Various studies suggest that on average that's what investors and traders seem to do. If inflation is steady to lower in the last 3 to 5 years, inflationary expectations will be looking for a stable or slightly lower inflation rate and will have a small downward effect on long-term interest rates.

Credit demand depends on how strong the economy is and will be. If everyone is rushing out to buy cars and houses and businesses are investing, credit demand is rising and interest rates will follow suit. One way to judge is to compare recent growth in real GDP with interest rates. Try plotting GDP growth and 10-year interest rates on the same chart. You may want to slide one ahead of the other to see if one anticipates the other. In general, if the economy is getting stronger or is growing faster than its long-term average, interest rates will begin to climb.

Some forecasters place a lot of importance on the budget deficit. My own sense and experience suggest that the budget deficit doesn't have any discernible impact on interest rates. However, market expectations of major changes in budget policy or in other government policies may affect long-term interest rates. If the market is convinced that the government is really going to balance the budget (heard that one before?), some investors might assume that Uncle Sam—one of the largest borrowers—

was tightening his belt and would borrow less money. Then interest rates would fall.

So look through these different issues and then write down what the long-term interest rate is likely to be in 3 to 6 months. (It helps to check what it is now.) The difference between the two rates—the 10-year T-note rate less the Fed funds rate—is the yield spread, sometimes called the slope of the yield curve. A yield curve is shown in Fig. 8-1. Some interest rate theories and forecasting techniques place much more emphasis on the yield spread than the suggestions given here. Yield spreads are very important, as we will see when we look at the GDP figures. But for this kind of systematic but nonmathematical forecasting, models of the yield spread don't seem to be the best approach. If you are still with me, don't worry. Interest rates are one of the two worst things to forecast—the other is foreign exchange, which we don't deal with.

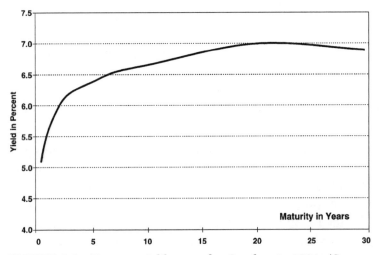

FIGURE 8-1 Treasury yield curve for October 1, 1996. (*Source:* U.S. Bureau of Economic Analysis.)

INFLATION

The most widely used inflation measure is the consumer price index. It is released each month by the Bureau of Labor Statistics. While there is considerable detail—the monthly report runs to 10 or more pages—the only number that most people really care about is the "inflation rate." This is usually stated as the change in the consumer price index over the last 12 months. A 1-month change is too volatile to be meaningful for most economic and investment questions.

News reports often mention the "core" inflation rate as well as the overall rate. The core rate is the change in the CPI after foodstuffs and energy commodities have been eliminated. This number tends to be a steadier, less volatile figure. To forecast inflation a good place to start is with the core rate. Look at its trend over the last 1 to 3 years and project it forward. You'll get a good idea of how much inflation the economy is expecting and what the current price pressures are. If the economy has been growing quickly or if the Federal Reserve seems unusually concerned about inflation, you may want to nudge up the trend-based projection of the core rate. But the core rate should be a starting point for inflation projections.

However, don't forget about food and energy, unless you don't want to eat or worry about having to take only ice-cold showers! Both of these categories are volatile and we are interested only in unusually large moves. The routine ups and downs wash out in the averages. If oil prices rise 50 cents a barrel, that's not likely to be very exciting. But a sustained climb of a dollar or two a barrel each quarter will hit the CPI. The same thing is true of food prices, but here we need to watch how important a particular food really is. If orange juice prices soar in a freeze, it may not make much difference in the CPI, since orange juice is only a small part of the average family budget. If food and energy prices seem to be pushing your forecasts all over the map every month, step back and see what the numbers look like without them. In general, inflation tends to respond to trends unless the economy is moving one way and inflation is moving the other.

GENERAL ECONOMY

There is little in the economy that escapes the economy. Moreover, having a forecast for overall GDP growth can be helpful with much of the other stuff. Most large-scale computer models build GDP up from its component parts. While such an approach is useful in these kinds of models, it is not the easiest one for investors who want to spend a little time examining the economy. A better approach is to go back to the yield spread described in the interest rates section. When short-term rates are way under long-term rates, the Fed is trying to lower interest rates and stimulate the economy. At the other extreme, if short rates are above long rates and the yield curve is "inverted," the Fed is trying to stop the economy. Since the Fed often gets its way with the economy, the yield spread can tell us a lot about the future path of economic growth. Figure 8-2 shows the yield spread and real GDP growth. The GDP growth is moved forward by about six quarters so that what we see is the link between the current yield spread and growth one to one and a half years later. This time lag may not be the magical right number, but looking at the yield spread can tell us a lot about future GDP growth. Of course, the number should make sense—as should all the forecasts. If the economy is crumbling and the yield spread is very wide, you will have doubts about whether it will turn around in time for the

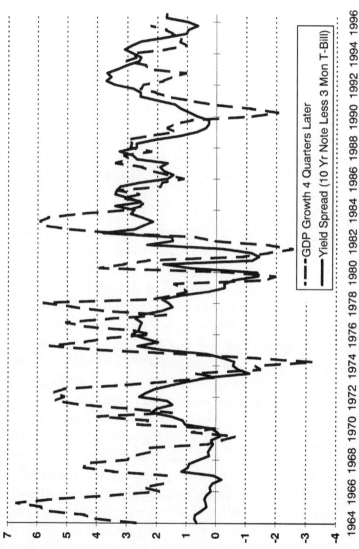

FIGURE 8-2 Yield spread and GDP growth. (*Source:* U.S. Bureau of Economic Analysis, Federal Reserve Bank of St. Louis.)

forecasts to be proved right. Many times it will and there are real opportunities to make money, but you should go through all the other measures carefully to see if you missed something in your calculations.

Unemployment

For most of us, the unemployment rate is the most interesting measure of the labor markets. While many economists tend to look at the number of jobs being created, we will stick with the unemployment rate for this discussion. Here there is a widely accepted approach to forecasting unemployment called "Okun's Law," after economist Arthur Okun, who was chairman of John F. Kennedy's Council of Economic Advisers. Among his more serious studies Okun suggested some useful, quick approaches to economic forecasting. One was to use two quarters of declining GDP as the benchmark for a recession rather than wait for several quarters for every bit of data to be analyzed. This rule is widely used today; often people don't realize it is a shortcut. Okun also suggested that the way to gauge unemployment was to compare the current unemployment rate with what it would be if the economy were operating at full capacity and how far below capacity the economy really is.

This is a bit easier said than done, but it does work. To figure the economy's capacity, look at its long-term trend growth. Over the last 20 years this has been about 2.7 percent. Now, take a point about 20 years ago when GDP was high but not quite at a peak. Project that level at the 2.7 percent annual growth rate. That is a rough measure in billions of constant dollars of the potential level of GDP. Calculate the percentage difference between that number and the current GDP. This is the GDP gap, the amount that GDP is below full capacity. (The gap could be a negative number, since the economy can grow very fast for brief periods and might actually exceed its long-run potential for a few quarters.)

Now the unemployment rate should be the same percentage above its full capacity level as the overall economy is below it. Of course, this requires knowing the full capacity or "full employment" unemployment rate. That number is often a matter of political debate. Currently most economists would choose a number between 5 and 6 percent, close to the actual rate of unemployment. But a few would argue that the number should really be 4 percent, or even a bit less!

An alternative way to judge the employment picture is to do the percentage gap analysis for the current quarter and, using your forecast of GDP found earlier, the same analysis for four to six quarters out. If the gap is falling, the unemployment rate will fall toward the full-employment level. If the gap is growing, unemployment is rising. This will give you some direction without having to fight the politicians over exactly what full employment is.

Earnings

Earnings, or corporate profits, are both important and difficult to forecast. If you are looking at a single company, factors specific to that company must be considered as well as the general economy. If the company is followed by analysts on Wall Street, a good place to start is with their work. It should give you an idea of what broad economic factors matter as well as what is specified to the company in question. Some of the overall economic factors may be sales in the company's industry and prices of key inputs.

The specific factors have to do with the company's business. Suppose you are looking at an oil company. Certainly the prices of crude oil and oil products like gasoline and heating oil make a big difference to an oil company's profits—but how? Here you need to know something about the company in particular. If the company is "crude-rich," meaning it produces more crude oil than it refines and sells the surplus crude to other oil companies, it will do well when crude oil prices push higher but prices of oil products lag. This might be the case during a Middle East crisis, when general business activity sags because of worries over a possible war or extended political crisis. Alternatively, if the company is crude-poor and buys crude oil to keep its refineries running, it will do well in periods when demand pushes oil product prices higher and crude oil prices lag as producers compete for the business.

The best way to forecast a single company's price is to know as much about the company and its financial fortunes as the company's own chief financial officer. Next best is to know it as well as a first-rate stock analyst (who should know it as well as the chief financial officer). Third, and the technique used by many stock analysts, is to call the company's investor relations manager and ask what he or she thinks. In any of these, you can decide if the forecast is consistent with other things you know about the economy. It is much easier for a company to make more money (higher profits) when its sales are rising than when they are falling. Likewise, it is harder to raise profits if costs are rising. So look at what's happening to revenues and costs first of all. Profits, even in a single company, are more complicated than whether revenues rose more, or less, than costs. But to explore things further you will need to look at the company over a number of years, not just at one moment in time.

For tracking the overall economy and for watching the stock market, the profits that matter may relate more to corporations as a group than to one or two particular companies. There are two general approaches to looking at overall profits and earnings. The first is "bottom up." Since Wall Street analysts, taken as a group, track hundreds of companies, we could add up the earnings estimates for all these companies and find out what the whole stock market will do. That sounds difficult, but there are some investment services that do just that. The results, usually published as "analysts' estimates," give a measure of overall profits or earnings. The most common figure used is earnings per share for the S&P 500. This figure is a measure of the earnings of all the stocks in the Standard & Poor's 500 index.

An alternative to the bottom-up figures are "top-down" numbers. These are estimates done by looking at the overall economy and trends in the economy rather than at the individual companies in the stock market. Forecasters use detailed mathematical or econometric models to derive profit numbers from the other economic factors (wages, sales, and so on) that the model estimates. This approach is often too complex for easy use. A simpler way is to identify various patterns and indicators of earnings trends.

One of the best broad-based indicators is how well the economy is doing and has been doing. Earnings are often measured as the percentage change from the same period (usually a quarter) a year ago. If you make the same calculation for real gross national product, you can see a pattern in which the changes in GDP tend to lead the changes in profits by about two to three quarters. (See Fig. 8-3.) This suggests that watching the trend in the overall economy will reveal a lot about where profits are heading. Since profits are what is left after the company pays for everything else, it is no surprise that profits do better in good times and magnify the size of other changes.

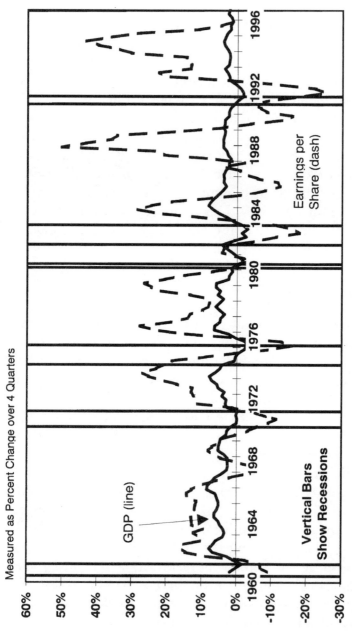

FIGURE 8-3 Real GDP and corporate earnings growth. (*Source:* U.S. Bureau of Economic Analysis, Standard and Poor's.)

There are also some reasons for profits to lag a little behind GDP. No company likes to report falling profits. When companies suspect times may be getting tougher—they see inventories pile up or sales slow—they will begin tightening their belts. They will take longer to hire new people, be slower to order supplies and materials, or even wait a little bit before paying their bills. All this tends to soften, for a time, the impact of falling business in falling profits. Further, for a lot of companies, accounting is not as simple as adding up the numbers in the ledgers. There are numerous adjustments and judgments to be made. In other words, it is quite easy, and completely legal and proper, to "manage earnings." This is a fancy way of saying that when times get tough, some companies can easily maintain appearances for a quarter or two even though things are falling all around them.

Now, before you indict a company you just invested in for managing earnings or cooking the books, recognize that some kinds of businesses do well in poor times. Ironically, economic forecasting may be one of them! When everyone is doing well and profits are easy to come by, there is no reason to spend money to find out where to make more money—it's almost growing on trees. But when times are tough, it is worthwhile spending money to identify where there are some good times left. Of course, if times get very tough, anything that is not absolutely essential is likely to be trimmed back.

Watching GDP and broad economic trends is useful to track profits. But a number of other economic indicators are much less useful. Neither interest rates nor inflation is likely to reveal much about earnings trends. Other measures, such as unemployment, merely echo the GDP numbers. One approach worth looking at is to combine the top-down,

GDP-related figures with what you glean from surveys of analysts—the so-called bottom-up numbers. Here there is a peculiar seasonal pattern worth noting as well. Most companies report earnings and other financial results on a calendar year. Therefore, most analysts are interested in forecasting earnings for a calendar year. In November it is relatively easy to forecast the full-year results, since three of the four quarterly numbers have been reported. But at the beginning of the year, in January, it is very difficult—there are only forecasts and no real numbers. So as the year wears on, the analysts' bottom-up numbers should become more accurate. While they do, they often get lower and lower as well. Early in the year look at what the Wall Street analysts say but trust to GDP trends. Late in the year, pay more attention to the analysts but don't forget where GDP is going.

STOCKS

Of all, or most, of the topics discussed here, stocks are the ones that people want to forecast the most. If you look at investment studies, this makes sense. The biggest reason for the success, or failure, of an investor is the choice he or she makes between putting the money in stocks or in bonds. Some analyses suggest that this choice accounts for as much as three-quarters of the variation in how rich or poor an investor becomes. So being able to forecast the stock market is a big part of the game. Forecasting interest rates—and remember that when interest rates rise, bond prices fall—accounts for another large part of an investor's success.

Forecasting stocks day to day or week to week is a combination of luck and rolling the dice. But over longer periods of time, the market will often mount a sustained advance or decline. These longer-term moves are not random. Rather, they are governed by a combination of investors' expectations of interest rates and of corporate earnings. When you buy stocks, you are buying a share of tomorrow's corporate earnings. How much that share is going to be worth depends first on what those earnings will be. Second, it depends on the discount factor.

The discount factor is a fancy way of reminding ourselves that a dollar next year is worth something less than a dollar today. How much less is the discount factor. Mathematically it is linked to the rate of interest. If you say a dollar today is the same as a dollar next year, give me that dollar today. I'll invest it in Treasury bills, turn it into $1.06 by waiting a year, and give the dollar back to you. I keep the 6 cents as profit. Not much, but not much work or risk either! Equivalently, you could discount the dollar from next year to today (divide by 1 + 6%, or 1.06 in this example) and give me $.94 today. Now there is no profit and the sum is discounted.

Stocks are discount machines. High earnings mean higher stock prices; lower interest rates mean higher stock prices. If you want to try your hand at building some simple models, this is a good—and maybe rewarding—place to start. Ideally the S&P 500 should be measured as the discounted value of all future earnings. Since we don't know what people expect for future earnings, let's start where they would start with a forecast of the future—with today's earnings. Of course, if we knew all the future earnings, we would need to know future interest rates as well. We don't, so let's settle for today's interest rates.

Now, when you discount something, you divide by 1 plus the interest rate. It's the division that creates the relation in which higher interest rates (dividing by a larger number) means lower stock prices. Anyone who has suffered through, or enjoyed, at least a simple course in statistics has seen how to fit an equation to data. If you avoided statistics but learned how to use a computer spreadsheet program, use the Help-Search feature to find something called regression analysis. With this and some data on the S&P 500 and interest rates, you can try building a rudimentary stock market forecasting model, as shown in Figs. 8-4 and 8-5. (The data can be found at the St. Louis Fed's Web site listed in the Appendix.) There are no guarantees with this model, but it can provide some interesting insights to the way the market is moving at any moment.

If you want to play the market, but find equations about as exciting as investing in money market funds, there are some other things to look at or try. A few measures of the stock market that seem to relate to the value of stocks are worth watching from time to time. The idea behind all these gauges is that the market has a normal range. As long as it is in the normal range, it will probably keep moving in the same direction. But when things go beyond the norm, the market will reverse course and push things back to the norm.

The three measures, in order of popularity, are the price-to-earnings (P/E) ratio, dividend yields, and the price-to-book ratio. From time to time some analysts argue for other measures, but these three seem to persevere. P/E is the ratio of the stock's price to its earnings. A similar measure can be constructed for the overall market by comparing the level of the S&P 500 index with the earnings per share on the index. Roughly speaking, this number is likely to be between 10 and 20 times. In other words, if earnings are $35 per share and the market has a "multiple" (Wall Street jargon for the P/E) of 18.5, then the market would be at about 650. Suppose the P/E climbs to 22 or 24, as it did in the summer of 1987 before the market crash. Such a high P/E suggests

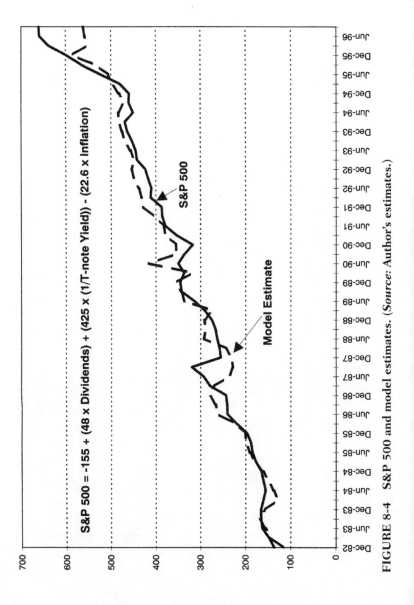

FIGURE 8-4 S&P 500 and model estimates. (*Source:* Author's estimates.)

S&P 500 = -155 + (48 x Dividends) + (425 x (1/T-note Yield)) - (22.6 x Inflation)

S&P 500

Model Estimate

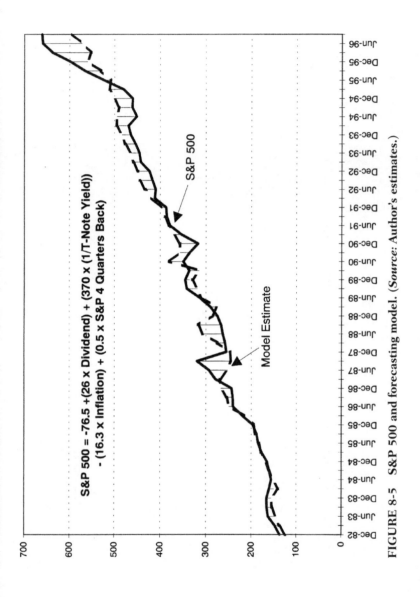

S&P 500 = -76.5 + (26 × Dividend) + (370 × (1/T-Note Yield)) - (16.3 × Inflation) + (0.5 × S&P 4 Quarters Back)

S&P 500

Model Estimate

FIGURE 8-5 S&P 500 and forecasting model. (*Source:* Author's estimates.)

that we are living on borrowed time. A P/E under 10, last seen before the bull market that began in the summer of 1982, is a sign that the market is poised to pick up.

Some analysts use the "Rule of 20," although they sometimes argue that the number is really not 20, but 21 or 22. The Rule of 20 is that the sum of the P/E on the market and inflation should be 20 (or 22). If the market P/E is 17 times earnings and inflation is 3 percent, the Rule of 20 is satisfied. What it tells us is that the market can afford a higher P/E when inflation is low than when it is high.

Of course, the timing between the ratio crossing some benchmark and the market's reaction may be variable. One of the most variable is the dividend yield. This measure is similar to P/E except that it uses dividends, not earnings, and is inverted. It is the dividend divided by the stock price with the result stated as a percentage. For instance, if a stock is priced at $100 and pays a dividend of $4 per year, the yield is 4 percent. Again, the number can be calculated for the market as well as for a stock. As of early 1997, the dividend yield on the S&P 500 approached its fourth year at record lows. Since a low dividend yield means that dividends are small and stock prices are high, the low yield is a sign that stock prices could fall. So far they haven't. In fact, for much of the late 1960s—the end of one of the great bull markets in modern times—dividend yields were at record lows. For the record, analysts used to say that you should worry if the S&P 500 dividend yield is under 3 percent. Currently it is close to about 2 percent.

Price-to-book ratios can also be used, but here the numbers are probably less reliable, because book values—which depend on accounting rules and depreciation procedures—often don't reflect what is really happening in a company.

One more comment on the indicator game: The indicators often don't tell the full story. For instance, the lower inflation is, the higher the P/E can be. This can be seen by simply plotting a chart of inflation rates and annual P/E's and realizing that lower inflation tends to be associated with higher P/E's. The reason is that the P/E is a little like the inverse of an interest rate. The earnings-to-prices ratio (an upside-down P/E) represents the amount of money a stock throws off, just as a bond's coupon is the amount of money the bond throws off. High inflation tends to push interest rates up. High inflation also makes for high earnings-to-price ratios or low P/E's. So, given the relatively moderate current inflation rate of about 3 percent, a P/E of 18 is not too far out of line. If inflation were 8 percent, the P/E of 18 would signal disaster.

EXPORTS AND IMPORTS

The best advice on exports says less about how to forecast them than about how not to. People seem to believe that a change in the dollar's foreign exchange value has an immediate effect on imports and exports. For most goods, the dollar's foreign exchange value makes very little difference. Other factors are far more important than foreign exchange rates.

Some goods tend to be priced in dollars all over the world, so that changes in the value of the dollar don't affect our imports. Oil is a primary example, but most commodities follow a similar pattern. Likewise, some countries have currencies that follow the dollar up and down. When the dollar moves against the Japanese yen, some people get excited about shifts in imports from Asia. But most of Asia other than Japan is almost on a dollar standard. Korea,

Taiwan, Singapore, and others have currencies that tend to track with the dollar.

Of course, there are many countries where the currency fluctuates against the dollar and where there is a lot of trade with the United States. Japan is one of the largest, but it is followed by much of Europe, including such economic leaders as England and Germany. Even here the dollar makes only a little difference to imports and exports. There are two general reasons. First, even when the dollar moves against the yen, the prices of Japanese goods available in the United States don't jump around. Manufacturers, wholesalers, and retailers all tend to hold their prices constant. They absorb the foreign exchange losses (and reap the foreign exchange gains) in order to provide consistent prices to customers and maintain market share. Only when the currencies move by substantial amounts will the wholesale and retail prices react quickly. Often prices respond with a long time lag—as much as 6, 12, or even 18 months later.

Second, not only the price of an import or export matters. The overall market is much more important. In boom times, imports rise along with everything else. As the imports grow, the trade position worsens and a trade deficit either appears or grows. But it is a general economic boom that is driving the imports, not the currency. The same is true with exports. When our trading partners' economies do well, our exports grow. When our trading partners' economies are in recession, so are our exports. So if you want to forecast imports and exports, don't look at currencies.

One last comment on trade and forecasting. If you want to forecast when protectionist sentiment—arguments to use tariffs to keep foreign goods out and prevent foreigners from stealing American jobs—will be on the rise, look at the employment numbers. When people think that times are tough and they want someone to blame for their troubles, especially someone faceless and far away, protectionism is an easy sell. When we are enjoying economic growth and growing world trade, protectionist arguments fall on deaf ears.

FORECASTING AND ECONOMY WATCHING

As a professional economic forecaster—if that isn't an oxymoron—I have no choice but to claim that a short chapter on forecasting can barely begin to look at the issues. Probably the best lesson about forecasting is to look at the economy in light of what has been discussed here and look for the inconsistencies. The economy tends to grow at a modest pace until it runs into something. That something could be the economy's own capacity limits, it could be excessive optimism that leads to rising prices and inventories, it could even be a war. When that happens, things don't add up correctly and the economy takes a new turn to a new direction. If you see what doesn't add up, and how it might rearrange itself to add up, you are on the way to a profitable forecast. Last of all, don't forget some history. The economy seldom if ever repeats itself, but knowing what has happened before often shows that the seemingly impossible has already happened, maybe more than once.

GUIDE TO FURTHER READING

This section is not a bibliography or a balanced guide for those who wish to read more about economics and the economy. Instead, it is a rather opinionated, personal, and idiosyncratic reading list about economics and the economy. No pretense is made about balance, and there is no fairness doctrine. This section comes from being (believe it or not) really interested in economics. It also comes from the second most common question I get after admitting to being an economist: "I really should know something about the economy. What should I read?" As to the most common question, it is "What will the stock market do next?" The second question is much much easier to answer, especially if reliability is any consideration at all.

Now that you have made it to the end of the first book I recommend, some others should be mentioned. We will look at both old media and new. Old media are newspapers, magazines, and books. New media include the Internet and the World Wide Web. Radio and television are excluded from the list. These are important sources of news, but it is hard to turn on the TV or the radio to research some specific question. Maybe when we really do get 500-channel cable TV, there will be one or more economics channels. However, I doubt it—and hope we can avoid that much predigested economics.

OLD MEDIA

NEWSPAPERS

Newspaper preferences are probably dominated by geography and political philosophy as much as anything else. For economic content, *The Wall Street Journal* is always a key source, as is *The New York Times*. Their editorial philosophies are significantly different and should be watched. The *Journal* loses some perspective when it digs into supply-side economics and tax simplification. On the other hand, the *Journal*'s editorial pages often carry views completely opposed to its own editorials. Both papers provide a lot of interesting economics. Another publication worth looking at is the *Financial Times*. The *FT* carries a lot more economics than the U.S. papers do and often tackles subjects that most American papers would consider too economic or too dull. Debates over policies at the Bank of England or the long-term outlook for inflation are common in the *FT*, while American papers focus on gossip about the Fed and last month's consumer price report. In short, all are worth a look.

As a New Yorker now working on Wall Street, I can't claim to read many other papers often enough to recommend or discourage them. When I talk to reporters from *USA Today* they are usually well informed and perceptive. But after the first 30 seconds of discussion, I begin to wonder why we're still talking: The average article they write is 3.2 sound bites long. If you think economics takes a little thought and a few details beyond the headlines, *USA Today* may raise more questions than it answers. Chartists, technicians, and stock market lovers should look at *Investors' Business Daily.* The economic analysis is close to that in the *Journal,* the *Times,* and the *FT*—and the stock charts are much better.

MAGAZINES

When we turn to magazines, one stands out. Not because of its name, *The Economist,* published in the UK, is my first choice. It is a bastion of free-market capitalist economics, and it is proud of it. The editorials are in the front of the magazine, not buried in some obscure corner. The level of economic analysis, especially for long surveys or special short-review articles on economic topics, is first rate.

There are other magazines of course. *Business Week* (published by the publisher of this book and the corporation that includes my employer, Standard & Poor's) covers a fair amount of economics as well as business topics. Despite the parenthetical note, *Business Week* is a better economic read than its competitors, *Forbes* and *Fortune. Barron's* has always seemed to be Wall Street's gossip sheet as much as anything else. Its commentaries are a bit to the right of *The Wall Street Journal.*

There are more specialized journals for economics than anyone would want to think about, but most are rather expensive and sometimes difficult reading besides. One good source of information—in terms of both price and readability—is a group of publications by the regional Federal Reserve banks. In addition to the Fed's board of governors, headquartered in Washington, there are 12 regional banks located around the country. The locations were chosen in 1913, so some may not seem logical today. All the regional Feds publish a lot of material; some have developed specialities of their own over time.

One of the best general economic reviews is a monthly collection of charts called *Economic Trends,* published by the Cleveland Federal Reserve. The price is also right—free for the asking. International economics often gets big play in publications from the New York Fed. Issues relating to monetary policy are well covered by the St. Louis, Chicago, Atlanta, and Kansas City Fed banks. The Boston Fed covers a broad range of issues and sometimes publishes articles about the financial markets. The Minneapolis Fed is a good source for discussions of mathematical models. All the Fed banks are worth a look. All are on the World Wide Web, as noted below.

BOOKS

Books on economics are far too numerous to mention in any detail, but some books and some authors do stand out. Among well-known economist-authors of the past are Adam Smith, David Ricardo, and John Maynard Keynes. There are also the very much alive Milton Friedman, Paul Samuelson, Paul Krugman, Jeremy Siegel, and Burton Malkiel. The difficulty with many economics tomes is that they are not novels for reading at the beach. On the contrary, after perusing a few of the great works of economics, you may become convinced that the phrase "dismal science" was coined by a book reviewer.

Adam Smith pretty much started modern economics in 1776 (an easy year to remember). His *Wealth of Nations* may be a bit dated in spots but is not totally irrelevant, even now. Even rougher going, but more interesting when conquered, is David Ricardo's *Principles of Economics*. One of Ricardo's contributions, and one of the more difficult ideas in economics, is something called economic rent. It is distantly related to the common meaning of rent as in paying the landlord. Briefly, if you rent a house on the best street in town, you pay a large premium for being on the best street. The size of the premium paid over the rent of similar house in a more ordinary location depends on the demand for houses in posh neighborhoods, not on the cost of building the house. The premium is the economic rent. The same idea applies to selling anything when the supply is fixed and the price exceeds the production costs. As Ricardo commented: "Rent is high because corn is high, not corn is high because rent is high." Corn referred to British wheat crops in an era when first-quality farmland was in limited supply. Rent referred to the costs of renting land to grow crops.

The difficulty with Keynes is that his most significant piece of economics may be one of the worst written of all his books. *The General Theory of Employment Interest and Money* was written in a mad dash of creativity and teaching in 1934–1935 as a response to the Great Depression. Between various events, including the Depression, World War II, the Bretton Woods Conference and the establishment of the International Monetary Fund, and the postwar world economic order, Keynes never really got back to rewriting his basic ideas. He died in 1946. The result is that the *General Theory* is not an elegant book to read. Moreover, economists have created a mini-industry of reinterpreting the *General Theory* to the extent that almost any economic theory proposed today can be traced back to Keynes's book. If this sounds a little like tracing everything back to the Bible, you aren't all wrong.

Nothing seems to generate interest in economics like a crash or financial crisis. Crashes and crises are also popular topics with both economists and historians. One of the best accounts of some fabled crashes and certainly some of the best analysis of what happens in a crash is *Manias, Panics, and Crashes: A History of Financial Crises* by Charles Kindleberger. Kindleberger is an outstanding economic historian. His review gives a mix of theory to understand what happens when markets crumble and anecdotes about some of the more exciting crumbles of the last century or two. Among the classic reviews of market manias is Charles MacKay's *Extraordinary Popular Delusions and the Madness of Crowds*. Originally published in 1841, MacKay's book is frequently reprinted and usually finds its way into the business-books sections of large bookstores.

Books on the stock market and how to get rich are certainly too numerous to list. There are a few that do stand out. While his name has vanished into history, the most fabled investor of the first half of this century was Bernard Baruch. Baruch made his first few fortunes in the rough-and-tumble decades that preceded the great crash of 1929; he also managed to hang on to his fortune through the crash. Among bits of intelligence Baruch cited for escaping the devastation of 1929 was MacKay's book. One of the more interesting accounts of Baruch's investment battles is his autobiography, *My Own Story.*

The most celebrated investor of the current age is Warren Buffett. One aspect of his celebrity is the plethora of books on Buffett the investor, the man, the individual, and the capitalist. While many of these are worth reading, it is doubtful that any of them will turn someone into as skillful, or fortunate, an investor as Buffett has proved to be. But the books do demonstrate that investors who follow their own analyses and their own counsel often do far far better than those who jump from fad to fad.

There are more analytical approaches to Wall Street than reading assorted Tales of Great Investors. One classic, Burton Malkiel's *A Random Walk Down Wall Street,* has grown in length and gained in appeal through several editions. Malkiel explains the results of the last few decades of economic and financial research and offers concrete advice for investing. He is a strong believer in index funds and passive investing. Another good read on finance, economics, and the stock market is *Stocks for the Long Run* by Jeremy Siegel. If you want to be convinced that stocks are the place to be, this is the book to read. Investing with Siegel may not provide stories for cocktail parties but it will provide nice returns. More and more investors seem to prefer mutual funds. If you like the Malkiel-Siegel approach but want to put it into practice with funds, *Bogle on Mutual Funds* by John Bogle is the ticket. Bogle is chairman of Vanguard Funds and there are moments when he may be too much of a salesman for his own company. But, if you can set that aside, it is a worthy book.

Back in the economics arena, Paul Krugman manages to turn out new books rather than new editions. Two recent ones are *The Age of Discontent* and *Peddling Prosperity.* His comments about economic policy, trade, competitiveness, and deficit issues are especially interesting. Krugman manages to replace philosophical diatribes about capitalism with solid economic analysis. He is unusually skillful at skewering sacred cows and rarely pulls his punches. Few readers will find that all their pet projects escape him. Another example of applying economics to current political issues and discovering that things are not always what they seem is Robert Eisner's *The Misunderstood Economy.*

Eisner's view of the federal budget deficit is quite different from most of what we see and hear.

Two of the most famous (or infamous) economist-authors around today are Paul Samuelson and Milton Friedman. More people may have slugged through or given up on Samuelson's textbook, *Economics*, than on almost any other. If you make it through, it is really quite comprehensive. Samuelson's other writings are largely for professionals and academics and are as comprehensive and accurate as the textbook. Milton Friedman's writings include some more popular and also more political work.

A word or two about bonds might also be in order. For those interested in junk bonds, almost anything by Edward Altman should be worthwhile reading. Altman, a finance professor at NYU's School of Business, is the pioneer researcher on the true returns that investors can earn on junk bond portfolios. Without his research, junk bonds would still be nothing more than a few fallen angels. Last on the financial book list is a thin volume on bonds that has sold continuously since it was first published in 1971. Homer and Leibowitz's *Inside the Yield Book* is probably the best introduction to bonds and that end of the financial markets. In this most mathematical corner of the financial world, here is one book that never goes beyond high school algebra. Though it is 25 years old, it anticipates most of the bond market innovations that appeared *after* it was published, including zero-coupon bonds, stripping coupons, and even some of the derivative securities that have plagued markets in the last few years. After reading more bond books than I care to admit to, I still find that this one gives the best intuitive understanding of the bond game.

One of the largest sources of economic information—though some would argue misinformation—is the government. While government documents are gradually moving from the old media of print to the new media of CD-ROM and the Web, one or two items are worth mentioning. Each January or February the government publishes the *Economic Report of the President* and *The Budget*. The *Economic Report* is sometimes worth reading for an explanation of the administration's thinking on the economy. The data tables are always useful for checking your idea of history against the cold facts. *The Budget* is worth one look to recognize how big, complex, and confused it really is. Don't buy it—the price for all the parts and appendixes is approaching the national debt. If you want a more critical review of the budget, the place to look is the Congressional Budget Office (CBO). CBO is Congress's analytical answer to the White House budget number crunchers. Even in this increasingly partisan age, CBO's publications are good economics rather than bad politics.

NEW MEDIA

In today's wired world one of the newest and richest sources of information for the curious is the Internet and its World Wide Web. Unlike most authors of books, magazines, and newspaper articles on the Internet, I am not going to spend much time telling you how to get on the Web or what software or hardware you need. If you don't know what the Web is, this isn't the place to find out—try the local newsstand or library. If you know what the Web is, but you're not on it, buy one of the myriad computer magazines that comes in a plastic bag with a free info disk for America Online or CompuServe or a similar service.

What this section will do is suggest some places on the Web to look if you want to learn more about economics and the economy. Dividing up places to look on the Web is difficult because there are so many and they are so varied. Moreover, more interesting pages seem to show up all the time. Without doubt some of what follows is out of date or inaccurate. One caveat. These comments are not the result of an organized hunt or a scientific survey. The next few pages should be read as a diary of a would-be Web surfing economist looking for an interesting bit of information or some clue to what the economy will do next. Happy hunting!

WHERE TO HUNT

Veteran Web surfers know about search tools such as Yahoo and Lycos (http://www.Yahoo.com;http://www.lycos.com). Investors also know about Yahoo, which went public early in 1996. But there are some special places to look for information on economics. The key one is an ever-evolving Web document called *Resources for Economists on the Internet* by Bob Goffe (http://econwpa.wustl.edu/EconFAQ.html). Serious economic surfers should consult this early and often. It is a gold mine of information and is continuously updated. In some cases it tends toward academic users, but it is a very good general resource and guide.

One comment you may doubt after getting this far into this book is that (some) economists have a sense of humor. Whether we do or not, there is an Economist Jokes page on the Web. It may not be as funny as your favorite late-night talk show, but it is more erudite and probably less painful (http://www.etla.fi/pkm/joke.html).

INVESTMENTS

One thing that is definitely growing on the web is Investment information and people who want to help you invest your money, usually for a fee, a commission, or some other piece of the action. Many major stockbrokers and mutual fund companies have Web pages. These are good places to look for information on specific mutual funds or other investments. Rather than list a lot of Web addresses, I suggest that you search for some discount brokers and large fund companies—Charles Schwab, Fidelity, Vanguard, and so forth. Beyond these detailed inquiries, you can search for more general information on the economy and the financial markets.

DATA

Understanding the economy often requires some numbers and data. Data are readily available on the Web. If you are looking for some basic economic information about things like interest rates, inflation, and gross domestic product, a good place to start is the Federal Reserve Bank of St. Louis. This regional Fed bank maintains a Web site (and old-fashioned BBS) called FRED, for something like *Federal Reserve economic data*. FRED is a small but very rich gold mine of data. You can find numerous data series for interest rates, exchange rates, stock market indexes, and major economic indicators like GDP, industrial production, and the money supply. The St. Louis Fed (http://www.stls.frb.org) is known as the most monetarist of all the regional Fed banks, and offers a wealth of data on the money supply. Some of the data series go back to the 1920s or before. Further, with only a little effort, you can get the data into a spreadsheet program like Excel or Lotus 1-2-3 and begin drawing charts or building economic models. Most of the Fed banks are linked to one another. Others include the New York Fed (http://www.ny.frb.org) and the Minneapolis Fed (http://www.mpls.frb.org), where you can find the Federal Open Market Committee (FOMC) minutes.

For very current data, one of the best places to look is the federal government. The Bureau of Economic Analysis in the Commerce Department runs a computer bulletin board called the EBB, or Economic Bulletin Board. It also runs a large Web site, STAT-USA. Either of these has current economic releases. "Current" is just that. The monthly employment report from the Bureau of Labor Statistics is released at 8:30 a.m. on the first Friday of the month. It is on the EBB at 8:30.5—but things can get crowded, since most of Wall Street is on-line downloading the release by 8:31. For those who don't need instant service or who don't want to pay the EBB fees, the University of Michigan has a Web site that mirrors the entire EBB on a 24-hour delay. For the EBB, call (202) 482-1986 (that's the voice number, not the modem line) or look at the Web site (http://www.bea.doc.org) for information from the Bureau of Economic Analysis.

While a lot of economic data comes from the government, some still comes from the private sector. The S&P 500 is one example. Other financial market indexes—such as bond indexes published by investment banks like Salomon Brothers, Lehman Brothers, and Merrill Lynch—can often be found on the Web. Likewise, indicators such as the Russell 2000 stock indexes are available in one form or another. Most of these indexes are copyrighted and there may be some restrictions on their use. However, using them for your own private analyses shouldn't be a problem.

MORE ECONOMIC INFORMATION

You may want more than simply files of numbers. You want someone else's analysis as a comparison with your own. One good place to begin is the Cleveland Federal Reserve. The Cleveland Fed publishes a monthly call *Economic*

Trends. It is on the Web and also available by old-fashioned U.S. mail—and the price is right: free. *Economic Trends* is an excellent monthly chartbook of economic commentary and analysis, often written with a wry sense of humor we might not expect from a central banker (http://www.clev.frb. org/research/index.htm). (No, it isn't cited on the Economist Jokes page, at least not yet.)

Though somewhat drier, the analysis in the Federal Open Market Committee minutes and the Fed's *Beige Book* review of the economy is equally important to understanding the economy and the Fed. Both of these are available on the Minneapolis Federal Reserve Web page. The Minneapolis Fed's site is called Woodrow, named for Woodrow Wilson, the President who signed the law that created the Federal Reserve system. Most of the regional Federal Reserve banks have Web sites, and they are all hot-linked to one another. The various Feds seem to specialize in different kinds of information. St. Louis has the richest data, and only Minneapolis has the FOMC minutes. Most of the regional Fed banks list or publish a lot of their own research papers and a fair amount of regional economic data. If you want to find out what local economic conditions are in some part of the country—maybe you're thinking about moving and want to check on home values and incomes—the regional Fed bank Web page is a good place to start.

A few other special items can be found on various Fed bank pages. Data on foreign exchange and indexes of the U.S. dollar's value can be found on the Atlanta and Dallas Fed pages. Philadelphia and Atlanta both do regional indexes of economic activity that are usually available at their Web sites. The New York Fed offers a lot of detailed data on U.S. Treasury securities, including current prices.

Other analyses of current economic conditions are sprinkled around the Web. A couple that are worth looking at are Ed Yardeni's charts. Yardeni is the chief economist at C. J. Lawrence, a unit of Deutsche Bank Morgan Grenfell. (http://www.webcom.com/~yardeni/). His Web pages include a number of files of long-term charts of the stock and bond markets and the economy. People with a love of charts showing decades of history should take a look. Ongoing commentaries can also be found on the Bank of America's pages.

Standard & Poor's maintains a Web site with both data on the Standard & Poor's indexes and commentaries on financial markets and the economy. Additional information, including Standard & Poor's stock reports, is available for a modest fee (http://www.stockinfo.standardpoor.com/).

MORE SERIOUS STUDY

Of course, a lot of what's on the Web is more academic and requires more consideration and study. There is a wealth of academic stuff up there as well. A few items are worthy of mention. William Sharpe, a Nobel laureate in economics and a professor at Stanford University, has a Web page with a lot of good stuff. It includes some articles he has published, materials for courses he teaches, and other projects he is working on. Some of the material is at a fairly advanced level, but a lot of it is of general interest to anyone curious about the ideas of modern financial economics (http://gsb-www.stanford.edu/~wfsharpe/home.htm). After you wander around Stanford, another San Francisco spot to look at is Berkeley—specifically, the Web pages for the University of California's School of Information Management Sciences and the pages for Hal Varian, the dean. Hal Varian is an economist who has done a lot of work on the economics of markets and firms, known as microeconomics. His recent work includes some interesting studies of the Internet itself and how it will, or won't, prosper in a profit-oriented capital-ist world (http://www.sims.berkeley.edu/~hal).

Another interesting bit of academia is a history of money written by a Welshman named Gavyn Davies (http://www.ex.ac.uk/!RDavies/arian/money.html). From the selec-tions on the Web, it should be an interesting read. As you might expect, many of the classics of economics—especially when they are old enough for the copyrights to have expired—are on the Web. Adam Smith's *Wealth of Nations* is there, at least once if not several times. (Try http://www.duke.edu/~atm2/SMITH/ for the *Wealth of Nations*.)

The list could go on and on. Part of the challenge of the Web is finding what no one else (well, no one else except for the author of the page) put up there. Between *Resources for Economists on the Internet,* Yahoo, Lycos, and the rest, it should be an interesting hunt.

INDEX

ABOUT THE AUTHOR

David M. Blitzer is vice president and chief economist of Standard & Poor's. He is frequently quoted in the national business press and is a regular guest on CNN, CNBC, and the Nightly Business Report. His economic analyses and forecasts are used by Standard & Poor's analysts and managers as well as by many investors and corporations. Dr. Blitzer writes S&P's monthly economic review, Trends & Projections, and writes for other S&P publications.